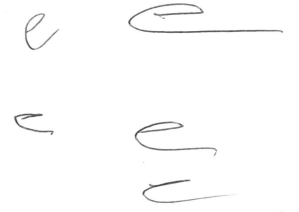

Prentice Hall

GRAMMAR HANDBOOK

Grade 9

Upper Saddle River, New Jersey

Boston, Massachusetts

Chandler, Arizona

Glenview, Illinois

Prentice Hall Grammar Handbook Consulting Author
We wish to thank Jeff Anderson who guided the pedagogical approach to grammar instruction utilized in this handbook.

Grateful acknowledgment is made to the following for copyrighted material:

Alfred A. Knopf, Inc.
"Dream Deferred" from *The Collected Poems of Langston Hughes* by Langston Hughes. Copyright © 1994 by The Estate of Langston Hughes.

Longman Publishing Group, A Division of Pearson Education, Inc.
"Writing in a Second Language" from *Writing: A Guide for College and Beyond (2nd Edition)* by Lester Faigley. Copyright © 2010 by Pearson Education, Inc.

Note: Every effort has been made to locate the copyright owner of material reproduced in this component. Omissions brought to our attention will be corrected in subsequent editions.

4000714097

Credits

Cover
Photos provided by istockphoto.com

Illustrations
Tom Garret

Photographs
All interior photos provided by Shutterstock, Inc.

ISBN-13: 978-0-13-363842-4
ISBN-10: 0-13-363842-1
2 3 4 5 6 7 8 9 10 V064 13 12 11 10

GRAMMAR

CONTENTS

USAGE

MECHANICS

Numbered tags like this **EL1** are used on instruction pages of the Grammar Handbook to indicate where to find a related tip in the English Learner's Resource.

CHAPTER 1

THE PARTS *of* SPEECH

Use the various parts of speech to form sentences that are strong in structure and meaning.

WRITE GUY *Jeff Anderson, M.Ed.*

WHAT DO YOU NOTICE?

Notice different parts of speech as you zoom in on this sentence from "Uncle Marcos," an excerpt from *The House of the Spirits* by Isabel Allende.

MENTOR TEXT

All that remained on earth were the comments of the amazed crowd below and a multitude of experts, who attempted to provide a reasonable explanation of the miracle.

Now, ask yourself the following questions:

- What is the function of the verb *were* in the sentence?
- Which words are adjectives, and which nouns do they modify?

The verb *were* functions as a linking verb that connects the subject *all* to the nouns *comments* and *multitude*. Linking verbs serve to connect the subject of a sentence to words that identify or describe it. The word *amazed* is used as an adjective modifying the noun *crowd*, and the adjective *reasonable* modifies the noun *explanation*.

Grammar for Writers Each part of speech plays an important role in crafting clear and meaningful sentences. Use each part of speech to its best advantage to improve the quality of your writing.

I'm pretty lukewarm about it.

Do you think the word cool is a good adjective?

1

1.1 Nouns and Pronouns

Nouns and pronouns make it possible for people to label everything around them.

Nouns

The word *noun* comes from the Latin word *nomen*, which means "name."

RULE 1.1.1

> **A noun** is the part of speech that names a person, place, thing, or idea.

Nouns that name a *person* or *place* are easy to identify.

PERSON	Uncle Mike, neighbor, girls, Bob, swimmer, Ms. Yang, Captain Smith
PLACE	library, Dallas, garden, city, kitchen, James River, canyon, Oklahoma

The category *thing* includes visible things, ideas, actions, conditions, and qualities.

VISIBLE THINGS	chair, pencil, school, duck, daffodil, fort
IDEAS	independence, democracy, militarism, capitalism, recession, freedom
ACTIONS	work, research, exploration, competition, exercise, labor
CONDITIONS	sadness, illness, excitement, joy, health, happiness
QUALITIES	kindness, patience, ability, compassion, intelligence, drive

Concrete and Abstract Nouns

Nouns can also be grouped as *concrete* or *abstract*. A **concrete noun** names something you can see, touch, taste, hear, or smell. An **abstract noun** names something you cannot perceive through any of your five senses.

CONCRETE NOUNS	person, cannon, road, city, music
ABSTRACT NOUNS	hope, improvement, independence, desperation, cooperation

See Practice 1.1A

Collective Nouns

A **collective noun** names a *group* of people or things. A collective noun looks singular, but its meaning may be singular or plural, depending on how it is used in a sentence.

COLLECTIVE NOUNS			
army	choir	troop	faculty
cast	class	crew	legislature

Do not confuse collective nouns—nouns that name a collection of people or things acting as a unit—with plural nouns.

Compound Nouns

A **compound noun** is a noun made up of two or more words acting as a single unit. Compound nouns may be written as separate words, hyphenated words, or combined words.

COMPOUND NOUNS	
Separate	life preserver coffee table bird dog
Hyphenated	sergeant-at-arms self-rule daughter-in-law
Combined	battlefield dreamland porthole

Check a dictionary if you are not sure how to write a compound noun.

Common and Proper Nouns

Any noun may be categorized as either *common* or *proper*.
A **common noun** names any one of a class of people, places,
or things. A **proper noun** names a specific person, place, or thing.
Proper nouns are capitalized, but common nouns are not.
(See Chapter 10 for rules of capitalization.)

COMMON NOUNS	building, writer, nation, month, leader, place, book, war
PROPER NOUNS	Jones, Virginia, *Leaves of Grass,* Revolutionary War, White House, Mark Twain, France, June

A noun of direct address—the name of a person to whom you
are directly speaking—is always a proper noun, as is a family
title before a name. In the examples below, common nouns are
highlighted in yellow, and proper nouns are highlighted in orange.

COMMON NOUNS	My **aunt** is a **pilot**.
	Our **coach** is never late.
	My favorite person is my **uncle**.
DIRECT ADDRESS	Please, **Dad**, tell us about your trip.
	Mom, can you pick me up?
	Jake, please bring your fruit salad when you come to the party.
FAMILY TITLE	**Aunt Sarah** works for **NASA**.
	Grandma makes great pies, but her blueberry pie is my favorite.
	My favorite person is **Uncle Barry**.

See Practice 1.1B

PRACTICE 1.1A ▶ Identifying and Labeling Nouns as Concrete or Abstract

Read each sentence. Then, write the noun or nouns in each sentence, and label them *concrete* or *abstract*.

EXAMPLE   No one knows the identity of the robber.

ANSWER   *identity* — abstract

              robber — concrete

1. It seems very few mosquitoes display much intelligence.

2. Her loyalty always impresses her friends.

3. Very few visitors understand the culture.

4. Rarely does Martha miss the bus.

5. Strangely, nobody heard a sound coming from the television.

6. After a long time, Franco finally appeared.

7. All the volunteers developed strong friendships.

8. If it is not too much trouble, can you help Max?

9. His cat was known for its curiosity.

10. Brent called me twice about his excitement.

PRACTICE 1.1B ▶ Recognizing Kinds of Nouns (Collective, Compound, Proper)

Read each sentence. Then, write whether the underlined noun is *collective*, *compound*, or *proper*.

EXAMPLE   Cars were moving along the freeway.

ANSWER   *compound*

11. My family was late for the awards show.

12. The weather becomes warmer in April.

13. Many of the speakers were early for the fundraiser.

14. One team flew across the country for the tournament.

15. After two hours, he finally received his suitcase.

16. At the end of the summer, I'm going to Virginia.

17. Sheila had meatloaf for dinner.

18. Does anyone know who wrote *To Kill A Mockingbird*?

19. A crowd gathered near the entrance.

20. They scored a touchdown to win the game.

SPEAKING APPLICATION

Take turns with a partner. Tell about what you did over the weekend, using both concrete and abstract nouns. Your partner should listen for and name each type of noun that you use.

WRITING APPLICATION

Write four sentences. Each sentence should have a collective, compound, proper, or common noun.

Pronouns

Pronouns help writers and speakers avoid awkward repetition of nouns.

> **Pronouns** are words that stand for nouns or for words that take the place of nouns.

Antecedents of Pronouns Pronouns get their meaning from the words they stand for. These words are called **antecedents.**

> **Antecedents** are nouns or words that take the place of nouns to which pronouns refer.

The arrows point from pronouns to their antecedents.

EXAMPLES   **Michael** said **he** lost **his** watch at the fair.

When the **Lees** moved, **they** gave **their** pets to me.

Attending the state fair is tiring, but **it** is fun!

Antecedents do not always appear before their pronouns, however. Sometimes an antecedent follows its pronoun.

EXAMPLE   Because of **its** carnival, **Rottweil**, Germany, is my favorite city.

There are several kinds of pronouns. Most of them have specific antecedents, but a few do not.

See Practice 1.1C

Personal Pronouns The most common pronouns are the
personal pronouns.

1.1.4 RULE

> **Personal pronouns** refer to the person speaking
> (first person), the person spoken to (second person), or the
> person, place, or thing spoken about (third person).

PERSONAL PRONOUNS		
	SINGULAR	PLURAL
First Person	I, me my, mine	we, us our, ours
Second Person	you your, yours	you your, yours
Third Person	he, him, his she, her, hers it, its	they, them their, theirs

In the first example below, the antecedent of the personal
pronoun is the person speaking. In the second, the antecedent of
the personal pronoun is the person being spoken to. In the last
example, the antecedent of the personal pronoun is the thing
spoken about.

FIRST
PERSON
My name is not Jorge.

SECOND
PERSON
When **you** left, **you** forgot **your** coat.

THIRD
PERSON
Don't judge a book by **its** cover.

Reflexive and Intensive Pronouns These two types of pronouns
look the same, but they function differently in sentences.

1.1.5 RULE

> A **reflexive pronoun** ends in *-self* or *-selves* and indicates that
> someone or something in the sentence acts for or on itself.
> A reflexive pronoun is essential to the meaning of a sentence.
> An **intensive pronoun** ends in *-self* or *-selves* and simply adds
> emphasis to a noun or pronoun in the sentence.

REFLEXIVE AND INTENSIVE PRONOUNS		
	SINGULAR	PLURAL
First Person	myself	ourselves
Second Person	yourself	yourselves
Third Person	himself, herself, itself	themselves

REFLEXIVE   The settlers prepared **themselves** for the approaching winter.

INTENSIVE   John Smith **himself** wrote an account of the meeting.

See Practice 1.1D

Reciprocal Pronouns **Reciprocal pronouns** show a mutual action or relationship.

RULE 1.1.6

The **reciprocal pronouns** *each other* and *one another* refer to a plural antecedent. They express a mutual action or relationship.

EXAMPLES   The two dogs shook water all over **each other**.

The class collected autographs from **one another**.

See Practice 1.1E

Demonstrative Pronouns **Demonstrative pronouns** are used to point out one or more nouns.

RULE 1.1.7

A **demonstrative pronoun** directs attention to a specific person, place, or thing.

There are four demonstrative pronouns.

DEMONSTRATIVE PRONOUNS	
SINGULAR	PLURAL
this, that	these, those

Demonstrative pronouns may come before or after their antecedents.

BEFORE   **That** is the **ranch** I would like to own.

AFTER   I hope to visit **Butte** and **Helena**. **Those** are my first choices.

One of the demonstrative pronouns, *that*, can also be used as a relative pronoun.

Relative Pronouns

Relative pronouns are used to relate one idea in a sentence to another. There are five relative pronouns.

> A **relative pronoun** introduces an adjective clause and connects it to the word that the clause modifies.

RULE 1.1.8

RELATIVE PRONOUNS				
that	which	who	whom	whose

EXAMPLES   We read a **book** **that** contained an account of the settlers' experiences.

The **settlers** **who** had written it described their hardships.

The **winter**, **which** they knew would be harsh, was fast approaching.

See Practice 1.1F

Read each sentence. Then, write the pronoun in each sentence and its antecedent.

EXAMPLE   Did Julie forget to bring her lunch?

ANSWER   *her, Julie*

1. Jonathan asked his father for help.
2. This is not the movie that Alicia ordered.
3. The pig has broken out of its sty.
4. The Smiths enjoyed themselves at the concert.
5. The boat with its sail spread wide won the race.
6. The twins rented a video game with their money.
7. The princess wore a pink dress to her ceremony.
8. Lauren bought herself a new comic book at the store.
9. The girls said they would be early.
10. The choir just sang its final song.

Read each sentence. Then, write the pronoun in each sentence, and label it *personal, reflexive,* or *intensive*.

EXAMPLE   Lance promised himself to work harder next summer.

ANSWER   *himself* — reflexive

11. It is time to make myself some lunch.
12. Students, just keep telling yourselves that learning is fun!
13. Franklin finished his homework before watching the game.
14. The host herself showed up late to the party.
15. Terrance forgot his books on the bus.
16. The defensive player scored a touchdown himself.
17. The thirsty actors poured themselves some water.
18. The coach was ready with her whistle and clipboard.
19. I mowed the lawn myself.
20. The students congratulated themselves on performing so well.

SPEAKING APPLICATION

Take turns with a partner. Tell about your favorite character in a movie, using at least two pronouns that refer to that character. Your partner should identify both the pronouns you used and their antecedents.

WRITING APPLICATION

Write a brief paragraph about something you've done on a holiday. Use a personal, a reflexive, and an intensive pronoun in your paragraph.

PRACTICE 1.1E ▷ **Identifying Reciprocal Pronouns**

Read each sentence. Then, write the reciprocal pronoun in each sentence.

EXAMPLE   The students congratulated each other.

ANSWER   *each other*

1. The committee members complimented one another.

2. Tammy and William respect each other.

3. After a long summer, they kept in touch with each other.

4. Don and Chung greeted each other.

5. Betsy, Carmen, and Helen were embarrassed that they had forgotten one another's names.

6. The toddlers played with one another at daycare.

7. They see each other often.

8. We gave presents to one another.

9. They don't speak to each other often because they are both very busy.

10. Barbara, Julian, and Caitlin always greet one another.

PRACTICE 1.1F ▷ **Recognizing Demonstrative and Relative Pronouns**

Read each sentence. Then, write the pronoun or pronouns in each sentence, and label them *demonstrative* or *relative*.

EXAMPLE   The man who goes by the name of Bobby owns this building.

ANSWER   *who* — relative

    this — demonstrative

11. That is Emmett's favorite song.

12. These certainly will increase in value.

13. That man whose name was picked won a prize.

14. Local vendors brought jewelry and displayed these at the fair.

15. Janice was the person who told Maria about the sale.

16. The ten guests whom I invited came and brought presents.

17. Julio has a cousin who lives in New Hampshire.

18. This is a perfect example of why you shouldn't watch television while doing your homework.

19. The pieces that covered the playing board fell onto this pillow.

20. Sandy's neighbor borrowed those serving dishes a few weeks ago.

SPEAKING APPLICATION

Take turns with a partner. Describe an enjoyable weekend you have had. Show that you understand reciprocal pronouns by using some in your response. Your partner should listen for and identify the reciprocal pronouns that you use.

WRITING APPLICATION

Using sentence 18 as your first sentence, write a short paragraph about what you think happened, using a demonstrative and a relative pronoun in your paragraph.

Interrogative Pronouns

Interrogative pronouns are used to ask questions.

RULE 1.1.9

An **interrogative pronoun** is used to begin a question.

The five interrogative pronouns are *what*, *which*, *who*, *whom*, and *whose*. Sometimes the antecedent of an interrogative pronoun is not known.

EXAMPLE   **Who** picked up the children?

See Practice 1.1G

Indefinite Pronouns

Indefinite pronouns sometimes lack specific antecedents.

RULE 1.1.10

An **indefinite pronoun** refers to a person, place, or thing that may or may not be specifically named.

INDEFINITE PRONOUNS				
SINGULAR			PLURAL	BOTH
another	everyone	nothing	both	all
anybody	everything	one	few	any
anyone	little	other	many	more
anything	much	somebody	others	most
each	neither	someone	several	none
either	nobody	something		some
everybody	no one			

Indefinite pronouns sometimes have specific antecedents.

NO SPECIFIC ANTECEDENT   **Many** have visited Gettysburg.

SPECIFIC ANTECEDENTS   **One** of the **students** sang.

Indefinite pronouns can also function as adjectives.

ADJECTIVE   **Few** orchestras are as famous as this one.

See Practice 1.1H

PRACTICE 1.1G > **Recognizing Interrogative Pronouns**

Read each sentence. Then, write the correct interrogative pronoun needed in each sentence.

EXAMPLE   _____ will happen next?

ANSWER   *What*

1. _____ of the candidates is leading in the polls?

2. _____ was chosen as team captain?

3. _____ is Diane making for the bake-off?

4. _____ child is causing all that commotion?

5. _____ of these colors do you think works the best?

6. With _____ did Malik go to the dance?

7. _____ is your favorite topping on a pizza?

8. _____ will start in the big game tonight?

9. To _____ does this bag belong?

10. _____ of these hats did your sister knit?

PRACTICE 1.1H > **Identifying Indefinite Pronouns**

Read each sentence. Then, write the indefinite pronoun in each sentence.

EXAMPLE   Did anyone remember to bring a radio?

ANSWER   *anyone*

11. Some of the players refused to leave the field.

12. My teacher knows everything about current events.

13. None of the answers were obvious.

14. Tiffany is always thinking of others.

15. Both of my friends promised to keep things a secret.

16. My uncle will worry about anything.

17. Most of the fans were cheering.

18. Two weeks before the debate, most of the tickets had been sold.

19. She can do little in this situation.

20. Has anyone seen this movie lately?

SPEAKING APPLICATION

With a partner, take turns interviewing each other. Ask at least five questions that begin with interrogative pronouns.

WRITING APPLICATION

Replace the indefinite pronouns in sentences 12, 13, and 16 with different indefinite pronouns.

1.2 Verbs

Every complete sentence must have at least one **verb**, which may consist of as many as four words.

A verb is a word or group of words that expresses time while showing an action, a condition, or the fact that something exists.

Action Verbs and Linking Verbs

Action verbs express action. They are used to tell what someone or something does, did, or will do. **Linking verbs** express a condition or show that something exists.

An action verb tells what action someone or something is performing.

ACTION
VERBS

Mia **learned** about winter sports.

The radio **blared** the broadcast of the hockey game.

We **chose** two books about Texas.

They **remember** the film about China.

The action expressed by a verb does not have to be visible. Words expressing mental activities—such as *learn*, *think*, or *decide*—are also considered action verbs.

The person or thing that performs the action is called the *subject* of the verb. In the examples above, *Mia*, *radio*, *we*, and *they* are the subjects of *learned*, *blared*, *chose*, and *remember*.

> A **linking verb** is a verb that connects its subject with a noun, pronoun, or adjective that identifies or describes the subject.

LINKING
VERBS

The man **is** a famous hockey player.

The ice surface **seems** smooth.

EL6

The verb *be* is the most common linking verb.

THE FORMS OF *BE*			
am	am being	can be	have been
are	are being	could be	has been
is	is being	may be	had been
was	was being	might be	could have been
were	were being	must be	may have been
		shall be	might have been
		should be	shall have been
		will be	should have been
		would be	will have been
			would have been

Most often, the forms of *be* that function as linking verbs express the condition of the subject. Occasionally, however, they may merely express existence, usually by showing, with other words, where the subject is located.

EXAMPLE   The skater **is** on the rink.

Other Linking Verbs A few other verbs can also serve as linking verbs.

OTHER LINKING VERBS		
appear	look	sound
become	remain	stay
feel	seem	taste
grow	smell	turn

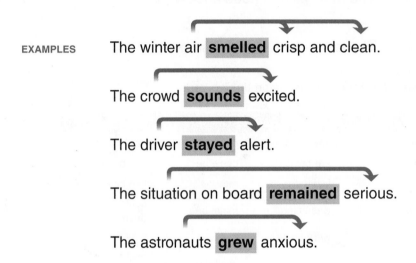

EXAMPLES   The winter air **smelled** crisp and clean.

The crowd **sounds** excited.

The driver **stayed** alert.

The situation on board **remained** serious.

The astronauts **grew** anxious.

Some of these verbs may also act as action—not linking—verbs. To determine whether the word is functioning as an action verb or as a linking verb, insert *am*, *are*, or *is* in place of the verb. If the substitute makes sense while connecting two words, then the original verb is a linking verb.

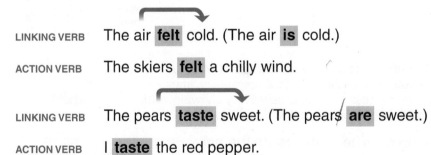

LINKING VERB   The air **felt** cold. (The air **is** cold.)

ACTION VERB   The skiers **felt** a chilly wind.

LINKING VERB   The pears **taste** sweet. (The pears **are** sweet.)

ACTION VERB   I **taste** the red pepper.

See Practice 1.2A
See Practice 1.2B

PRACTICE 1.2A ▷ Identifying Action and Linking Verbs

Read each sentence. Write the action verb in each sentence.

EXAMPLE   I tasted squid for the first time.

ANSWER   *tasted*

1. The bus turned left into the service area.
2. Our neighbor grows beautiful roses.
3. Dad played with the children.
4. The detective looked at the clues.
5. They wandered through the forest.

Read each sentence. Write the linking verb in each sentence.

EXAMPLE   Cold water is refreshing.

ANSWER   *is*

6. The crowd became restless.
7. I grew interested in coins a year ago.
8. The two remained friends all year.
9. We all felt cooler after a dip in the ocean.
10. Each bird's call sounds different.

PRACTICE 1.2B ▷ Distinguishing Between Action and Linking Verbs

Read each sentence. Then, write the verb in each sentence, and label it *action* or *linking*.

EXAMPLE   The vegetables tasted salty.

ANSWER   *tasted* — linking

11. Fred smelled the bouquet of flowers.
12. The bridge looked sturdy enough.
13. The guard sounded the alarm.
14. The candidate appeared confident.
15. The farmer grows wheat in these fields.
16. Levi tasted the sweet and sour pork at the Chinese restaurant.
17. The skunk smelled awful.
18. She performs at the music fair each summer.
19. I turned the volume down on the television.
20. Aunt Judy feels fine after her illness last week.

SPEAKING APPLICATION

Take turns with a partner. Tell about something fun you did recently, using both action verbs and linking verbs. Your partner should listen for and name three verbs that you use.

WRITING APPLICATION

Use sentences 17 and 20 as models to write sentences of your own. Replace the verb in each sentence with another action verb or linking verb.

Transitive and Intransitive Verbs

All verbs are either **transitive** or **intransitive,** depending on whether or not they transfer action to another word in a sentence.

EL9

> A **transitive verb** directs action toward someone or something named in the same sentence. An **intransitive verb** does not direct action toward anyone or anything named in the same sentence.

The word toward which a transitive verb directs its action is called the *object* of the verb. Intransitive verbs never have objects. You can determine whether a verb has an object by asking *whom* or *what* after the verb.

TRANSITIVE   Jack **shot** the puck.
(Shot what? puck)

We **ate** the chicken.
(Ate what? chicken)

INTRANSITIVE   The team **practiced** on the outdoor field.
(Practiced what? [no answer])

The fan **shouted** loudly.
(Shouted what? [no answer])

> Because linking verbs do not express action, they are always intransitive. Most action verbs can be either transitive or intransitive, depending on the sentence. However, some action verbs can only be transitive, and others can only be intransitive.

TRANSITIVE   I **wrote** a letter from New Mexico.

INTRANSITIVE   The secretary **wrote** quickly.

| ALWAYS TRANSITIVE | California grapes **rival** those of France. |

| ALWAYS INTRANSITIVE | She **winced** at the sound of his voice. |

See Practice 1.2C

EL5

Verb Phrases

A verb that has more than one word is a **verb phrase.**

> A **verb phrase** consists of a main verb and one or more helping verbs.

1.2.6 RULE

Helping verbs are often called auxiliary verbs. One or more helping verbs may precede the main verb in a verb phrase.

| VERB PHRASES | I **will be taking** a horse-and-carriage ride. |

| | I **should have been watching** when I crossed the road. |

All the forms of *be* listed in this chapter can be used as helping verbs. The following verbs can also be helping verbs.

OTHER HELPING VERBS			
do	have	shall	can
does	has	should	could
did	had	will	may
		would	might
			must

A verb phrase is often interrupted by other words in a sentence.

| INTERRUPTED VERB PHRASE | I **will** definitely **be taking** a horse-and-carriage ride through the snow. |

| | **Should** I **take** a horse-and-carriage ride through the snow? |

See Practice 1.2D

Read each sentence. Then, write the action verb in each sentence, and label it *transitive* or *intransitive*.

EXAMPLE   Dana entered her poem in the contest.

ANSWER   *entered* — transitive

1. The chef prepared spectacular desserts.
2. The monkeys swung from tree to tree.
3. We divided the rest of the sandwich among us.
4. Mr. Anderson lives alone.
5. Icicles hung from the roof.
6. We saw Grandma last night.
7. The fans cheered from the bleachers.
8. We crawled carefully to the fence.
9. A stray dog followed us home from the park.
10. The quarterback ran down the field.

Read each sentence. Then, write the verb phrase in each sentence.

EXAMPLE   I have been studying for hours.

ANSWER   *have been studying*

11. You should have come with us.
12. We are going to Arizona this summer.
13. David could not see his brother in the fog.
14. Nguyen does know the words to the song.
15. Cameron might come to the party after all.
16. Basketball was invented in 1891.
17. This sewing machine does work.
18. I have seen that portrait before.
19. Elise will perform a solo at the recital.
20. I am talking on my cellphone.

SPEAKING APPLICATION

Take turns with a partner. Tell about what you did last summer, using both transitive and intransitive verbs. Your partner should listen for and name three transitive or intransitive verbs that you use.

WRITING APPLICATION

Write three sentences with verb phrases. The first sentence should have one helping verb. The second sentence should have two helping verbs. The third should have three helping verbs.

1.3 Adjectives and Adverbs

Adjectives and **adverbs** are the two parts of speech known as *modifiers*—that is, they slightly change the meaning of other words by adding description or making them more precise.

Adjectives

An **adjective** clarifies the meaning of a noun or pronoun by providing information about its appearance, location, and so on.

> An **adjective** is a word used to describe a noun or pronoun or to give it a more specific meaning.

An adjective answers one of four questions about a noun or pronoun: *What kind? Which one? How many? How much?*

EXAMPLES **green** fields (What kind of fields?)

that garden (Which garden?)

six roses (How many roses?)

extensive rainfall (How much rainfall?)

When an adjective modifies a noun, it usually precedes the noun. Occasionally, the adjective may follow the noun.

EXAMPLES The expert was **tactful** about my limited knowledge.

I considered the expert **tactful**.

An adjective that modifies a pronoun usually follows it. Sometimes, however, the adjective precedes the pronoun as it does in the example on the next page.

AFTER They were **brokenhearted** by the early frost.

BEFORE **Brokenhearted** by the early frost, they left for Florida.

More than one adjective may modify a single noun or pronoun.

EXAMPLE We hired a **competent, enthusiastic** gardener.

Articles Three common adjectives—*a, an,* and *the*—are known as **articles.** *A* and *an* are called **indefinite articles** because they refer to any one of a class of nouns. *The* refers to a specific noun and, therefore, is called the **definite article.**

INDEFINITE EXAMPLES	DEFINITE EXAMPLES
a daisy	the stem
an orchid	the mask

Remember that *an* is used before a vowel sound; *a* is used before a consonant sound.

EXAMPLES **a** one-horse town (*w* sound)

a union (*y* sound)

an honest man (no *h* sound)

See Practice 1.3A

Nouns Used as Adjectives Words that are usually nouns sometimes act as adjectives. In this case, the noun answers the questions *What kind?* or *Which one?* about another noun.

NOUNS USED AS ADJECTIVES	
flower	flower garden
lawn	lawn mower

See Practice 1.3B

Proper Adjectives Adjectives can also be proper. **Proper adjectives** are proper nouns used as adjectives or adjectives formed from proper nouns. They usually begin with capital letters.

PROPER NOUNS	PROPER ADJECTIVES
Monday	Monday morning
San Francisco	San Francisco streets
Europe	European roses
Rome	Roman hyacinth

Compound Adjectives Adjectives can be compound. Most are hyphenated; others are combined or are separate words.

HYPHENATED **rain-forest** plants

water-soluble pigments

COMBINED **airborne** pollen

evergreen shrubs

See Practice 1.3C   SEPARATE **North American** rhododendrons

Pronouns Used as Adjectives Certain pronouns can also function as adjectives. The seven personal pronouns, known as either **possessive adjectives** or **possessive pronouns**, do double duty in a sentence. They act as pronouns because they have antecedents. They also act as adjectives because they modify nouns by answering *Which one?* The other pronouns become adjectives instead of pronouns when they stand before nouns and answer the question *Which one?*

> **A pronoun is used as an adjective if it modifies a noun.**

Possessive pronouns, demonstrative pronouns, interrogative pronouns, and indefinite pronouns can all function as adjectives when they modify nouns.

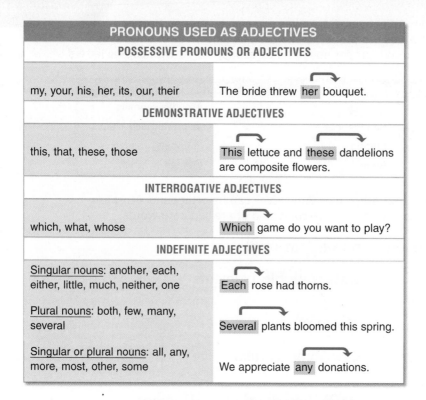

PRONOUNS USED AS ADJECTIVES	
POSSESSIVE PRONOUNS OR ADJECTIVES	
my, your, his, her, its, our, their	The bride threw her bouquet.
DEMONSTRATIVE ADJECTIVES	
this, that, these, those	This lettuce and these dandelions are composite flowers.
INTERROGATIVE ADJECTIVES	
which, what, whose	Which game do you want to play?
INDEFINITE ADJECTIVES	
Singular nouns: another, each, either, little, much, neither, one	Each rose had thorns.
Plural nouns: both, few, many, several	Several plants bloomed this spring.
Singular or plural nouns: all, any, more, most, other, some	We appreciate any donations.

Verb Forms Used as Adjectives Verb forms used as adjectives usually end in -*ing* or -*ed* and are called **participles.**

EXAMPLE   I pruned the **wilting** flowers.

Nouns, pronouns, and verb forms function as adjectives only when they modify other nouns or pronouns. The following examples show how their function in a sentence can change.

	REGULAR FUNCTION	AS AN ADJECTIVE
Noun	The deck was slippery.	I sat in the deck chair.
Pronoun	This was an idyllic life.	This life was idyllic.
Verb	The ice melted in the sun.	The melted ice made a puddle.

See Practice 1.3D

PRACTICE 1.3A > Recognizing Adjectives and Articles

Read each sentence. Then, write the adjective in each sentence.

EXAMPLE   Dad baked an apple pie.

ANSWER   *apple*

1. The runner set a new record.
2. The passenger remained calm.
3. The house floods during heavy rains.
4. No one knew the answer to the last question.
5. The speaker raised an interesting point.

Read each sentence. Then, write the article(s) in each sentence.

EXAMPLE   I saw an ostrich and a penguin.

ANSWER   *an, a*

6. The students were eager to volunteer.
7. The lifeguard raised a white flag.
8. The dog came to the woman.
9. The wicker basket contained an apple.
10. Uncle Harry gave Erin a present.

PRACTICE 1.3B > Identifying Nouns Used as Adjectives

Read each sentence. Then, write the noun that is used as an adjective in each sentence.

EXAMPLE   She is running for a town office.

ANSWER   *town*

11. Dairy products can be good for you.
12. Each camper had insect repellent.
13. We have a birdbath in our rose garden.
14. Melissa had a delicious lettuce salad for lunch.
15. The apartment building is very high.
16. We put the breakfast dishes away.
17. Emma missed her ballet class last week.
18. Rocco is a player on the football team.
19. The television show has too many commercials.
20. My sister is going to day camp this summer.

SPEAKING APPLICATION

Take turns with a partner. Tell about your favorite movie. Your partner should listen for and name four adjectives and four articles that you use.

WRITING APPLICATION

Write three sentences that contain nouns used as adjectives.

PRACTICE 1.3C Recognizing Proper and Compound Adjectives

Read each sentence. Then, write the adjective in each sentence, and label it as either *proper* or *compound*.

EXAMPLE   The decision had far-reaching effects.

ANSWER   *far-reaching* — compound

1. My mother grows African violets.
2. She is very closemouthed about her life.
3. The restaurant serves soft-shell crab.
4. Emily took a ride on her Shetland pony.
5. The program was started by a farsighted group.
6. We shared a triple-decker sandwich.
7. The Italian restaurant makes lasagna.
8. Do not turn onto the one-way street.
9. England flourished during the Elizabethan period.
10. He is my next-door neighbor.

PRACTICE 1.3D Recognizing Pronouns and Verbs Used as Adjectives

Read each sentence. Then, write the pronoun or verb used as an adjective in each sentence.

EXAMPLE   Some students still have tickets for the game.

ANSWER   *some*

11. All citizens have a duty to vote.
12. The sinking ship was lost at sea.
13. We visited several natural history museums.
14. Please mail those letters.
15. The boiling water was ready.
16. A bouncing bunny hopped through the field.
17. Several teachers attended the game.
18. That movie was so funny!
19. We camped in a few parks during the trip.
20. The spoiled food was thrown into the garbage.

SPEAKING APPLICATION

With a partner, name four adjectives that are proper or compound. Then, each of you should use one of the adjectives in a sentence.

WRITING APPLICATION

Write four sentences that use pronouns as adjectives. Then, write four sentences that use verbs as adjectives.

Adverbs

Adverbs, like adjectives, describe other words or make other words more specific.

> An **adverb** is a word that modifies a verb, an adjective, or another adverb.

When an adverb modifies a verb, it will answer any of the following questions: *Where? When? In what way? To what extent?*

An adverb answers only one question when modifying an adjective or another adverb: *To what extent?* Because it specifies the degree or intensity of the modified adjective or adverb, such an adverb is often called an **intensifier.**

The position of an adverb in relation to the word it modifies can vary in a sentence. If the adverb modifies a verb, it may precede or follow it or even interrupt a verb phrase. Normally, adverbs modifying adjectives and adverbs will immediately precede the words they modify.

ADVERBS MODIFYING VERBS	
Where?	**When?**
The plant grew here.	She never raked the leaves.
The bushes were planted there.	Later, we toured the greenhouses.
The snake slid underground.	The boat sails daily to the city.
In what way?	**To what extent?**
He officially announced it.	The bees were still buzzing loudly.
She was graciously helping.	He always did it right.
Jeff left quickly after the party.	Be sure to wash completely after painting.

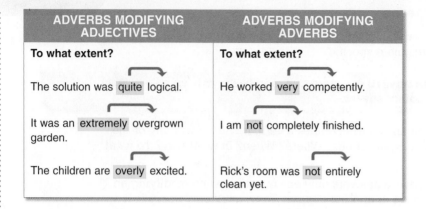

ADVERBS MODIFYING ADJECTIVES	ADVERBS MODIFYING ADVERBS
To what extent?	**To what extent?**
The solution was quite logical.	He worked very competently.
It was an extremely overgrown garden.	I am not completely finished.
The children are overly excited.	Rick's room was not entirely clean yet.

Adverbs as Parts of Verbs Some verbs require an adverb to complete their meaning. Adverbs used this way are considered part of the verb. An adverb functioning as part of a verb does not answer the usual questions for adverbs.

EXAMPLES   The tractor **backed up** alongside the field.

Please **point out** which band instrument is yours.

Jennifer had to **run out** at lunch to pick up her car.

See Practice 1.3E

Nouns Functioning as Adverbs

Several nouns can function as adverbs that answer the questions *Where?* or *When?* Some of these words are *home, yesterday, today, tomorrow, mornings, afternoons, evenings, nights, week, month,* and *year.*

NOUNS USED AS ADVERBS	
NOUNS	AS ADVERBS
Evenings are restful times.	I work evenings.
My home is miles from here.	Let's head home.
Yesterday was a lovely day.	I saw them yesterday at the show.

Adverb or Adjective?

Adverbs usually have different forms from adjectives and thus are easily identified. Many adverbs are formed by the addition of -*ly* to an adjective.

ADJECTIVES   Our professor looked **pensive**.

Teri walked through the **open** door.

ADVERBS   The professor looked at her notes **pensively**.

We discussed the matter **openly**.

Some adjectives, however, also end in -*ly*. Therefore, you cannot assume that every word ending in -*ly* is an adverb.

ADJECTIVES   an **ugly** scene

a **nightly** bloom

a **lovely** shell

curly edges

Some adjectives and adverbs share the same form. You can determine the part of speech of such words by checking their function in the sentence. An adverb will modify a verb, adjective, or adverb; an adjective will modify a noun or pronoun.

ADVERB   The concert ran **late**.

ADJECTIVE   We enjoyed the **late** dinners in Spain.

ADVERB   The fish swam **straight** through the channel.

See Practice 1.3F   ADJECTIVE   The path was **straight**.

PRACTICE 1.3E > **Recognizing Adverbs**

Read each sentence. Then, write the adverb in each sentence.

EXAMPLE   The snow completely covered our car.

ANSWER   *completely*

1. The play began promptly.

2. A new mall is nearby.

3. Let's stop here and rest.

4. I opened the door cautiously.

5. The woman put her packages down.

6. We threw away our trash.

7. That was an extremely funny comedian.

8. Juan was somewhat tired after the game.

9. Hardly any students bought tickets for the play.

10. The actor was extraordinarily talented.

PRACTICE 1.3F > **Identifying Adverbs and the Words They Modify**

Read each sentence. Then, write the adverb in each sentence and the word it modifies.

EXAMPLE   I am going home.

ANSWER   *home, going*

11. The baseball season starts tomorrow.

12. Sarah took the test early.

13. Who finished first in the contest?

14. My grandparents arrived yesterday from Florida.

15. I ran fast and scored a run.

16. Please go downstairs and feed the cat.

17. We arrived later than our friends.

18. My dad works nights at the factory.

19. We have only one chance to pass the test.

20. Tim worked hard to finish his project.

SPEAKING APPLICATION

Take turns with a partner. Tell about something that you enjoy doing. Your partner should name adverbs that you use to describe where, when, in what way, and to what extent you do the activity.

WRITING APPLICATION

Use sentence 12 as a model to write three sentences of your own. Replace the adverb in sentence 12 with other adverbs.

1.4 Prepositions, Conjunctions, and Interjections

Prepositions and conjunctions function in sentences as connectors. **Prepositions** express relationships between words or ideas, whereas **conjunctions** join words, groups of words, or even entire sentences. **Interjections** function by themselves and are independent of other words in a sentence.

Prepositions and Prepositional Phrases

Prepositions make it possible to show relationships between words. The relationships may involve, for example, location, direction, time, cause, or possession. A preposition may consist of one word or multiple words. (See the chart on the next page.)

> **A preposition** relates the noun or pronoun that appears with it to another word in the sentence.

RULE 1.4.1

Notice how the prepositions below, highlighted in pink, relate to the words highlighted in yellow.

LOCATION Inventions **are made** **around** the **world**.

TIME Some inventions **last** **for** **centuries**.

CAUSE Tina is **late** **because of** the **train**.

> **A prepositional phrase** is a group of words that includes a preposition and a noun or pronoun.

RULE 1.4.2

The noun or pronoun with a preposition is called the **object of the preposition.** Objects may have one or more modifiers. A prepositional phrase may also have more than one object. In the example below, the objects of the prepositions are highlighted in blue, and the prepositions are in pink.

EXAMPLE Eric and Alisha applied **for** **jobs** **on** **Tuesday**.

PREPOSITIONS			
aboard	before	in front of	over
about	behind	in place of	owing to
above	below	in regard to	past
according to	beneath	inside	prior to
across	beside	in spite of	regarding
across from	besides	instead of	round
after	between	into	since
against	beyond	in view of	through
ahead of	but	like	throughout
along	by	near	till
alongside	by means of	nearby	to
along with	concerning	next to	together with
amid	considering	of	toward
among	despite	off	under
apart from	down	on	underneath
around	during	on account of	until
aside from	except	onto	unto
as of	for	on top of	up
as	from	opposite	upon
atop	in	out	with
barring	in addition to	out of	within
because of	in back of	outside	without

See Practice 1.4A

Preposition or Adverb?
Many words may be used either as prepositions or adverbs.
Words that can function in either role include *around, before,
behind, down, in, off, on, out, over,* and *up.* If an object
accompanies the word, the word is used as a preposition.

PREPOSITION   The Machine Age developed **around** a
group of inventions .

ADVERB   My thoughts went **around and around** .

See Practice 1.4B

PRACTICE 1.4A **Identifying Prepositions and Prepositional Phrases**

Read each sentence. Then, write the prepositional phrase in each sentence, and underline the preposition.

EXAMPLE   The girls are playing in the back yard.

ANSWER   *~~In~~ the back yard* phrase

1. Most players on our team practice every day.

2. Each boy told a story about his pet.

3. Trish made a gift for Michelle.

4. Our neighbors have friends from many different states.

5. The computer I saw in the catalog was the newest model.

6. The main difference between my brother and me is that I am taller.

7. My aunt and uncle live above a restaurant.

8. Sanjay painted a picture of a beach.

9. We climbed aboard the sailboat.

10. We visited their fishing cabin at the lake.

PRACTICE 1.4B **Distinguishing Between Prepositions and Adverbs**

Read each sentence. Then, label each underlined word as a *preposition* or an *adverb*.

EXAMPLE   We planted flowers <u>around</u> the fountain.

ANSWER   *preposition*

11. I like to work <u>outside</u>. *its telling where you are*

12. Palm trees swayed <u>outside</u> the hotel.

13. Two eager fans ran <u>past</u> the guard.

14. As we cheered, the runners raced <u>past</u>.

15. Skyscrapers towered <u>above</u>.

16. The jet roared <u>above</u> the clouds.

17. We put our boots <u>on</u> quickly.

18. A small boat floated <u>on</u> the lake.

19. The catcher crouched <u>behind</u> home plate.

20. Carla went home and left her sweater <u>behind</u>.

SPEAKING APPLICATION

Take turns with a partner. Describe the locations of different objects in the room. Your partner should listen for and identify three prepositional phrases that you use and the preposition in each phrase.

WRITING APPLICATION

Write a sentence using the word *off* as a preposition. Then, write another sentence using *off* as an adverb.

Conjunctions

There are three main kinds of conjunctions: **coordinating, correlative,** and **subordinating.** Sometimes a type of adverb, the **conjunctive adverb,** is also considered a conjunction.

> A **conjunction** is a word used to connect other words or groups of words.

Coordinating Conjunctions The seven coordinating conjunctions are used to connect similar parts of speech or groups of words of equal grammatical weight.

COORDINATING CONJUNCTIONS						
and	but	for	nor	or	so	yet

EXAMPLES   My sister **and** brother ran the program.

Bob left early, **so** I left with him.

Correlative Conjunctions The five paired correlative conjunctions join elements of equal grammatical weight.

CORRELATIVE CONJUNCTIONS		
both . . . and	either . . . or	neither . . . nor
not only . . . but also	whether . . . or	

EXAMPLES   He saw **both** lions **and** tigers.

Neither John **nor** Joan came to the picnic.

I don't know **whether** to go to the movies **or** see a play.

Subordinating Conjunctions Subordinating conjunctions join two complete ideas by making one of the ideas subordinate to, or dependent upon, the other.

SUBORDINATING CONJUNCTIONS			
after	because	lest	till
although	before	now that	unless
as	even if	provided	until
as if	even though	since	when
as long as	how	so that	whenever
as much as	if	than	where
as soon as	inasmuch as	that	wherever
as though	in order that	though	while

The subordinate idea in a sentence always begins with a subordinating conjunction and makes up what is known as a subordinate clause. A subordinate clause may either follow or precede the main idea in a sentence.

EXAMPLES   We protect the wetlands **because** they are important to the ecosystem.

As soon as the volunteers arrived, the cleanup work began.

Conjunctive Adverbs Conjunctive adverbs act as transitions between complete ideas by indicating comparisons, contrasts, results, and other relationships. The chart below lists the most common conjunctive adverbs.

CONJUNCTIVE ADVERBS		
accordingly	finally	nevertheless
again	furthermore	otherwise
also	however	then
besides	indeed	therefore
consequently	moreover	thus

Punctuation With Conjunctive Adverbs Punctuation is usually required both before and after conjunctive adverbs.

EXAMPLES   The team was very successful. **Nevertheless**, they continued to practice very hard.

Sophia played several instruments well; **however**, her favorite is the piano.

I arrived late; **furthermore**, I forgot my books.

See Practice 1.4C

Interjections

Interjections express emotion. Unlike most words, they have no grammatical connection to other words in a sentence.

RULE 1.4.4

An **interjection** is a word that expresses feeling or emotion and functions independently of a sentence.

Interjections can express a variety of sentiments, such as happiness, fear, anger, pain, surprise, sorrow, exhaustion, or hesitation.

SOME COMMON INTERJECTIONS				
ah	dear	hey	ouch	well
aha	goodness	hurray	psst	whew
alas	gracious	oh	tsk	wow

EXAMPLES   **Ouch**! That machine is very hot.

Wow! This is great!

Oh! Go away.

Whew! We worked hard cleaning the mountain trail.

See Practice 1.4D

Read each sentence. Then, write the conjunction
in each sentence, and label it as *coordinating*,
correlative, *subordinating*, or *conjunctive adverb*.

EXAMPLE After walking home in the rain, we
were not only wet but also tired.

ANSWER *not only ... but also* — correlative

1. A package arrived while we were out.

2. Jake said he would be here, yet he didn't
show up.

3. The coach was kind but firm.

4. Jen likes her new school; besides, she was
ready for a change.

5. The team needs both a pitcher and an
outfielder.

6. I did my homework while they watched
television.

7. Kevin sleeps later than I do.

8. Neither Jamal nor Keisha knows where
Trina is.

9. Tran won the race; therefore, he will go to
the state track meet.

10. Class will begin as soon as the teacher
arrives.

Read each sentence. Then, write an interjection
that shows the feeling expressed in the sentence.

EXAMPLE _____! This soup is awful!

ANSWER *Eek*

11. _____, we never found the ball.

12. _____! I hurt my knee!

13. _____, isn't that Marcy over there?

14. _____! I've been hoping for a new baseball
mitt!

15. _____! That was the best concert I've ever
been to.

16. _____! I'm stuck!

17. _____, I knew I wouldn't get the part.

18. _____, I can't believe it's raining again.

19. _____! Our team won the game!

20. _____! I'm really tired!

SPEAKING APPLICATION

Take turns with a partner. Tell about
something that you did with a friend. Your
partner should name conjunctions that you
use and identify the kind of conjunction.

WRITING APPLICATION

Write three sentences using interjections.

1.5 Words as Different Parts of Speech

Words are flexible, often serving as one part of speech in one sentence and as another part of speech in another.

Identifying Parts of Speech

To *function* means "to serve in a particular capacity." The function of a word may change from one sentence to another.

> **The way a word is used in a sentence determines its part of speech.**

The word *well* has different meanings in the following sentences.

As a Noun	Our well ran dry.
As a Verb	After falling off her bicycle, tears welled in Jill's eyes.
As an Adjective	She does not feel well today.

Nouns, Pronouns, and Verbs A **noun** names a person, place, or thing. A **pronoun** stands for a noun. A **verb** shows action, condition, or existence.

The chart below reviews the definition of each part of speech.

PARTS OF SPEECH	QUESTIONS TO ASK YOURSELF	EXAMPLES
Noun	Does the word name a person, place, or thing?	Our visit to the Grand Canyon delighted Rosa.
Pronoun	Does the word stand for a noun?	They gave some to him.

PARTS OF SPEECH	QUESTIONS TO ASK YOURSELF	EXAMPLES
Verb	Does the word tell what someone or something did? Does the word link one word with another word that identifies or describes it? Does the word show that something exists?	We played baseball. The woman was a lawyer. Mother appeared happy. The family is here.

See Practice 1.5A

The Other Parts of Speech An **adjective** modifies a noun or pronoun. An **adverb** modifies a verb, an adjective, or another adverb. A **preposition** relates a noun or pronoun that appears with it to another word. A **conjunction** connects words or groups of words. An **interjection** expresses emotion.

PARTS OF SPEECH	QUESTIONS TO ASK YOURSELF	EXAMPLES
Adjective	Does the word tell *what kind, which one, how many, or how much?*	Those three apples are an unusual color.
Adverb	Does the word tell *where, when, in what way,* or *to what extent?*	Go home. Leave now. Drive very slowly. I am thoroughly tired.
Preposition	Is the word part of a phrase that includes a noun or pronoun?	Near our house, the carnival was in full swing.
Conjunction	Does the word connect other words in the sentence or connect clauses?	Both you and I will go because they need more people; besides, it will be fun.
Interjection	Does the word express feeling or emotion and function independently of the sentence?	Hey, give me that! Wow! That's amazing!

See Practice 1.5B

PRACTICE 1.5A > **Identifying Nouns, Pronouns, and Verbs**

Read each sentence. Then, label the underlined word in each sentence as a *noun*, *pronoun*, or *verb*.

EXAMPLE   <u>We</u> visited a sheep ranch.

ANSWER   *pronoun*

1. Our school's new library is a big <u>hit</u> with students.
2. Lightning <u>hit</u> the tree and caused a fire.
3. Jared asked for a computer for <u>his</u> birthday.
4. <u>She</u> asked the teacher a question.
5. I hope no one <u>spots</u> the stain on my shirt.
6. The puppies have <u>spots</u> on their backs.
7. Did you see <u>our</u> car in the parking lot?
8. The team is practicing at the <u>park</u>.
9. Mom <u>parks</u> her car in the driveway.
10. Will <u>you</u> help Sean take out the trash?

PRACTICE 1.5B > **Recognizing All the Parts of Speech**

Read each sentence. Then, for each sentence, write the part of speech of the underlined word.

EXAMPLE   Nobody is absent today <u>but</u> Erin.

ANSWER   *preposition*

11. <u>Pedro</u> plays baseball, but I don't.
12. <u>Since</u> it's raining, let's watch a movie.
13. <u>Hey</u>, why didn't I see you at lunch?
14. I lost my notebook yesterday, <u>and</u> it's been missing ever since.
15. I <u>ate</u> a late dinner and went to bed.
16. William arrived <u>late</u> again.
17. <u>After</u> school we played basketball.
18. Fireworks are set off <u>after</u> a player hits a home run.
19. We have an <u>early</u> test tomorrow.
20. Did <u>you</u> find your locker yet?

SPEAKING APPLICATION

Take turns with a partner. Tell about something that you did earlier today. Your partner should identify the nouns, pronouns, and verbs that you use.

WRITING APPLICATION

Write the part of speech of each word in sentence 18.

BASIC SENTENCE PARTS

Use strong subjects and verbs in your writing, and use vivid complements to add description.

WRITE GUY *Jeff Anderson, M.Ed.*

WHAT DO YOU NOTICE?

Uncover different sentence parts as you zoom in on this sentence from the essay "Single Room, Earth View" by Sally Ride.

MENTOR TEXT

> Spectacular as the view is from 200 miles up, the Earth is not the awe-inspiring "blue marble" made famous by the photos from the moon.

Now, ask yourself the following questions:

- What is the simple subject of the sentence?
- Which noun in the sentence further explains the word *Earth*?

Earth is the simple subject of the sentence. A complement is a group of words that helps complete the meaning of a sentence. The noun *marble* helps explain what the Earth is *not* like and serves as a complement called a predicate nominative, which is a noun or pronoun that gives more detail about the subject.

Grammar for Writers Think of complements as adding details that perfect, or complement, your sentences. Use complements to add clarity and variety to your writing.

My sentence gets a compliment, but I don't?

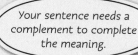

Your sentence needs a complement to complete the meaning.

2.1 Subjects and Predicates

A **sentence** is a group of words that expresses a complete unit of thought. *The cereal in the bowl* is not a complete unit of thought because you probably wonder what the writer wanted to say about the cereal. *The cereal in the bowl is soggy,* however, does express a complete unit of thought.

2.1.1

A sentence is a group of words that has two main parts: a complete subject and a complete predicate. Together, these parts express a complete thought or paint a complete picture.

The **complete subject** contains a noun, pronoun, or group of words acting as a noun, plus its modifiers. These words tell *who* or *what* the sentence is about. The **complete predicate** consists of the verb or verb phrase, plus its modifiers. These words tell what the complete subject is or does.

COMPLETE SUBJECTS	COMPLETE PREDICATES
Snakes	slither.
A bell-clanging streetcar	moved through the turn.
Wood or cellulose	makes a delicious meal for a termite.
The candidate's approach to fiscal problems	impressed the voters attending the rally.

Sometimes, part of the predicate precedes the complete subject.

EXAMPLES

At midnight , **the cluster of spiders**
complete   complete subject

spun webs .
predicate

Yesterday **my social studies class**
complete   complete subject

visited a Wild West exhibit .
predicate

See Practice 2.1A

Simple Subjects and Predicates

The most essential parts of a sentence are the **simple subject** and the **simple predicate.** These words tell you the basics of what you need to know about the topic of the sentence. All of the other words in the sentence give you information about the simple subject and simple predicate.

> The **simple subject** is the essential noun, pronoun, or group of words that acts as a noun in a complete subject. The **simple predicate** is the essential verb or verb phrase in a complete predicate.

2.1.2 RULE

Note: When sentences are discussed in this chapter, the term *subject* will refer to a simple subject, and the term *verb* will refer to a simple predicate.

SUBJECTS	VERBS
Small mice	fit nicely into coat pockets.
Many horror films	have used bugs to terrifying effect.
Jugs of sweet cider	were covering the table.
A colorful flag	hung above the porch.
The writer's children	published all of his early poetry.
Studies of insects	have certainly revealed much about their behavior.

In the last example, the simple subject is *studies,* not *insects; insects* is the object of the preposition *of.* Objects of prepositions never function as simple subjects. In this same example, the simple predicate is a verb phrase. In addition, the word *certainly* is not part of the simple predicate because it does not provide essential information.

See Practice 2.1B

PRACTICE 2.1A > Recognizing Complete Subjects and Predicates

Read each sentence. Then, write whether the underlined word or group of words in each sentence is the *complete subject* or the *complete predicate*.

EXAMPLE   The shoes with the green laces <u>are mine</u>.

ANSWER   *complete predicate*

1. <u>Roses</u> are the most popular flower.

2. <u>The first talent show performer</u> was really funny.

3. Most of the dogs on our block <u>are friendly</u>.

4. The person who collects the most newspapers <u>wins</u>.

5. The coaches <u>expect another tough game from Harrison High</u>.

6. <u>The first spelling bee champion from our school</u> was a sophomore.

7. <u>Thomas Delgado</u> used to be a teacher here.

8. <u>Many wild animals</u> become dependent on food provided by people.

9. We <u>may need to call the librarian for help</u>.

10. Who <u>sells tickets to the play</u>?

PRACTICE 2.1B > Identifying Simple Subjects and Predicates

Read each sentence. The complete subject is underlined. The rest of the sentence is the complete predicate. Write the simple subject and simple predicate in each sentence.

EXAMPLE   <u>That tall boy in math class</u> is on the basketball team.

ANSWER   *boy, is*

11. <u>That book that we both liked</u> was made into a movie.

12. <u>Kyle</u> nominated me for class president.

13. <u>The second Saturday of each month</u> is when our club meets.

14. <u>The speaker</u> arrived on time.

15. <u>Coyotes</u> often howl from the hilltops.

16. <u>Exchange students from all over the world</u> have come to our school.

17. <u>Our huge, fancy tower of blocks</u> fell.

18. <u>Pies</u> are popular Thanksgiving desserts.

19. <u>Several teachers from my school</u> are going to New York City.

20. <u>The quiet stranger from abroad</u> participated in the fundraiser.

SPEAKING APPLICATION

Take turns with a partner. Tell about something interesting that happened to you. Your partner should tell the complete subject and complete predicate in each of your sentences.

WRITING APPLICATION

Write a paragraph about a favorite place. In each sentence, underline the simple subject, and double underline the simple predicate.

Fragments

A **fragment** is a group of words that does not contain either a complete subject or a complete predicate, or both. Fragments are usually not used in formal writing. You can correct a fragment by adding the parts needed to complete the thought.

> A **fragment** is a group of words that lacks a subject or a predicate, or both. It does not express a complete unit of thought.

FRAGMENTS	COMPLETE SENTENCES
the basket of apples (complete predicate missing)	The basket of apples was eaten quickly. (complete predicate added)
thrive in the rain forests (complete subject missing)	Tarantulas thrive in the rain forests. (complete subject added)
from the barn (complete subject and predicate missing)	Flies from the barn swarmed into the house. (subject and complete predicate added)

In conversations, fragments usually do not present a problem because tone of voice, gestures, and facial expressions can add the missing information. A reader, however, cannot ask a writer for clarification.

Fragments are sometimes acceptable in writing that represents speech, such as the dialogue in a play or short story. Fragments are also sometimes acceptable in elliptical sentences.

> An **elliptical sentence** is one in which the missing word or words can be easily understood.

EXAMPLES   Until later.

Why such a sad face?

Don't be late!

Locating Subjects and Verbs

To avoid writing a fragment, look for the subject and verb in a sentence. To find the subject, ask, "Which word tells *what* or *who* this sentence is about?" Once you have the answer (the subject), then ask, "What does the subject do?" or "What is being done to the subject?" This will help you locate the verb.

In some sentences, it's easier to find the verb first. In this case, ask, "Which word states the action or condition in this sentence?" This question should help you locate the verb. Then ask, "*Who* or *what* is involved in the action of the verb?" The resulting word or words will be the subject.

EXAMPLE   Grasshoppers often feed on corn and grass.

To find the subject first, ask, "Which word or words tell what or whom this sentence is about?"

ANSWER   Grasshoppers (*Grasshoppers* is the subject.)

Then ask, "What do grasshoppers do?"

ANSWER   feed (*Feed* is the verb.)

To find the verb first, ask, "Which word or words state the action or condition in the sentence?"

ANSWER   feed (*Feed* states the action, so it is the verb.)

Then ask, "Who or what feeds?"

ANSWER   Grasshoppers (*Grasshoppers* is the subject.)

To easily locate the subject and verb, mentally cross out any adjectives, adverbs, and prepositional phrases you see. These words add information, but they are usually less important than the simple subject and verb.

EXAMPLE   ~~Green~~ **technology** **should grow** ~~rapidly in~~
              simple subject   verb phrase
       ~~the next ten years.~~

Sentences With More Than One Subject or Verb

Some sentences contain a **compound subject** or a **compound verb,** or a subject or verb with more than one part.

> A **compound subject** consists of two or more subjects. These subjects may be joined by a conjunction such as *and* or *or*.

RULE 2.1.5

EXAMPLES   The **campers** and **hikers** repelled the mosquitoes with insect spray.

Flies, **gnats**, and **bees** are always buzzing around the garbage can.

Neither the **horse** nor the **driver** looked tired.

> A **compound verb** consists of two or more verbs. These verbs may be joined by a conjunction such as *and, but, or,* or *nor*.

RULE 2.1.6

EXAMPLES   I neither **saw** them nor **heard** them.

Randy **left** school and **ran** to the gym.

She **sneezed** and **coughed** all day.

Some sentences contain both a compound subject and a compound verb.

EXAMPLES   My **father** and **brother** **swatted** at the fly but **smacked** each other in the head instead.

The **dog** and **cat** **eyed** each other, **circled** warily, and then **advanced** into combat.

See Practice 2.1C
See Practice 2.1D

PRACTICE 2.1C > Locating Subjects and Verbs

Read each sentence. Then, write the subject and the verb in each sentence. Underline the subject.

EXAMPLE A fifteen-year-old boy from our state entered and won the poetry contest.

ANSWER *boy; entered, won*

1. The curious horse in the stable sniffed and nibbled at Jan's popcorn.

2. Will and Ken showed me how to solve the problem.

3. The beautiful geese were honking as they flew overhead.

4. The girl and boy with the best voices got the solo parts.

5. The classrooms on the first floor are all dark.

6. The frightened fawn ran when we approached.

7. The tour guide lost his boot in the deep snow.

8. All the musicians in the concert arrived and began rehearsing.

9. The new player from Hilton High hit a home run and stole a base.

10. Stargazers in our club saw several shooting stars.

PRACTICE 2.1D > Fixing Sentence Errors

Read each fragment. Then, use each fragment in a sentence.

EXAMPLE swimming in the lake

ANSWER *Josie went swimming in the lake.*

11. to meet the president

12. which my uncle brought from Turkey

13. who left

14. the student

15. likes getting up early in the morning

16. went to the park

17. the taste of fresh-baked bread

18. the most frightening thing about earthquakes

19. playing my favorite song

20. our car

SPEAKING APPLICATION

Take turns with a partner. Tell about your favorite possessions. Your partner should name the subject and verb in each of your sentences.

WRITING APPLICATION

Write three original fragments. Exchange papers with a partner. Your partner should turn your fragments into sentences.

2.2 Hard-to-Find Subjects

While most sentences have subjects that are easy to find, some present a challenge.

Subjects in Declarative Sentences Beginning With *Here* or *There*

When the word *here* or *there* begins a declarative sentence, it is often mistaken for the subject.

> ***Here*** and ***there*** are never the subject of a sentence.

Here and *there* are usually adverbs that modify the verb by pointing out *where* something is located. However, *there* may occasionally begin a sentence simply as an introductory word.

In some sentences beginning with *here* or *there*, the subject appears before the verb. However, many sentences beginning with *here* or *there* are **inverted.** In an inverted sentence, the subject follows the verb. If you rearrange such a sentence in subject–verb order, you can identify the subject more easily.

INVERTED   There **are** the **buses**. (verb–subject order)

REARRANGED   The **buses are** there. (subject–verb order)

SENTENCES BEGINNING WITH *HERE* OR *THERE*	SENTENCES REARRANGED IN SUBJECT–VERB ORDER
There are the downtown buildings.	The downtown buildings are there.
Here is the ticket for your trip.	The ticket for your trip is here.
There is money in the cash register.	Money is in the cash register there.

> In some declarative sentences, the subject is placed after the verb in order to give the subject greater emphasis.

Because most sentences are written in subject–verb order, changing that order makes readers stop and think. Inverted sentences often begin with prepositional phrases.

SENTENCES INVERTED FOR EMPHASIS	SENTENCES REARRANGED IN SUBJECT–VERB ORDER
Toward the elevated train rushed the evening commuters .	The evening commuters rushed toward the elevated train.
Around the corner careened the speeding car .	The speeding car careened around the corner.

Subjects in Interrogative Sentences

Some interrogative sentences use subject–verb order. Often, however, the word order of an interrogative sentence is verb–subject.

EXAMPLES   Which **car** **gets** the best mileage?
(subject–verb order)

Where **are** **we** going?
(verb–subject order)

In interrogative sentences, the subject often follows the verb.

An inverted interrogative sentence can begin with an action verb, a helping verb, or one of the following words: *how, what, when, where, which, who, whose,* or *why.* Some interrogative sentences divide the helping verb from the main verb. To help locate the subject, mentally rearrange the sentence into subject–verb order.

INTERROGATIVE SENTENCES	REARRANGED IN SUBJECT–VERB ORDER
Is the City Zoo open in the morning?	The City Zoo is open in the morning.
Do they own that house?	They do own that house.
Where will the dance be held ?	The dance will be held where?

Subjects in Imperative Sentences

The subject of an imperative sentence is usually implied rather than specifically stated.

> In imperative sentences, the subject is understood to be *you*.

RULE 2.2.4

IMPERATIVE SENTENCES	SENTENCES WITH *YOU* ADDED
First, visit the Sears Tower.	First, [you] visit the Sears Tower.
After the tour, come home right away.	After the tour, [you] come home right away.
Mia, show me the map.	Mia, [you] show me the map.

In the last example, the name of the person being addressed, *Mia*, is not the subject of the imperative sentence. Instead, the subject is still understood to be *you*.

Subjects in Exclamatory Sentences

In some **exclamatory sentences,** the subject appears before the verb. In others, the verb appears first. To find the subject, rearrange the sentence in subject–verb order.

> In exclamatory sentences, the subject often appears after the verb, or it may be understood.

RULE 2.2.5

EXAMPLES   What **does he know**!
(He does know what.)

Go now!
(Subject understood: **[You] go** now!)

In other exclamatory sentences, both the subject and verb may be unstated.

EXAMPLES   Fire! ([**You watch** out for the] fire!)

See Practice 2.2A
See Practice 2.2B

Snakes! ([**I see**] snakes!)

PRACTICE 2.2A > **Identifying Hard-to-Find Subjects**

Read each sentence. Then, write the subject of each sentence.

EXAMPLE   How far does this path go?

ANSWER   *path*

1. Do you know the phone number of the restaurant?
2. Has your teacher asked you to turn in your report?
3. There is the new principal.
4. Here are the documents you asked for.
5. How were the pyramids built?
6. There has never been a hotter summer.
7. What instrument do you play in the band?
8. There are few places available to rent at this time of year.
9. Here comes the nurse with your medicine.
10. How fast was the train traveling?

PRACTICE 2.2B > **Locating Hard-to-Find Verbs**

Read each sentence. Then, write the verb in each sentence.

EXAMPLE   Eat at the restaurant I told you about.

ANSWER   *Eat*

11. Do you believe what you're seeing?
12. How could you do such a thing!
13. In the woods are many brooks and streams.
14. Before the game, tell me about yourself.
15. Leave us alone, please.
16. Is that a tarantula?
17. Hey, give that back!
18. Where is my hat?
19. Can you tell me where the elevator is?
20. Come inside right away.

SPEAKING APPLICATION

With a partner, take turns asking questions. Your partner should name the subject in each of your responses.

WRITING APPLICATION

Write three exclamatory sentences. Underline the subject, and double underline the verb in each sentence.

2.3 Complements

Some sentences are complete with just a subject and a verb or with a subject, verb, and modifiers: *The crowd cheered.* Other sentences need more information to be complete.

The meaning of many sentences, however, depends on additional words that add information to the subject and verb. For example, although *The satellite continually sends* has a subject and verb, it is an incomplete sentence. To complete the meaning of the predicate—in this case, to tell *what* a satellite sends—a writer must add a **complement.**

> A **complement** is a word or group of words that completes the meaning of the predicate of a sentence.

RULE 2.3.1

There are five kinds of complements in English: **direct objects, indirect objects, object complements, predicate nominatives,** and **predicate adjectives.** The first three occur in sentences that have transitive verbs. The last two are often called **subject complements.** Subject complements are found only with linking verbs. (See Chapter 1 for more information about action and linking verbs.)

Direct Objects

Direct objects are the most common of the five types of complements. They complete the meaning of action verbs by telling *who* or *what* receives the action.

> A **direct object** is a noun, pronoun, or group of words acting as a noun that receives the action of a transitive verb.

RULE 2.3.2

EXAMPLES   I visited the Air and Space Museum .
                                    direct object

Sticks and leaves clogged the gutters .
                                    direct object

Direct Objects and Action Verbs The direct object answers the question *Whom?* or *What?* about the action verb. If you cannot answer the question *Whom?* or *What?* the verb may be intransitive, and there is no direct object in the sentence.

EXAMPLES

Owls **can see** in the dark.
(Ask, "Owls can see *what*?" No answer; the verb is intransitive.)

The satellite **spun** beyond the atmosphere.
(Ask, "The satellite spun *what*?" No answer; the verb is intransitive.)

In some inverted questions, the direct object may appear before the verb. To find the direct object easily, rearrange inverted questions in subject–verb order.

INVERTED QUESTION

Which **books** **did** **they** **read**?
　　　direct object

REARRANGED IN SUBJECT– VERB ORDER

They **did read** which **books**?
　　　　　　　　　　　direct object

Some sentences have more than one direct object, known as a **compound direct object**. If a sentence contains a compound direct object, asking *Whom?* or *What?* after the action verb will yield two or more answers.

EXAMPLES

The astronauts **wore** **helmets** and
　　　　　　　　　　direct object
spacesuits.
direct object

The band **has played** **fairs** and **concerts**
　　　　　　　　　direct object　　direct object
over the last four months.

In the last example, *months* is the object of the preposition *over*. The object of a preposition is never a direct object.

Indirect Objects

Indirect objects appear only in sentences that contain transitive verbs and direct objects. Indirect objects are common with such verbs as *ask, bring, buy, give, lend, make, show, teach, tell,* and *write.* Some sentences may contain a compound indirect object.

> An **indirect object** is a noun or pronoun that appears with a direct object. It often names the person or thing that something is given to or done for.

2.3.4 | RULE

EXAMPLES **NASA gave** the **astronauts** a course
indirect object
correction .
direct object

I showed my **mom** and **dad** the tennis **poster** .
compound indirect object   direct object

To locate an indirect object, make sure the sentence contains a direct object. Then, ask one of these questions after the verb and direct object: *To* or *for whom?* or *To* or *for what?*

EXAMPLES The **teacher taught** our **class music** .
(The teacher taught music *to whom*? ANSWER: our class)

We made our **dog** a **raincoat** .
(Made a raincoat *for what*? ANSWER: our dog)

An indirect object almost always appears between the verb and the direct object. In a sentence with subject–verb order, the indirect object never follows the direct object, nor will it ever be the object of the preposition *to* or *for.*

EXAMPLES **Paul sent** the **poster** to **me** .
direct object object of preposition

Paul sent me the **poster** .
indirect object   direct object

Paul gave Doug a **review** of the movie.
indirect object direct object

See Practice 2.3A

Object Complements

While an indirect object almost always comes *before* a direct object, an **object complement** almost always *follows* a direct object. The object complement completes the meaning of the direct object.

RULE 2.3.5

> An **object complement** is an adjective or noun that appears with a direct object and describes or renames it.

A sentence that contains an object complement may seem to have two direct objects. However, object complements occur only with such verbs as *appoint, call, consider, declare, elect, judge, label, make, name, select,* and *think.* The words *to be* are often understood before an object complement.

EXAMPLES   The **organizers** of the dance **declared** **it**
           direct object
successful .
object complement

The **president** **appointed** **him** **ambassador**
                          direct object object complement
to China.

I **consider** **Dave** a strong **swimmer** and a
                  direct object   object complement
graceful **diver** .
         object complement

Subject Complements

Linking verbs require **subject complements** to complete their meaning.

RULE 2.3.6

> A **subject complement** is a noun, pronoun, or adjective that appears with a linking verb and gives more information about the subject.

There are two kinds of subject complements: **predicate nominatives** and **predicate adjectives.**

Predicate Nominatives

The **predicate nominative** refers to the same person, place, or thing as the subject of the sentence.

> A **predicate nominative** is a noun or pronoun that appears with a linking verb and renames, identifies, or explains the subject. Some sentences may contain a compound predicate nominative.

RULE 2.3.7

EXAMPLES **Ann Pace** **is** a **scientist** with NASA.
predicate nominative

The **winner** **will be** **you**.
predicate nominative

John Glenn **was** a former **senator** and former **astronaut**.
compound predicate nominative

Predicate Adjectives

A **predicate adjective** is an adjective that appears with a linking verb. It describes the subject in much the same way that an adjective modifies a noun or pronoun. Some sentences may contain a compound predicate adjective.

> A **predicate adjective** is an adjective that appears with a linking verb and describes the subject of the sentence.

RULE 2.3.8

EXAMPLES Your **reasoning** **seems** **logical**.
predicate adjective

The **swimmer** **was** **fast**.
predicate adjective

The **storm** **sounded** **loud** and **thunderous**.
compound predicate adjective

The **uniforms** **are** **green** and **white**.
compound predicate adjective

See Practice 2.3B

PRACTICE 2.3A > Identifying Direct and
Indirect Objects

Read each sentence. Then, write whether the
underlined word or words in each sentence are a
direct object or an *indirect object*.

EXAMPLE   Please fill this <u>pitcher</u>.

ANSWER   *direct object*

1. Which <u>books</u> and <u>magazines</u> do you read?

2. My teammates gave <u>me</u> a party.

3. The principal gave <u>us</u> a lecture on safety.

4. They all attended <u>the ceremony</u> and <u>the party</u>.

5. I wrote <u>my grandparents</u> and <u>my uncle</u> a letter.

6. Who can send <u>invitations</u> for the party?

7. Tina gave <u>the teacher</u> a note from her doctor.

8. The school will send <u>our parents</u> our grades.

9. The author of that play has won an <u>award</u>.

10. Too little exercise can cause <u>illness</u>.

PRACTICE 2.3B > Locating Object and Subject
Complements

Read each sentence. Then, write the complement
in each sentence, and label it as an *object
complement* or a *subject complement*.

EXAMPLE   The victory left us joyful.

ANSWER   *joyful* — object complement

11. That has always been my favorite song.

12. The tea made me sleepy.

13. Everest is the mountain to climb.

14. Caryn thinks tennis and baseball are the hardest sports.

15. Ed became a teacher because he likes working with children.

16. The mayor appointed Mr. Zaragosa constable.

17. The principal found the student believable.

18. We call our lake cabin "The Castle."

19. The elderly actor is still a fan favorite.

20. My grandmother's special dish is beef stew.

SPEAKING APPLICATION

**Take turns with a partner. Tell about a family
event. Your partner should name the direct
object and indirect object, if any, in each of
your sentences.**

WRITING APPLICATION

**Use sentences 11 and 12 as models to write
sentences of your own. Underline and label the
complement in each sentence.**

CHAPTER 3

PHRASES *and* CLAUSES

Use phrases and clauses to make your sentences more descriptive and dynamic.

WRITE GUY *Jeff Anderson, M.Ed.*

WHAT DO YOU NOTICE?

Seek out phrases as you zoom in on these lines from the play *The Tragedy of Romeo and Juliet* by William Shakespeare.

MENTOR TEXT

> The boy gives warning something doth approach.
> What cursèd foot wanders this way tonight…?

Now, ask yourself the following questions:

- Which phrase in the sentence contains a form of a verb that functions as a noun?
- Which phrase includes a form of a verb that acts as an adjective?

The phrase *gives warning* contains the gerund *warning*. A gerund is a form of a verb that functions as a noun and ends in *-ing*. Because the phrase *gives warning* includes a gerund, it is a gerund phrase. *Cursèd* is a participle that acts as an adjective modifying the noun *foot*. A participle is a form of a verb ending in *-ing* or *-ed* that acts as an adjective. Since the phrase *cursèd foot* contains a participle, it is a participial phrase.

Grammar for Writers Phrases and clauses allow a writer to expand on meaning. See if there are sentences in your writing that could benefit from adding a phrase or clause.

Phrases get to have all the fun.

This phrase adds humor, and this one adds suspense.

3.1 Phrases

When one adjective or adverb cannot convey enough information, a phrase can contribute more detail to a sentence. A **phrase** is a group of words that does not include a subject and verb and cannot stand alone as a sentence.

There are several kinds of phrases, including **prepositional phrases, appositive phrases, participial phrases, gerund phrases,** and **infinitive phrases.**

Prepositional Phrases

A **prepositional phrase** consists of a preposition and a noun or pronoun, called the object of the preposition. *Over their heads, until dark,* and *after the baseball game* are all prepositional phrases. Prepositional phrases often modify other words by functioning as adjectives or adverbs.

Sometimes, a single prepositional phrase may include two or more objects joined by a conjunction.

EXAMPLES
between the **window** and the **wall**
preposition   object   object

with the **wind** and the freezing **rain**
preposition   object   object

beside the underground **stream** and **rocks**
preposition   object   object

See Practice 3.1A

Adjectival Phrases
A prepositional phrase that acts as an adjective is called an **adjectival phrase.**

RULE 3.1.1

An **adjectival phrase** is a prepositional phrase that modifies a noun or pronoun by telling *what kind* or *which one*.

ADJECTIVES	ADJECTIVAL PHRASES
A beautiful painting hung in the palace.	A painting of great beauty hung in the palace. *(What kind of painting?)*
Mary had a paperbag lunch.	Mary had lunch from a paperbag. *(What kind of lunch?)*

Like one-word adjectives, adjectival phrases can modify subjects, direct objects, indirect objects, or predicate nominatives.

MODIFYING
A SUBJECT

The mansion **across the road** has been abandoned.

MODIFYING
A DIRECT OBJECT

Let's take a picture **of the Eiffel Tower**.

MODIFYING AN
INDIRECT OBJECT

I gave the people **on the bus** a tour.

MODIFYING
A PREDICATE
NOMINATIVE

France is a country **with many charms**.

A sentence may contain two or more **adjectival phrases.** In some cases, one phrase may modify the preceding phrase. In others, two phrases may modify the same word.

EXAMPLES

MODIFIES   MODIFIES

We bought tickets **for the trip** **to Paris**.

MODIFIES

The painting **of the zoo** **in the museum** is old.

Adverbial Phrases

> An **adverbial phrase** is a prepositional phrase that modifies a verb, an adjective, or an adverb by pointing out *where, why, when, in what way,* or *to what extent.*

ADVERBS	ADVERBIAL PHRASES
She ran swiftly. (Ran *in what way?*)	She ran with speed.
I was frightened then. (Frightened *when?*)	I was frightened at the time.
The birds flew overhead. (Flew *where?*)	The birds flew over our house.

Adverbial phrases can modify verbs, adjectives, or adverbs.

MODIFYING
A VERB

The ball rolled **across the floor** .

MODIFYING
AN ADJECTIVE

Charlie was annoyed **beyond belief** .

MODIFYING
AN ADVERB

He buried the thought deep **in his mind** .

An adverbial phrase may either follow the word it modifies or be located elsewhere in the sentence. Often, two adverbs in different parts of a sentence can modify the same word.

MODIFIES

EXAMPLES

A village flooded **during the storm** .

MODIFIES

During the storm , a village flooded.

MODIFIES   MODIFIES

After dinner we all gathered **in the living room** .

See Practice 3.1B

PRACTICE 3.1A ► Identifying Prepositional Phrases

Read each sentence. Write the prepositional phrase in each sentence, and underline the preposition.

EXAMPLE   The flowering plants in the front yard need water.

ANSWER   *in the front yard*

1. Only one of us can play the guitar.
2. Several houses on our street have pools.
3. Each student will write a story about a different city.
4. My mother collects teapots from different places.
5. The dress in the shop window is very pretty.
6. There is a difference between right and wrong.
7. Someone just sold the house down the street.
8. Emma made a statue of a bird.
9. The top of the wall is concrete.
10. Their house on the beach is amazing.

PRACTICE 3.1B ► Identifying Adjectival and Adverbial Phrases

Read each sentence. Write the adjectival or adverbial phrase. Then, identify each phrase as *adjectival* or *adverbial*.

EXAMPLE   The price of the guitar was much too high.

ANSWER   *of the guitar* — adjectival

11. You can put that box of magazines down here.
12. The house on the corner is haunted.
13. The shapes of the objects are very different.
14. This coupon is valid for another year.
15. Did you close the window in the bedroom?
16. You deserve a vacation for all the hours that you've worked.
17. We arrived at the theater late.
18. I enjoyed your story about your vacation.
19. Something moved down the hall.
20. We sometimes drive far beyond the city limits.

SPEAKING APPLICATION

Take turns with a partner. Describe the classroom. Your partner should listen for and identify three prepositions that you use.

WRITING APPLICATION

Using sentences 11, 14, and 18 as models, write three sentences of your own. Use the same prepositions, but change the other words.

Appositives and Appositive Phrases

The term *appositive* comes from a Latin verb that means "to put near or next to."

Appositives Using **appositives** in your writing is an easy way to give additional meaning to a noun or pronoun.

RULE 3.1.3

> An **appositive** is a group of words that identifies, renames, or explains a noun or pronoun.

As the examples below show, appositives usually follow immediately after the words they explain.

EXAMPLES   Some villagers, **the old-timers**, prefer to travel the dirt roads.

The home team, **the Cougars**, won the season title.

Notice that commas are used in the examples above because these appositives are **nonessential.** In other words, the appositives could be omitted from the sentences without altering the basic meaning of the sentences.

Some appositives, however, are not set off by any punctuation because they are **essential** to the meaning of the sentence.

EXAMPLES   The artist **Monet** was a French painter.
(The appositive is essential because it identifies which specific artist.)

My brother **Hermando** is a graceful dancer.
(The appositive is essential because you might have several brothers.)

Note About Terms: Sometimes, the terms *nonrestrictive* and *restrictive* are used in place of *nonessential* and *essential.*

Appositive Phrases When an appositive is accompanied by its own modifiers, it is called an **appositive phrase.**

> An **appositive phrase** is a noun or pronoun with modifiers that adds information by identifying, renaming, or explaining a noun or pronoun.

3.1.4 RULE

Appositives and appositive phrases may follow nouns or pronouns used in almost any role within a sentence. The modifiers within an appositive phrase can be adjectives, adjective phrases, or other groups of words functioning as adjectives.

EXAMPLES Ms. James, **my English teacher**, assigned an essay.

Fred explained numismatics, **the hobby of coin collecting**.

ROLES OF APPOSITIVE PHRASES IN SENTENCES	
Identifying a Subject	Ernest Hemingway, a famous author, wrote in a terse style.
Identifying a Direct Object	The chef prepared lasagna, an Italian dish.
Identifying an Indirect Object	I brought my brother, a boy of six, a souvenir from my trip.
Identifying an Object Complement	I chose the color purple, an unusual color for a house.
Identifying a Predicate Nominative	My favorite food is cassoulet, a hearty stew.
Identifying the Object of a Preposition	Store the onions in the cellar, a cool, dry place.

Compound Appositives Appositives and appositive phrases can also be compound.

EXAMPLES The entire team—**guards**, **forwards**, and **centers**—practiced together.

All computers, **desktops** and **laptops**, are on sale this month.

I used my favorite colors, **pink**, **lavender**, and **green**, to make the quilt.

See Practice 3.1C

Grammar and Style Tip When **appositives** or **appositive phrases** are used to combine sentences, they help to eliminate unnecessary words. One way to streamline your writing is to combine sentences by using an appositive phrase.

TWO SENTENCES	COMBINED SENTENCE
Marseilles is located on the Mediterranean Sea. The city is an important French seaport.	Marseilles, an important French seaport, is located on the Mediterranean Sea.
The minuet was danced in the seventeenth century. The dance includes many intricate steps and turns.	The minuet, a seventeenth-century dance, includes many intricate steps and turns.
California is on the West Coast. It is one of our largest states.	California, one of our largest states, is on the West Coast.

Read aloud the pairs of sentences in the chart. Notice how the combined sentences, which began as two choppy sentences, include the same information. However, they flow much more smoothly once the information in both sentences is clearly linked.

See Practice 3.1D

PRACTICE 3.1C Identifying Appositives and Appositive Phrases

Read each sentence. Then, write the appositive or appositive phrase in each sentence.

EXAMPLE   Michael, my brother, is very kind.

ANSWER   *my brother*

1. Anna Maria, a new student from Nicaragua, likes science class.

2. The Hays High Steppers, our school dance team, will be holding auditions this afternoon.

3. My sister Mona deserves a second chance.

4. My friend Johnna just got a new car.

5. Our neighbor Mr. Brodie planted a new garden.

6. Her brother Kenny is learning how to play the piano.

7. Nigel, her cousin, will be attending veterinary school in the spring.

8. Her parents are sending her on a European trip, a generous gift.

9. Our teacher, Mrs. Wu, is teaching the class about gerunds.

10. She is practicing calligraphy, a form of writing.

PRACTICE 3.1D Using Appositives and Appositive Phrases to Combine Sentences

Read each pair of sentences. Then, combine the sentences using an appositive or an appositive phrase.

EXAMPLE   The book is a novel. The book is an extremely slow read.

ANSWER   *The book, a novel, is an extremely slow read.*

11. Mrs. Hughes is a reporter. Mrs. Hughes confirmed the story.

12. My favorite teacher is Mrs. Ladner. She will retire next year.

13. The mechanic drove my car into the garage. The car is a sporty model.

14. The newspaper had an ad about a part-time job. The newspaper is a big-city daily.

15. Dad's specialty is chili. It won a blue ribbon.

16. Edward ordered his favorite dinner. His favorite dinner is enchiladas.

17. The new bicycle path is near the lake. The bicycle path is four feet wide.

18. The marching band performed on the field. The marching band is made up of all seniors.

19. The centerpiece was beautiful. It was an arrangement of roses.

20. The unicorn is a mythical animal. It is a strange creature with one horn.

SPEAKING APPLICATION

Take turns with a partner. Tell about your favorite book or story. Use three appositives or appositive phrases in your sentences. Your partner should identify the appositives or appositive phrases that you use.

WRITING APPLICATION

Write two pairs of sentences. Then, combine each pair with an appositive or an appositive phrase.

Verbal Phrases

When a verb is used as a noun, an adjective, or an adverb, it is called a **verbal.** Although a verbal does not function as a verb, it retains two characteristics of verbs: It can be modified in different ways, and it can have one or more complements. A verbal with modifiers or complements is called a **verbal phrase.**

Participles

Many of the adjectives you use are actually verbals known as **participles.**

RULE 3.1.5

> A **participle** is a form of a verb that can act as an adjective.

The most common kinds of participles are **present participles** and **past participles.** These two participles can be distinguished from one another by their endings. Present participles usually end in *-ing (frightening, entertaining).* Past participles usually end in *-ed (frightened, entertained),* but many have irregular endings, such as *-t* or *-en (burnt, written).*

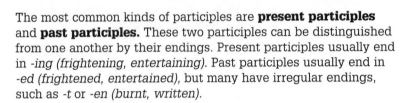

PRESENT PARTICIPLES	PAST PARTICIPLES
The limping hiker favored his aching ankle.	Confused, Nan returned to her interrupted work.

Like other adjectives, participles answer the question *What kind?* or *Which one?* about the nouns or pronouns they modify.

EXAMPLES   Irma's **shining** eyes betrayed her excitement.
(*What kind* of eyes? Answer: *shining* eyes)

The **shattered** window needs replacement.
(*Which* window? Answer: *shattered* window)

Participles may also have a **present perfect** form.

EXAMPLES   **Having decided**, Madeleine acted quickly.

Being greeted by his friends, François shakes hands all around.

Verb or Participle? Because **verbs** often have endings such as *-ing* and *-ed,* you may confuse them with **participles.** If a word ending in *-ed* or *-ing* expresses the action of the sentence, it is a verb or part of a verb phrase. If it describes a noun or pronoun, it is a participle.

> A **verb** shows an action, a condition, or the fact that something exists. A **participle** acting as an adjective modifies a noun or a pronoun.

3.1.6 RULE

ACTING AS VERBS	ACTING AS ADJECTIVES
The dog is snarling at the plumber. (What is the dog doing?)	The snarling dog attacked the plumber. (Which dog?)
The mimes delighted their audience. (What did the mimes do?)	Delighted, the audience applauded the mimes. (What kind of audience?)

See Practice 3.1E

Participial Phrases
A participle can be expanded by adding modifiers and complements to form a **participial phrase.**

> A **participial phrase** is a participle modified by an adverb or adverbial phrase or accompanied by a complement. The entire participial phrase acts as an adjective.

3.1.7 RULE

The following examples show different ways that participles may be expanded into phrases.

WITH AN ADVERB

Traveling quickly , we completed the trip in two hours.

WITH AN ADVERB PHRASE

Traveling at breakneck speed , we completed the trip in two hours.

WITH A COMPLEMENT

Avoiding stops , we completed the trip in two hours.

A participial phrase that is nonessential to the basic meaning of a sentence is set off by commas or other forms of punctuation. A participial phrase that is essential is not set off by punctuation.

NONESSENTIAL PHRASES	ESSENTIAL PHRASES
There is Craig, standing at the bus stop .	The boy standing at the bus stop is Craig.
Painted in 1497 , the mural is Leonardo's masterpiece.	The mural painted in 1497 is the one that needs the most repair.

In the first sentence on the left side of the chart above, *standing by the bus stop* merely adds information about Craig, so it is nonessential. In the sentence on the right, however, the same phrase is essential because many different boys might be in view.

In the second sentence on the left, *Painted in 1497* is an additional description of *mural,* so it is nonessential. In the sentence on the right, however, the phrase is essential because it identifies the specific mural that is being discussed.

RULE 3.1.8

> **Participial phrases** can often be used to combine information from two sentences into one.

TWO SENTENCES
We were exhausted by the climb up Mont Blanc. We rested by the side of the trail.

COMBINED
Exhausted by the climb up Mont Blanc , we rested by the side of the trail.

TWO SENTENCES
We ate sandwiches. We shared stories about our adventure.

COMBINED
Eating sandwiches , we shared stories about our adventure.

Notice how part of the verb in one sentence is changed into a participle in the combined sentence.

See Practice 3.1F

PRACTICE 3.1E > Identifying Participles

Read each sentence. Show that you understand verbals (participles) by writing whether the underlined word is a *verb* or a *participle*. If the word is a participle, write whether it is a *present* or a *past* participle. Use the word in a new sentence.

EXAMPLE   The <u>annoyed</u> customer spoke loudly to the manager.

ANSWER   *participle, past; The annoyed driver beeped his car horn.*

1. The plane has been <u>delayed</u> by snow.
2. A <u>growing</u> child needs a healthy diet.
3. You can find what you need on the <u>following</u> pages.
4. Brilliant red roses were <u>growing</u> by the fence.
5. The white car was <u>following</u> too closely.
6. Some spots in the grass are <u>becoming</u> dry.
7. This restaurant has a wide but <u>unappealing</u> menu.
8. The plane is <u>arriving</u> at gate 20.
9. The <u>painted</u> house looked wonderful.
10. The home team was <u>winning</u> at halftime.

PRACTICE 3.1F > Recognizing Participial Phrases

Read each sentence. Write the participial phrase in each sentence. Then, write *E* for *essential* or *N* for *nonessential*.

EXAMPLE   The train arriving on track 13 is two hours late.

ANSWER   *arriving on track 13 — E*

11. All the food cooked in that restaurant is homemade.
12. Found at a garage sale, the statue was in good shape.
13. Looking worn out, the football players rested.
14. Katie is the girl sweeping the floor.
15. Excited by the flashing lights, the dog began to bark.
16. The tree growing beside the back door is a maple.
17. The cat, rubbing against the chair leg, purred contentedly.
18. Our house, shaded by trees, stays cool in the summer.
19. They boarded the bus packed with tourists.
20. Having spotted a wave, the surfers began paddling.

SPEAKING APPLICATION

Show that you understand verbals (participles). Tell a partner about movies you have seen recently. Use participles as you speak. Your partner should identify each participle and tell whether it is past or present.

WRITING APPLICATION

Write three sentences, using one of the following participial phrases in each sentence: *waking up late this morning; baked in a brick oven; spotting a friend.*

Gerunds

Many nouns that end in *-ing* are actually **verbals** known as **gerunds.** Gerunds are not difficult to recognize: They always end in *-ing,* and they always function as **nouns.**

> A **gerund** is a form of a verb that ends in *-ing* and acts as a **noun.**

FUNCTIONS OF GERUNDS	
Subject	Skiing is my favorite pastime.
Direct Object	The French people make visiting France a pleasure.
Indirect Object	Mr. Mendoza's lecture gave traveling a new dimension.
Predicate Nominative	My dad's favorite activity is fishing.
Object of a Preposition	His dog showed signs of careful training.
Appositive	Brady's profession, advertising, is very competitive.

Verb, Participle, or Gerund? Words ending in *-ing* may be parts of verb phrases, participles acting as adjectives, or gerunds.

> Words ending in *-ing* that act as **nouns** are called **gerunds.** Unlike verbs ending in *-ing,* gerunds do not have helping verbs. Unlike participles ending in *-ing,* they do not act as adjectives.

VERB	Kevin is **yawning** at his desk.
PARTICIPLE	The **yawning** boy was very tired.
GERUND	**Yawning** is contagious.
VERB	My sister was **sighing**, and that upset me.
PARTICIPLE	**Sighing**, my sister upset me.
GERUND	My sister's **sighing** upset me.

Gerund Phrases Like participles, gerunds may be joined by other words to make **gerund phrases.**

> A **gerund phrase** consists of a gerund and one or more modifiers or a complement. These phrases act together as a noun.

3.1.11 RULE

GERUND PHRASES	
With Adjectives	His constant, angry ranting made the general difficult to tolerate.
With an Adverb	Answering quickly is not always a good idea.
With a Prepositional Phrase	Many places in the city prohibit walking on the grass.
With a Direct Object	Pierre was incapable of reciting the poem.
With an Indirect and a Direct Object	The algebra teacher tried giving her students praise.

Note About Gerunds and Possessive Pronouns: Always use the possessive form of a personal pronoun in front of a gerund.

INCORRECT   We never listen to **him** boasting.

CORRECT   We never listen to **his** boasting.

INCORRECT   **Them** refusing to wear helmets is dangerous.

See Practice 3.1G   CORRECT   **Their** refusing to wear helmets is dangerous.

Infinitives
The third kind of verbal is the **infinitive.** Infinitives have many different uses. They can act as nouns, adjectives, or adverbs.

> An **infinitive** is a form of a verb that generally appears with the word *to* in front of it and acts as a noun, an adjective, or an adverb.

3.1.12 RULE

The teacher asked the students **to read quietly**.

INFINITIVES USED AS NOUNS	
Subject	To understand life requires maturity and acceptance.
Direct Object	The peasants decided to rebel.
Predicate Nominative	The soldier's only hope was to surrender.
Object of a Preposition	Our flight from Paris was boarding to leave.
Appositive	You have only one choice, to stay.

Unlike gerunds, infinitives can also act as adjectives and adverbs.

INFINITIVES USED AS MODIFIERS	
Adjective	The children showed a willingness to cooperate.
Adverb	Some people were unable to fight.

Prepositional Phrase or Infinitive? Although both **prepositional phrases** and **infinitives** often begin with *to,* you can tell the difference between them by analyzing the words that follow *to.*

RULE 3.1.13

> A **prepositional phrase** always ends with a noun or pronoun that acts as the object of the preposition. An **infinitive** always ends with a verb.

PREPOSITIONAL PHRASE	INFINITIVE
The soldier listened to the command.	A general's role in the army is to command.
We took the computer to the back of the room.	Make sure to back up your computer so you won't lose data.

Note About Infinitives Without *to*: Sometimes infinitives do not include the word *to*. When an infinitive follows one of the eight verbs listed below, the *to* is generally omitted. However, it may be understood.

VERBS THAT PRECEDE INFINITIVES WITHOUT *TO*			
dare	help	make	see
hear	let	please	watch

EXAMPLES

She doesn't dare **[to] go** without permission.

Please help me **[to] leave** this place now!

Juan helped Sam **[to] extinguish** the fire.

Infinitive Phrases Infinitives also can be joined with other words to form phrases.

> An **infinitive phrase** consists of an infinitive and its modifiers, complements, or subject, all acting together as a single part of speech.

3.1.14 RULE

INFINITIVE PHRASES	
With an Adverb	Jeffrey's family likes to eat early.
With an Adverb Phrase	To skate on the ice is not easy.
With a Direct Object	He hated to leave New York City.
With an Indirect and a Direct Object	They promised to show us the pictures from their trip. direct object / Indirect object / direct object
With a Subject and a Complement	I want her to determine her own goals. subject / complement

See Practice 3.1H

PRACTICE 3.1G ▷ Identifying Gerunds and Gerund Phrases

Read each sentence. Show that you understand the function of verbals (gerunds) by writing the gerund or gerund phrase. Then, use the gerund or gerund phrase in a new sentence.

EXAMPLE   Bertha enjoys hiking.

ANSWER   *hiking; We go hiking in the mountains.*

1. Jogging is a healthy activity.

2. The criminal went to court for stealing.

3. Keith's hobby, painting, keeps him busy.

4. Running across a busy street can be dangerous.

5. Vijay loves seeing good movies.

6. Driving through Texas will be the longest part of our trip.

7. Sarah was awarded a medal after winning the race.

8. Watching airplanes take off is fun.

9. Hitting a homerun is a baseball player's goal.

10. Brushing your teeth twice daily is what most dentists recommend.

PRACTICE 3.1H ▷ Identifying Infinitives and Infinitive Phrases

Read each sentence. Show that you understand verbals (infinitives) by writing each infinitive or infinitive phrase.

EXAMPLE   The music began to play.

ANSWER   *to play*

11. I took the train to get there early.

12. Would you like to ride bikes?

13. To sleep late on Saturday is impossible in my house.

14. I helped Margaret study for the test.

15. I think it is too late to eat.

16. I need to get some sleep.

17. To read one book a month is Seth's goal.

18. He had a research report to write.

19. To win the championship was our only desire.

20. Do you like to travel?

SPEAKING APPLICATION

Show that you understand the function of verbals (gerunds). Use gerunds in sentences to tell a partner about your favorite activities. Ask your partner to identify the gerunds as you speak.

WRITING APPLICATION

Show that you understand the function of verbals (infinitives). Write three sentences that use infinitives, and read your sentences to a partner. Ask your partner to identify the infinitives as you speak.

3.2 Clauses

Every **clause** contains a subject and a verb. However, not every clause can stand by itself as a complete thought.

> A **clause** is a group of words that contains a subject and a verb.

3.2.1 RULE

Independent and Subordinate Clauses

The two basic kinds of clauses are **independent** or **main clauses** and **subordinate clauses.**

> An **independent** or **main clause** can stand by itself as a complete sentence.

3.2.2 RULE

Every sentence must contain an independent clause. The independent clause can either stand by itself or be connected to other independent or subordinate clauses.

STANDING
ALONE

Ms. Colton teaches Spanish .
independent clause

WITH
ANOTHER
INDEPENDENT
CLAUSE

Ms. Colton teaches Spanish , and
independent clause

her sister teaches French .
independent clause

WITH A
SUBORDINATE
CLAUSE

Ms. Colton teaches Spanish , **while her sister**
independent clause   subordinate clause

teaches French .

When you subordinate something, you give it less importance.

> A **subordinate clause,** although it has a subject and verb, cannot stand by itself as a complete sentence.

3.2.3 RULE

Subordinate clauses can appear before or after an independent clause in a sentence or can even split an independent clause.

LOCATIONS OF SUBORDINATE CLAUSES	
In the Middle of an Independent Clause	The woman to whom I introduced you teaches Spanish.
Preceding an Independent Clause	Unless the rain stops soon, the river will flood those houses.
Following an Independent Clause	Brian asked that he be excused.

See Practice 3.2A

Like phrases, subordinate clauses can function as adjectives, adverbs, or nouns in sentences.

Adjectival Clauses

One way to add description and detail to a sentence is by adding an **adjectival clause.**

> An **adjectival clause** is a subordinate clause that modifies a noun or pronoun in another clause by telling *what kind* or *which one.*

An adjectival clause usually begins with one of the relative pronouns: *that, which, who, whom,* or *whose.* Sometimes, it begins with a relative adverb, such as *before, since, when, where,* or *why.* Each of these words connects the clause to the word it modifies.

> An **adjectival clause** often begins with a **relative pronoun** or a **relative adverb** that links the clause to a noun or pronoun in another clause.

The adjectival clauses in the examples on the next page answer the questions *What kind?* and *Which one?* Each modifies the noun in the independent clause that comes right before the adjectival clause. Notice also that the first two clauses begin with relative pronouns and the last one begins with a relative adverb.

EXAMPLES   I finished reading the book **that you loaned me**.

We gave the story, **which we found fascinating**, a second read.

In Italy, we visited the town **where my parents were born**.

Adjectival clauses can often be used to combine information from two sentences into one. Using adjectival clauses to combine sentences can indicate the relationship between ideas as well as add detail to a sentence.

TWO SENTENCES	COMBINED SENTENCES
This statue represents a Roman soldier. He is dressed for battle.	This statue represents a Roman soldier who is dressed for battle.
My brother ran the mile in less than five minutes. He is a junior in college.	My brother, who is a junior in college, ran the mile in less than five minutes.

Essential and Nonessential Adjectival Clauses Adjectival clauses, like appositives and participial phrases, are set off by punctuation only when they are not essential to the meaning of a sentence. Commas are used to indicate information that is not essential to the meaning of the sentence. When information in an adjectival clause is essential to the sentence, no commas are used.

NONESSENTIAL CLAUSES	ESSENTIAL CLAUSES
One of Dickens's best characters is Charles Darnay, who is a main character in *A Tale of Two Cities*.	The novel that everyone must read by Monday promises to be very exciting.
Jean McCurdy, who studied hard every evening for a month, won the statewide competition.	A student who studies regularly usually finds test-taking easy.

See Practice 3.2B

PRACTICE 3.2A > **Identifying Independent and Subordinate Clauses**

Read each sentence. Identify the underlined clause in each sentence as either *independent* or *subordinate*.

EXAMPLE   <u>Gertie practices</u> soccer every day.

ANSWER   *independent*

1. <u>While Dad was sleeping</u>, we cleaned the house.

2. Just as Terri came in the door, <u>the phone rang</u>.

3. Before you say it is all right, <u>ask your mother</u>.

4. Do you know <u>when the train should arrive</u>?

5. <u>Although she was better at music</u>, she loved science.

6. We all enjoyed the dinner <u>that Dad cooked for us</u>.

7. As far as scientists can tell, <u>there is no connection between these two events</u>.

8. <u>You were always singing</u> when you were little.

9. <u>If you adjust the blinds</u>, you won't be so hot.

10. Stay with us <u>as long as you want</u>.

PRACTICE 3.2B > **Identifying Adjectival Clauses**

Read each sentence. Then, write the adjectival clause in each sentence.

EXAMPLE   This is the street where I grew up.

ANSWER   *where I grew up*

11. Anyone who knows her can tell you how smart she is.

12. The theater company, which had just come to town, put on a great show.

13. The store that was having a sale was busy.

14. My friend, who is always on time, was late today.

15. Leah, whose locker is next to mine, can't find her lucky pen.

16. The bed where the roses grow needs to be watered.

17. I finished the test before the time was up.

18. I would like a dog that I could take for walks.

19. I'm not sure why Carlos left early.

20. The dancer, who looked familiar, was my mother's friend.

SPEAKING APPLICATION

Take turns with a partner. Say sentences that have independent and subordinate clauses. Your partner should identify the clauses as either independent or subordinate.

WRITING APPLICATION

Show that you understand restrictive relative clauses (essential) and nonrestrictive relative clauses (nonessential) by writing two sentences that use either type of clause. Then, read your sentences to a partner. Ask your partner to identify the clauses as you speak.

Relative Pronouns **Relative pronouns** help link a subordinate clause to another part of a sentence. They also have a function in the subordinate clause.

> **Relative pronouns** connect adjectival clauses to the words they modify and act as subjects, direct objects, objects of prepositions, or adjectives in the subordinate clauses.

3.2.6 RULE

To tell how a relative pronoun is used within a clause, separate the clause from the rest of the sentence, and find the subject and verb in the clause.

FUNCTIONS OF RELATIVE PRONOUNS IN CLAUSES	
As a Subject	A house that is built on a good foundation is built subject to last.
As a Direct Object	Mario, whom my sister met at college, is a poet. direct object (Reworded clause: my sister met *whom* at college)
As an Object of a Preposition	This is the book about which I read great reviews. object of preposition (Reworded clause: I read great reviews about *which*)
As an Adjective	The senator whose opinion was in question spoke adjective to the press.

Sometimes in writing and in speech, a relative pronoun is left out of an adjectival clause. However, the missing word, though simply understood, still functions in the sentence.

EXAMPLES   The heroes [**whom**] we studied were great women.

See Practice 3.2C   The suggestions [**that**] they made were ignored.

Relative Adverbs Like relative pronouns, **relative adverbs** help link the subordinate clause to another part of a sentence. However, they have only one use within a subordinate clause.

Relative adverbs connect adjectival clauses to the words they modify and act as adverbs in the clauses.

EXAMPLE Pat yearned for the day **when** she could walk without crutches.

In the example, the adjectival clause is *when she could walk without crutches.* Reword the clause this way to see that *when* functions as an adverb: *she could walk without crutches when.*

Adverbial Clauses

Subordinate clauses may also serve as adverbs in sentences. They are introduced by subordinating conjunctions. Like adverbs, **adverbial clauses** modify verbs, adjectives, or other adverbs.

Subordinate **adverbial clauses** modify verbs, adjectives, adverbs, or verbals by telling *where, when, in what way, to what extent, under what condition,* or *why.*

An adverbial clause begins with a subordinating conjunction and contains a subject and a verb, although they are not the main subject and verb in the sentence. In the chart that follows, the adverbial clauses are highlighted in orange. Arrows point to the words they modify.

ADVERBIAL CLAUSES	
Modifying a Verb	After you read about Rome , you should begin your report. (Begin *when?*)
Modifying an Adjective	Tricia seemed happy wherever she was . (Happy *where?*)
Modifying a Gerund	Driving a car if you do not have a license is illegal. (Driving *under what condition?*)

> **Adverbial clauses** begin with **subordinating conjunctions** and contain subjects and verbs.

EXAMPLE   **Although** it rained, the game was still played.
          subordinating
          conjunction

Recognizing the subordinating conjunctions will help you identify adverbial clauses. The following chart shows some of the most common subordinating conjunctions.

SUBORDINATING CONJUNCTIONS			
after	because	so that	when
although	before	than	whenever
as	even though	though	where
as if	if	unless	wherever
as long as	since	until	while

Whether an adverbial clause appears at the beginning, middle, or end of a sentence can sometimes affect the sentence meaning.

EXAMPLE   **Before the year was over**, Joel made plans to visit Rome.

Joel made plans to visit Rome **before the year was over**.

Like adjectival clauses, adverbial clauses can be used to combine the information from two sentences into one. The combined sentence shows a close relationship between the ideas.

TWO SENTENCES   **It rained**. They did not go out.

See Practice 3.2D

COMBINED   **Because** it rained, they did not go out.
           subordinating
           conjunction

PRACTICE 3.2C ⟩ **Identifying Relative Pronouns and Adjectival Clauses**

Read each sentence. Then, write the adjectival clause in each sentence, and underline the relative pronoun that introduces the clause.

EXAMPLE   The only student who could complete the race was Sophia.

ANSWER   *who could complete the race*

1. Lilacs, which are known for their scent, grow best in cold climates.

2. The new teacher, whom I have not met, starts tomorrow.

3. Before the store opened to the public, it only sold products to wholesalers.

4. My aunt, who is a substitute teacher, worked at my school Monday.

5. Miguel couldn't understand why the window wouldn't open.

6. The snow that fell last night has melted.

7. The rain, which had been falling all morning, finally stopped.

8. The park where I play basketball has put in new courts.

9. The cat that I found is a stray.

10. Sophia, whose father plays drums in a jazz band, is very musical.

PRACTICE 3.2D ⟩ **Recognizing Adverbial Clauses**

Read each sentence. Then, write the adverbial clause in each sentence.

EXAMPLE   That's the place where we first met.

ANSWER   *where we first met*

11. I remember the day when you started school.

12. Pluto is not a planet, although it was considered one for many years.

13. Although we were late, we still found good seats.

14. Dad waited while I ran into the store.

15. We ate dinner after the movie.

16. Mario wouldn't have changed his seat unless he couldn't see the screen.

17. Jane goes wherever Mary goes.

18. My dog barks if he sees a cat.

19. I always stretch before I exercise.

20. I didn't know where she went.

SPEAKING APPLICATION

With a partner, take turns telling each other about your favorite holiday. Use relative pronouns to introduce adjectival clauses in your description. Your partner should listen for and identify the relative pronouns.

WRITING APPLICATION

Write a sentence using the following adverbial clauses: *while I slept*; *because it was raining*; *after the show*.

Elliptical Adverbial Clauses Sometimes, words are omitted in adverbial clauses, especially in those clauses that begin with *as* or *than* and are used to express comparisons. Such clauses are said to be *elliptical.*

> An **elliptical clause** is a clause in which the verb or the subject and verb are understood but not actually stated.

RULE 3.2.10

Even though the subject or the verb (or both) may not appear in an elliptical clause, they make the clause express a complete thought.

In the following examples, the understood words appear in brackets. The sentences are alike, except for the words *he* and *him*. In the first sentence, *he* is a subject of the adverbial clause. In the second sentence, *him* functions as a direct object of the adverbial clause.

VERB UNDERSTOOD	His sister resembles their father more **than he** **[does]** .
SUBJECT AND VERB UNDERSTOOD	His sister resembles their father more **than [she** **resembles] him** .

When you read or write elliptical clauses, mentally include the omitted words to clarify the intended meaning.

See Practice 3.2E

Noun Clauses

Subordinate clauses can also act as nouns in sentences.

> A **noun clause** is a subordinate clause that acts as a noun.

RULE 3.2.11

A noun clause acts in almost the same way a one-word noun does in a sentence: It tells what or whom the sentence is about.

In a sentence, a noun clause may act as a subject, direct object, indirect object, predicate nominative, object of a preposition, or appositive.

EXAMPLES   **Whatever you lost** can be found in the office.
                    subject

My father remembered **what I wanted for my birthday** .
                                          direct object

The chart on the next page contains more examples of the functions of noun clauses.

Introductory Words

Noun clauses frequently begin with the words *that, which, who, whom,* or *whose*—the same words that are used to begin adjective clauses. *Whichever, whoever,* or *whomever* may also be used as introductory words in noun clauses. Other noun clauses begin with the words *how, if, what, whatever, where, when, whether,* or *why.*

Introductory words may act as subjects, direct objects, objects of prepositions, adjectives, or adverbs in noun clauses, or they may simply introduce the clauses.

SOME USES OF INTRODUCTORY WORDS IN NOUN CLAUSES	
FUNCTIONS IN CLAUSES	**EXAMPLES**
Adjective	She could not decide which kitten was her favorite .
Adverb	We want to know how we should dress .
Subject	I want the receipe from whoever made that delicious casserole .
Direct Object	Whatever my supervisor advised , I did.
No Function	The doctor determined that he had the flu .

Note that in the following chart the introductory word *that* in the last example has no function except to introduce the clause.

FUNCTIONS OF NOUN CLAUSES IN SENTENCES	
Acting as a Subject	Whoever is last must pay the penalty.
Acting as a Direct Object	Please invite whomever you want to the party.
Acting as an Indirect Object	His manner gave whomever met him a shock.
Acting as a Predicate Nominative	Our problem is whether we should stay or go.
Acting as an Object of a Preposition	Use the money for whatever purpose you choose.
Acting as an Appositive	The occupied country rejected our plea that orphans be cared for by the Red Cross.

Some words that introduce noun clauses also introduce adjectival and adverbial clauses. It is necessary to check the function of the clause in the sentence to determine its type. To check the function, try substituting the words *it, you, fact,* or *thing* for the clause. If the sentence retains its smoothness, you probably replaced a noun clause.

NOUN CLAUSE   I knew **that she would be late**.

SUBSTITUTION   I knew it.

In the following examples, all three subordinating clauses begin with *where,* but only the first is a noun clause because it functions in the sentence as a direct object.

NOUN CLAUSE   Mr. Wong told his students **where they would gather for the tour**.
(Told the students *what?*)

ADJECTIVAL CLAUSE   They took the soldier to a tent, **where a doctor examined his wound**.
(*Which* tent?)

ADVERBIAL CLAUSE   She lives **where the weather is warm all year.**
(Lives *where*?)

Note About Introductory Words: The introductory word *that* is often omitted from a noun clause. In the following examples, the understood word *that* is in brackets.

EXAMPLES   The assistant suggested **[that] you leave your name**.

After the coach chose her for the team, Ling knew **[that] she was going to have a very busy year**.

We remember **[that] you wanted to raise the flag in the morning**.

See Practice 3.2F

PRACTICE 3.2E Identifying Elliptical Adverbial Clauses

Read each sentence. Then, write the adverbial clause in each sentence. For the adverbial clauses that are elliptical, add the understood words in parentheses.

EXAMPLE   My essay received a higher grade than his essay.

ANSWER   *than his essay (did)*

1. My cousin is as tall as I.

2. A spider's silk is as strong as steel.

3. Bill is always as late as Nina.

4. Gillian's cousin is as smart as Gillian.

5. Stephen enjoys science class more than math class.

6. That monkey is as small as a mouse.

7. Aaron knows Dee better than I.

8. Vinnie spoke to Lauren more than to Daniel.

9. This restaurant has better food than that restaurant.

10. Nadia can run faster than Craig.

PRACTICE 3.2F Recognizing Noun Clauses

Read each sentence. Then, write the noun clause, and label it as a *subject, direct object, indirect object, predicate nominative,* or *object of a preposition.*

EXAMPLE   We were concerned about what we should perform next.

ANSWER   *what we should perform next —* object of a preposition

11. When the next showing will be held has only appeared online.

12. Tony sheepishly admitted that he had scored the winning touchdown.

13. Mrs. Baksh's one wish was that she could have a house of her own.

14. All of Kristen's classmates understood what she said.

15. The witnesses disagreed about how old the defendant had been.

16. What happened next made even me a believer.

17. The weatherman predicted that the storm would hit around midnight.

18. Do you know if our team won last night?

19. Mr. Newman explained why an owl is a symbol of wisdom.

20. Kemal wished that they would stay longer.

SPEAKING APPLICATION

Take turns with a partner. Say four elliptical clauses. Your partner should repeat your clauses, filling in the missing words.

WRITING APPLICATION

Using sentence 16 as your first sentence, write a paragraph about what happened next using at least three noun clauses in your paragraph. Underline the noun clauses in your sentences.

3.3 The Four Structures of Sentences

Independent and subordinate clauses are the building blocks of sentences. These clauses can be combined in an endless number of ways to form the four basic sentence structures: **simple, compound, complex,** and **compound-complex.**

A simple sentence contains a single independent or main clause.

Although a simple sentence contains only one main or independent clause, its subject, verb, or both may be compound. A simple sentence may also have modifying phrases and complements. However, it cannot have a subordinate clause.

In the following simple sentences, the subjects are highlighted in yellow, and the verbs are highlighted in orange.

ONE SUBJECT AND VERB

The **snow** **melted** .

COMPOUND SUBJECT

Ed and **I** **checked** our answers.

COMPOUND VERB

The **tree** **rotted** and **died** .

COMPOUND SUBJECT AND VERB

Neither the **driver** nor the **skier** **heard** or **saw** the other boat.

A compound sentence contains two or more main clauses.

The main clauses in a compound sentence can be joined by a comma and a coordinating conjunction *(and, but, for, nor, or, so, yet)* or by a semicolon (;). Like a simple sentence, a compound sentence contains no subordinate clauses.

EXAMPLE

A Sotho **bride** **carries** a beaded doll at her wedding, and **she** **keeps** the doll for a year.

See Practice 3.3A

A **complex sentence** consists of one independent or main clause and one or more subordinate clauses.

The independent clause in a complex sentence is often called the main clause to distinguish it from the subordinate clause or clauses. The subject and verb in the independent clause are called the subject of the sentence and the main verb. The second example shows that a subordinate clause may fall between the parts of a main clause. In the examples below, the main clauses are highlighted in blue, and the subordinate clauses are highlighted in pink.

EXAMPLES   **No one answered the phone when she called us**.

The bouquet of flowers that the bride carried didn't have any roses.

Note on Complex Sentences With Noun Clauses: The subject of the main clause may sometimes be the subordinate clause itself.

EXAMPLE   **That I wanted to go bothered them**.

A **compound-complex sentence** consists of two or more independent clauses and one or more subordinate clauses.

In the example below, the independent clauses are highlighted in blue, and the subordinate clauses are highlighted in pink.

EXAMPLE   **The roof leaks when it rains heavily, and we have to repaint the ceilings so that we cover any water stains**.

See Practice 3.3B

PRACTICE 3.3A ▷ Distinguishing Between Simple and Compound Sentences

Read each sentence. Then, label each sentence as either *simple* or *compound*.

EXAMPLE   The horse stomped the ground and kicked.

ANSWER   *simple*

1. Sharks and marlin are fish, but whales are not.

2. The contestants were in their spots, and the game was about to begin.

3. Mr. Thomas and Mrs. Chin are my favorite teachers.

4. Lorraine lifted herself off the couch and walked gingerly.

5. Jackson took the wrong route.

6. They learned a song with a number of verses.

7. The tremor from the earthquake caused the bed to shake.

8. The paint got onto his face and looked like a bruise.

9. Margo wore a new jacket, but her pants were worn and old.

10. The movie begins with a car chase.

PRACTICE 3.3B ▷ Identifying the Four Structures of Sentences

Read each sentence. Then, label each sentence as *simple, compound, complex,* or *compound-complex*.

EXAMPLE   Chicken and pasta are my favorite foods.

ANSWER   *simple*

11. The exit sign was clearly marked, but we still passed it.

12. The ball hit the uprights and bounced into the end zone.

13. The cowboys and field hands corralled the herd together.

14. The fixture that secures the fan is loose.

15. Allison went to the party, but Juan stayed home because he was sick.

16. The committee has not decided when the next meeting will take place.

17. Professor Mailer warned his students against untruthfulness.

18. Gerald took an earlier flight than I did, for he wanted to arrive in time for dinner.

19. Members must recite the oath, or they will not be allowed to enter.

20. Penelope wanted to go overseas, yet she couldn't justify spending all her money.

SPEAKING APPLICATION

With a partner, take turns describing the longest trip you have taken. Use both simple and compound sentences. Your partner should listen for and identify each sentence as simple or compound.

WRITING APPLICATION

Write a brief paragraph about your morning, using a variety of correctly structured sentences: simple, compound, complex, and compound-complex.

Cumulative Review Chapters 1–3

PRACTICE 1 ▶ Identifying Nouns

Read the sentences. Then, label each underlined noun as *concrete* or *abstract*. If the noun is concrete, label it *collective*, *compound*, or *proper*.

1. The <u>committee</u> decided to push the agenda until next week.
2. <u>Passersby</u> stopped to look at Tim's <u>artwork</u>.
3. <u>Daniel</u> exhibited much <u>bravery</u> rescuing the kitten.
4. The <u>team</u> enjoyed much <u>success</u> in the playoffs.
5. My <u>dream</u> is to work in the <u>White House</u>.

PRACTICE 2 ▶ Identifying Pronouns

Read the sentences. Then, label each underlined pronoun as *reciprocal*, *demonstrative*, *relative*, *interrogative*, or *indefinite*.

1. Does Frankie know who owns <u>that</u> house?
2. Is that the guy <u>whom</u> you took to the dance?
3. Gerald and Carlos greeted <u>each other</u>.
4. <u>Which</u> of the contestants won the prize?
5. <u>Some</u> of the students left early.

PRACTICE 3 ▶ Classifying Verbs and Verb Phrases

Read the sentences. Then, write the verb or verb phrase in each sentence. Label each as *action verb* or *linking verb*, and *transitive* or *intransitive*.

1. Nat remained under the shade of the tree.
2. Thomas will carry the box for me.
3. Out in the field, the corn grows quickly.
4. This perfume smells like lilacs.
5. Every day, Les drives me home.

PRACTICE 4 ▶ Identifying Adjectives and Adverbs

Read the sentences. Then, label the underlined word as an *adverb* or *adjective*. Write the word that is modified.

1. Weston is <u>noticeably</u> stronger than I.
2. A <u>healthy</u> portion of fruit will keep you fit.
3. You were <u>helpful</u> this morning at practice.
4. The theater is <u>regularly</u> full on weekends.
5. Samuel ordered an <u>enormous</u> salad.

PRACTICE 5 ▶ Using Conjunctions and Interjections

Read the sentences. Then, write the conjunction or interjection. Label conjunctions as *coordinating*, *correlative*, or *subordinating*.

1. Both my brother and I play tennis.
2. While I was standing in line, I read my book.
3. My word! Did you see that?
4. Neither the team nor the coach wanted to lose.
5. Nancy will buy either a dress or shoes.
6. Jared wants to stop at a restaurant, and he wants to see a movie.
7. The gym not only has a trainer but it also has a pool.
8. I wanted front row seats, so I ordered my tickets online.
9. Yikes! I can't eat all that cake.
10. Indeed! Of course I will go.

Continued on next page ▶

Cumulative Review Chapters 1–3

PRACTICE 6 Recognizing Direct and Indirect Objects and Object of a Preposition

Identify the underlined items as *direct object*, *indirect object*, or *object of a preposition*.

1. Has your teacher given <u>you</u> the assignment?
2. Running around the <u>pool</u> will not be allowed.
3. Has Kyle shown <u>Jason</u> his new car?
4. Jimmy told us his <u>plans</u> for the <u>summer</u>.
5. Mr. Williams told the <u>audience</u> some jokes.
6. The new owner offered <u>Louis</u> a higher <u>salary</u>.
7. Was Frank waiting around the <u>corner</u>?
8. I loaned <u>Stanley</u> and <u>Jim</u> my football.
9. Haley got <u>us</u> <u>tickets</u> to the movie.
10. Did someone put milk in my <u>tea</u>?

PRACTICE 7 Identifying Phrases

Write the phrases, and label them *prepositional*, *appositive*, *participial*, *gerund*, or *infinitive*.

1. A wonderful golden retriever, Bobo was my favorite.
2. I finally arrived home at midnight.
3. Sitting behind his desk, the teacher scanned the class.
4. I am hopeful that you appreciate my giving you this chance.
5. Joe has sworn never to ask for directions.
6. Being the class president made Stan feel proud.
7. Tom Benson, my next-door neighbor, borrowed my lawn mower.
8. Waiting near the train station, Courtney noticed her bag was missing.

9. That dress, to be perfectly honest, is so beautiful.
10. My legs cramped during the race.

PRACTICE 8 Recognizing Clauses

Label the underlined clauses in the following sentences *independent* or *subordinate*. Identify any subordinate clause as *adjectival*, *adverbial*, or *noun clause*. Then, label any adjectival clause *essential* or *nonessential*.

1. The new student <u>who sits in the front</u> always participates.
2. <u>Danny waited in the airport</u> for his brother's arrival.
3. <u>When the next audition will be held</u> has not been posted.
4. Gordon plays guitar <u>whenever he finds the time</u>.
5. <u>I want to be an astronaut</u>, but I need to improve my grades.
6. My cat will jump out <u>if the window is open</u>.
7. Maria, <u>who was dressed in a black gown</u>, waved from the balcony.
8. Harold enjoyed his trip to the zoo <u>even though the gorilla exhibit was closed</u>.
9. The real tragedy is <u>how the story ends</u>.
10. My best friend, Wendy, <u>who lives in Galveston</u>, visited me this weekend.

CHAPTER 4

EFFECTIVE SENTENCES

Use a combination of simple, compound, and complex sentences to add interest to your writing.

WRITE GUY *Jeff Anderson, M.Ed.*

WHAT DO YOU NOTICE?

Notice the complexity of this sentence as you zoom in on these lines from the epic poem the *Odyssey* by Homer.

MENTOR TEXT

> I might have made it safely home, that time,
> but as I came around Malea the current
> took me out to sea, and from the north
> a fresh gale drove me on, past Cythera.

Now, ask yourself the following questions:

- What are the main or independent clauses in this compound sentence?
- How does the poet combine these clauses into a single compound sentence?

The poet uses three main or independent clauses, groups of words that can stand alone as their own sentences. The first main clause is *I might have made it safely home, that time*, the second is *as I came around Malea the current took me out to sea*, and the third is *from the north a fresh gale drove me on, past Cythera*. The poet combines these clauses into one compound sentence using commas and the conjunctions *but* and *and*.

Grammar for Writers Writers craft sentences that work well together by varying the length and complexity of their sentences. Evaluate your sentences to see if they would be more effective if they were shorter or longer.

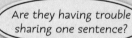

Are they having trouble sharing one sentence?

My main clauses are too independent.

4.1 The Four Functions of a Sentence

Sentences can be classified according to what they do—that is, whether they state ideas, ask questions, give orders, or express strong emotions.

Declarative sentences are used to declare, or state, facts.

> A **declarative sentence** states an idea and ends with a period.

DECLARATIVE London is a city in England.

To *interrogate* means "to ask." An **interrogative sentence** is a question.

RULE 4.1.2

> An **interrogative sentence** asks a question and ends with a question mark.

INTERROGATIVE In which countries do tigers live?

Imperative sentences give commands or directions.

RULE 4.1.3

> An **imperative sentence** gives an order or a direction and ends with either a period or an exclamation mark.

EL9

Most imperative sentences start with a verb. In this type of imperative sentence, the subject is understood to be *you*.

IMPERATIVE Follow the directions carefully.

Exclamatory sentences are used to express emotions.

RULE 4.1.4

> An **exclamatory sentence** conveys strong emotion and ends with an exclamation mark.

EXCLAMATORY This is an outrage!

See Practice 4.1A
See Practice 4.1B

PRACTICE 4.1A > **Identifying the Four Types of Sentences**

Read each sentence. Then, label each sentence *declarative, interrogative, imperative,* or *exclamatory.*

EXAMPLE   Stop in your tracks!

ANSWER   *imperative*

1. Has anyone here ever recorded a song in a studio?

2. Toast the bread until it is golden-brown.

3. Make sure you keep the receipt.

4. Which is harder to complete, a marathon or a triathlon?

5. The whale and the dolphin are both mammals.

6. Apply the bracket before hanging the painting.

7. What a horrible program that was!

8. Do NOT pass go.

9. Some Native Americans used smoke signals to communicate with one another.

10. Eating eggs provides you with protein.

PRACTICE 4.1B > **Punctuating the Four Types of Sentences**

Read each sentence. Then, label each sentence *declarative, interrogative, imperative,* or *exclamatory.* In parentheses, write the correct end mark.

EXAMPLE   Have you finished your work

ANSWER   *interrogative (?)*

11. What a great time this is

12. Did you see your schedule

13. Take a taxi toward downtown

14. Do you plan to travel

15. Phoenix has many interesting sights to see

16. Please take out the trash before it is too late

17. What a terrible day it was

18. This coffee shop has the best bagels

19. Who is the mayor of this city

20. My brother sometimes plays soccer at this venue

SPEAKING APPLICATION

Take turns with a partner. Say sentences that are declarative, interrogative, imperative, and exclamatory. Your partner should identify each type of sentence.

WRITING APPLICATION

Write a scripted dialogue between two people in an airport. Include declarative, interrogative, imperative, and exclamatory sentences in the script.

4.2 Sentence Combining

Too many short sentences can make your writing choppy and disconnected.

One way to avoid the excessive use of short sentences and to achieve variety is to combine sentences.

RULE 4.2.1

Sentences can be combined by using a compound subject, a compound verb, or a compound object.

TWO SENTENCES	Moira enjoyed watching the lions. Jon enjoyed watching the lions.
COMPOUND SUBJECT	Moira and Jon enjoyed watching the lions.
TWO SENTENCES	Lisa played the game. Lisa won a prize.
COMPOUND VERB	Lisa played the game and won a prize.
TWO SENTENCES	Scott saw the cheetah. Scott saw the hyena.
COMPOUND OBJECT	Scott saw the cheetah and the hyena.

See Practice 4.2A

RULE 4.2.2

Sentences can be combined by joining two main or independent clauses to create a compound sentence.

Use a compound sentence when combining ideas that are related but independent. To join main clauses, use a comma and a coordinating conjunction (*for, and, but, or, nor, yet,* or *so*) or a semicolon.

EXAMPLE	The antelope was looking for enemies. It did not notice the lion.
COMPOUND SENTENCE	The antelope was looking for enemies, but it did not notice the lion.

> **Sentences can be combined by changing one into a subordinate clause to create a complex sentence.**

4.2.3 RULE

To show the relationship between ideas in which one depends on the other, use a **complex sentence.** The subordinating conjunction will help readers understand the relationship. Some common subordinating conjunctions are *after, although, because, if, since, when,* and *while.*

EXAMPLE	We were frightened. We thought the lion we saw was hungry.
COMBINED WITH A SUBORDINATE CLAUSE	We were frightened **because we thought the lion was hungry** .

> **Sentences can be combined by changing one of them into a phrase.**

4.2.4 RULE

EXAMPLE	My team plays tomorrow. We play the Cougars.
COMBINED WITH PREPOSITIONAL PHRASE	My team plays **against the Cougars** tomorrow.

EXAMPLE	My team will play against the Cougars. They are an undefeated team.
COMBINED WITH APPOSITIVE PHRASE	My team will play against the Cougars, **an undefeated team** .

See Practice 4.2B
See Practice 4.2C

Read each set of sentences. Then, write one sentence that combines each set of sentences.

EXAMPLE   The player scored a basket in overtime. She won the game.

ANSWER   *The player scored a basket in overtime and won the game.*

1. Tom Mays went to law school. My mother went to law school.

2. The bald eagle symbolizes our country. The bird also symbolizes independence.

3. Dale will choose a ham sandwich. He will choose cole slaw.

4. Westlake is a neighborhood school. Loyola is a neighborhood school.

5. While on vacation, Jules visited a museum. Jules also visited an aquarium.

6. Wally wrote his essay over the weekend. Wally handed in his essay on Monday.

7. His manuscript was published last year. His manuscript was well-received by critics.

8. Brandon sprained his knee. Brandon sprained his ankle.

9. The diamond was stolen from the museum. The diamond was never recovered.

10. A small girl sits on the dock. A small girl fishes.

Read each set of sentences. Combine each set by turning one sentence into a phrase that adds detail to the other.

EXAMPLE   The women stand at the box office. They wait to buy tickets.

ANSWER   *The women standing at the box office wait to buy tickets.*

11. The sun rises between the trees. It is a breathtaking view.

12. Many movies have been made by that director. He is a hard-working man.

13. Mrs. Campbell approached the podium. Mrs. Campbell appeared excited.

14. The audience clapped for the actors. The actors were still wearing costumes.

15. The flames bend in the breeze. They look like tongues.

16. The ox pulls the cart. The ox works hard.

17. The wind blows. It makes leaves float down.

18. Tabitha lined up her shot carefully. She is the best player on the team.

19. The wooden fence was shattered by the storm. The storm was a real downpour.

20. The boat sprayed water onto the beach. The beach was crowded with sunbathers.

SPEAKING APPLICATION

Take turns with a partner. Tell two related sentences. Your partner should combine these two sentences to make one logical sentence.

WRITING APPLICATION

Write two sentences that relate to each other. Then, exchange papers with a partner. Your partner should combine the two sentences into one by turning one sentence into a phrase.

PRACTICE 4.2C Combining Sentences by Forming Compound or Complex Sentences

Read each pair of sentences. Then, combine the sentences, using the coordinating or subordinating conjunction indicated in parentheses.

EXAMPLE   I stay active. I jog every day. (because)

ANSWER   *I stay active because I jog every day.*

1. The team won the game. They didn't practice all week. (although)

2. I cleaned the closet. Boxes spilled out. (after)

3. We called for room service. No one responded. (but)

4. The pathway was slick. We could not keep our footing. (and)

5. Paul insisted on seeing the movie. He doesn't like westerns. (even though)

6. We could come back. We could stay here for the night. (or)

7. I couldn't say no. Who could resist the chance to meet a famous artist? (for)

8. I could read a suspense novel. I could read a magazine. (or)

9. Some of us study music. Others just enjoy listening to the radio. (but)

10. Planets are not stars. They can appear bright in the night sky. (yet)

SPEAKING APPLICATION

Take turns with a partner. Tell about a famous person whom you would like to meet, and explain why. Use at least three compound or complex sentences along with three coordinating or subordinating conjunctions in your description. Your partner should identify which of your sentences are compound or complex, as well as the types of conjunctions that you use.

WRITING APPLICATION

Write a paragraph about what makes you different from either your friends or your classmates. Use at least three compound or complex sentences, along with three coordinating or subordinating conjunctions.

4.3 Varying Sentences

Vary your sentences to develop a rhythm, to achieve an effect, or to emphasize the connections between ideas. There are several ways you can vary your sentences.

Varying Sentence Length

To emphasize a point or surprise a reader, include a short, direct sentence to interrupt the flow of long sentences. Notice the effect of the last sentence in the following paragraph.

EXAMPLE   The Jacobites derived their name from *Jacobus,* the Latin name for King James II of England, who was dethroned in 1688 by William of Orange during the Glorious Revolution. Unpopular because of his Catholicism and autocratic ruling style, James fled to France to seek the aid of King Louis XIV. In 1690, James, along with a small body of French troops, landed in Ireland in an attempt to regain his throne. His hopes ended at the Battle of the Boyne.

Some sentences contain only one idea and can't be broken. It may be possible, however, to state the idea in a shorter sentence. Other sentences contain two or more ideas and might be shortened by breaking up the ideas.

LONGER SENTENCE   Many of James II's predecessors were able to avoid major economic problems, but James had serious economic problems.

MORE DIRECT   Unlike many of his predecessors, James II was unable to avoid major economic problems.

LONGER SENTENCE   James tried to work with Parliament to develop a plan of taxation that would be fair and reasonable, but members of Parliament rejected his efforts, and James dissolved the Parliament.

SHORTER SENTENCES   James tried to work with Parliament to develop a fair and reasonable taxation plan. However, because members of Parliament rejected his efforts, James dissolved the Parliament.

Varying Sentence Beginnings

Another way to create sentence variety is to start sentences with different parts of speech.

WAYS TO VARY SENTENCE BEGINNINGS	
Start With a Noun	Bicycles are difficult to build.
Start With an Adverb	Naturally, bicycles are difficult to build.
Start With an Adverbial Phrase	Because of their complexity, bicycles are difficult to build.
Start With a Participial Phrase	Having tried to build several bicycles, I know how hard it is.
Start With a Prepositional Phrase	For the average person, bicycles are very difficult to build.
Start With an Infinitive Phrase	To build a high-performance bicycle was my goal.

See Practice 4.3A

Using Inverted Word Order

You can also vary sentence beginnings by reversing the traditional subject–verb order to create verb–subject order. You can reverse order by starting the sentence with a **participial phrase** or a **prepositional phrase.** You can also move a complement to the beginning of the sentence.

SUBJECT–VERB ORDER

The navy waited for the attack.

The royal armada sailed into the bay.

The booming of cannon fire filled the air.

The sound was deafening.

VERB–SUBJECT ORDER

Waiting for the attack was the navy.
   participial phrase

Into the bay sailed the royal armada.
prepositional phrase

Filling the air was the booming of cannon fire.
   participial phrase

Deafening was the sound.

See Practice 4.3B

predicate adjective

PRACTICE 4.3A > **Revising to Vary Sentence Beginnings**

Read each sentence. Rewrite each sentence to begin with the part of speech or phrase indicated in parentheses. You may need to add a word or phrase.

EXAMPLE   The teller counted five-dollar bills. (adverbs)

ANSWER   *Slowly and carefully, the teller counted the five-dollar bills.*

1. I haven't seen her since lunch. (preposition)

2. Mrs. Rosenthal watered her garden after sunset. (prepositional phrase)

3. The magnolia tree will be blooming soon. (adverb)

4. The river flooded the streets. (participial phrase)

5. My antique watch broke. (adverb)

6. The bicycle rider made it across the finish line. (participial phrase)

7. We will meet you at the park. (prepositional phrase)

8. We walked instead of driving. (infinitive phrase)

9. New condominiums will be built nearby. (adverb)

10. We watched fireflies. (adverb)

PRACTICE 4.3B > **Inverting Sentences to Vary Subject-Verb Order**

Read each sentence. Rewrite each sentence by inverting subject-verb order to verb-subject order.

EXAMPLE   The Memorial Day parade is coming.

ANSWER   *Here comes the Memorial Day parade.*

11. The new mayor is watching by the stands.

12. The boy watched cautiously.

13. Four laughing children ran ahead of the couple.

14. A lush meadow stretches between the creek and the dirt road.

15. Good news about the bank manager spread around town.

16. A story about the student of the year appeared on the front page.

17. The Statue of Liberty stands in New York harbor.

18. Restored colonial houses stood along the streets.

19. A beautiful rainbow appeared after the rain.

20. The custodian walked into the room with the keys.

SPEAKING APPLICATION

Take turns with a partner. Say the following phrases: *if you review your notes, when the storm ended, you need good balance.* Your partner should add words to the beginning of each phrase to form a sentence.

WRITING APPLICATION

Write three original sentences about something fun you did recently. Then, exchange papers with a partner. Your partner should invert the order of your sentences to vary their beginnings.

4.4 Avoid Fragments and Run-ons

Hasty writers sometimes omit crucial words, punctuate awkwardly, or leave their thoughts unfinished, causing two common sentence errors: **fragments** and **run-ons.**

Recognizing Fragments

Although some writers use them for stylistic effect, **fragments** are generally considered errors in standard English.

> **Do not capitalize and punctuate phrases, subordinate clauses, or words in a series as if they were complete sentences.**

Reading your work aloud to listen for natural pauses and stops should help you avoid fragments. Sometimes, you can repair a fragment by connecting it to words that come before or after it.

> **One way to correct a fragment is to connect it to the words in a nearby sentence.**

PARTICIPIAL FRAGMENT	inspired by the grace of the dancer
ADDED TO A NEARBY SENTENCE	**Inspired by the grace of the dancer**, Linda saw the performance again.
PREPOSITIONAL FRAGMENT	before her partner
ADDED TO A NEARBY SENTENCE	The ballerina came on stage **before her partner**.
PRONOUN AND PARTICIPIAL FRAGMENT	the one hanging in the closet
ADDED TO A NEARBY SENTENCE	The leotard I like is **the one hanging in the closet**.

Another way to correct a fragment is to add any sentence part that is needed to make the fragment a complete sentence.

Remember that every complete sentence must have both a subject and a verb and express a complete thought. Check to see that each of your sentences contains all of the parts necessary to be complete.

NOUN FRAGMENT

the troupe of lively young dancers

COMPLETED SENTENCES

The troupe of lively young dancers
subject

moved across the stage.
verb

We excitedly **watched**
subject   verb

the troupe of lively young dancers .
direct object

Notice what missing sentence parts must be added to the following types of phrase fragments to make them complete.

	FRAGMENTS	COMPLETED SENTENCES
Noun Fragment With Participial Phrase	the food eaten by us	The food was eaten by us.
Verb Fragment	will be at the rehearsal today	I will be at the rehearsal today.
Prepositional Fragment	in the hall closet	I put the shoes in the hall closet.
Participial Fragment	found under the desk	The books found under the desk are mine.
Gerund Fragment	teaching children to dance	Teaching children to dance is rewarding.
Infinitive Fragment	to see the new ballet	I expect to see the new ballet.

> You may need to attach a **subordinate clause** to a main clause to correct a fragment.

4.4.4 RULE

A **subordinate clause** contains a subject and a verb but does not express a complete thought and cannot stand alone as a sentence. Link it to a main clause to make the sentence complete.

ADJECTIVAL CLAUSE FRAGMENT	which was being performed outdoors
COMPLETED SENTENCE	I enjoyed watching the dance rehearsal, **which was being performed outdoors**.
ADVERBIAL CLAUSE FRAGMENT	after she practiced the new dance routine
COMPLETED SENTENCE	**After she practiced the new dance routine**, she was ready for the show.
NOUN CLAUSE FRAGMENT	whatever ballet we see in this theater
COMPLETED SENTENCE	We always enjoy **whatever ballet we see in this theater**.

Series Fragments A fragment is not always short. A long series of words still needs to have a subject and a verb and express a complete thought. It may be a long fragment masquerading as a sentence.

SERIES FRAGMENT	COMPLETE SENTENCE
after reading Steinbeck's novel, with its probing look at poverty and greed, in the style so typical of this master storyteller	After reading Steinbeck's novel, with its probing look at poverty and greed, in the style so typical of this master storyteller, I was able to prepare an interesting oral presentation.

See Practice 4.4A

Avoiding Run-on Sentences

A **run-on** sentence is two or more sentences capitalized and punctuated as if they were a single sentence.

RULE 4.4.5

> Use punctuation and conjunctions to correctly join or separate parts of a **run-on** sentence.

There are two kinds of **run-ons: fused sentences**, which are two or more sentences joined with no punctuation, and **comma splices**, which have two or more sentences separated only by commas rather than by commas and conjunctions.

FUSED SENTENCE — The dancers practiced every day they were soon the best in the state.

COMMA SPLICE — Only one package arrived in the mail, the other items never came.

As with fragments, proofreading or reading your work aloud will help you find run-ons. Once found, they can be corrected by adding punctuation and conjunctions or by rewording the sentences.

FOUR WAYS TO CORRECT RUN-ONS		
	RUN-ON	CORRECTION
With End Marks and Capitals	The dance was in full swing in the gym people crowded together.	The dance was in full swing. In the gym, people crowded together.
With Commas and Conjunctions	The paper needed cutting we could not locate the scissors.	The paper needed cutting, but we could not locate the scissors.
With Semicolons	Our city has many cultural activities, for example it hosts the National Ballet.	Our city has many cultural activities; for example, it hosts the National Ballet.
By Rewriting	The horse show began late, someone had misplaced the registration forms.	The horse show began late because someone had misplaced the registration forms.

See Practice 4.4B

PRACTICE 4.4A > Identifying and Correcting Fragments

Read each item. If an item contains a fragment, rewrite it to make a complete sentence. If an item is a complete sentence, write *correct*.

EXAMPLE   Riding on the *Orient Express*.

ANSWER   *Riding on the Orient Express
would be thrilling.*

1. To see the new airplane.
2. Which Cindy received for her birthday.
3. Who won the contest?
4. Enjoys riding her bike.
5. The smell of freshly mowed grass.
6. My notebook is missing.
7. What time is the party?
8. After searching high and low.
9. The play is so funny.
10. Known for its quick service and friendly atmosphere.

PRACTICE 4.4B > Revising to Eliminate Run-on Sentences

Read each sentence. Correct each run-on by correctly joining or separating the sentence parts.

EXAMPLE   The children played in the backyard, the swing amused them.

ANSWER   *The children played in the backyard. The swing amused them.*

11. We made three easy outs it was our team's turn at bat.
12. Laila did a wonderful job, we knew she would.
13. Hector wanted to be an actor, acting jobs were hard to get.
14. Math is easy for me I also do well in science.
15. The beach is very pretty, you can see into tide pools at low tide.
16. Shrimp eggs can survive for more than one year in the desert, rainwater brings them to life.
17. The trick amazed the group they had never seen anything like it.
18. Senator Gonzalez was the speaker he talked about citizenship.
19. Several committee members opposed the increase, they voted against it.
20. Many cactuses are odd-looking plants they have beautiful blossoms.

SPEAKING APPLICATION

Take turns with a partner. Say sentence fragments. Your partner should turn each fragment into a complete sentence.

WRITING APPLICATION

Rewrite the following run-on sentences as complete sentences:
The explorer followed the map he found the treasure.
We rounded the bend the castle came into view.

4.5 Misplaced and Dangling Modifiers

Careful writers put modifiers as close as possible to the words they modify. When modifiers are misplaced or left dangling in a sentence, the result may be illogical or confusing.

Recognizing Misplaced Modifiers

A **misplaced modifier** is placed too far from the modified word and appears to modify the wrong word or words.

RULE 4.5.1

> A **misplaced modifier** seems to modify the wrong word in the sentence.

MISPLACED MODIFIER | The man fell over a rock **running on the road**.

CORRECTION | The man **running on the road** fell over a rock.

MISPLACED MODIFIER | We heard the telephone ring **while watching television**.

CORRECTION | **While watching television**, we heard the telephone ring.

Recognizing Dangling Modifiers

With **dangling modifiers,** the word that should be modified is missing from the sentence. Dangling modifiers usually come at the beginning of a sentence and are followed by a comma. The subject being modified should come right after the comma.

RULE 4.5.2

> A **dangling modifier** seems to modify the wrong word or no word at all because the word it should modify has been omitted from the sentence.

See Practice 4.5A

DANGLING PARTICIPIAL PHRASE	Measuring carefully, the span over the river was closed accurately. *(Who did the measuring?)*
CORRECTED SENTENCE	Measuring carefully, **the engineer** accurately closed the span over the river.

Dangling participial phrases are corrected by adding missing words and making other needed changes.

Dangling infinitive phrases and elliptical clauses can be corrected in the same way. First, identify the subject of the sentence. Then, make sure each subject is clearly stated. You may also need to change the form of the verb.

DANGLING INFINITIVE PHRASE	To cross the river, the bridge toll must be paid. *(Who is crossing and must pay?)*
CORRECTED SENTENCE	To cross the river, **drivers** must pay the bridge toll.
DANGLING ELLIPTICAL CLAUSE	While sailing under the bridge, a school of porpoises was sighted. *(Who was sailing and sighted the porpoises?)*
CORRECTED SENTENCE	While sailing under the bridge, **we** saw a school of porpoises.

EL8

A dangling adverbial clause may also occur when the antecedent of a pronoun is not clear.

DANGLING ADVERBIAL CLAUSE	When she was ninety years old, Mrs. Smith's granddaughter planned a picnic near the bridge. *(Who is ninety, Mrs. Smith or her granddaughter?)*
CORRECTED SENTENCE	**When Mrs. Smith was ninety years old** , her granddaughter planned a picnic near the bridge.

See Practice 4.5B

PRACTICE 4.5A Identifying and Correcting Misplaced Modifiers

Read each sentence. Then, rewrite each sentence, putting the misplaced modifiers closer to the words they should modify. If a sentence is correct, write *correct*.

EXAMPLE   We pitched our tent in the mountains with a view of the lake.

ANSWER   *In the mountains, we pitched our tent with a view of the lake.*

1. Rafael waved at me from his car.

2. Mom came by while I was washing the windows with a casserole.

3. Mei ran through the rain slipping and sliding.

4. Maggie picked up the heavy package left by the delivery man with a groan.

5. Roger accidentally spent the rare coins on gasoline that his grandfather gave him.

6. Tim saw a bird soar in the sky while jogging.

7. Anita designs delightful clothing for children in prints and plaids.

8. Trying to avoid a tie score, the player made a desperate shot at the basket.

9. Earth revolves around the sun once a year.

10. Crossing the ford is easy on horseback.

PRACTICE 4.5B Identifying and Correcting Dangling Modifiers

Read each sentence. Then, rewrite each sentence, correcting any dangling modifiers by supplying missing words or ideas.

EXAMPLE   Hiking through the woods at night, many animal sounds were heard.

ANSWER   *Hiking through the woods at night, I heard many animal sounds.*

11. Born in Uganda, America seemed like a dream.

12. Running down the hallway, the elevator door closed.

13. After mopping the floor, the dog tracked mud through the kitchen.

14. To get the job, a test must be passed.

15. While climbing the mountain, a herd of goats was spotted.

16. Remaining calm, the entire building was evacuated.

17. When she was asleep, the babysitter carried the infant to her crib.

18. To reach the bottom of the canyon, safety must be considered.

19. Feeling exhausted, the road seemed to go on forever.

20. When he was three, Paul's father got a new job.

SPEAKING APPLICATION

Take turns with a partner. Tell about something interesting that you have done. Use modifiers in your sentences. Your partner should name the modifiers in your description, and tell whether they are correctly placed.

WRITING APPLICATION

Rewrite sentences 12, 15, and 18, replacing the verbs. Then, rewrite each sentence to correct the dangling modifier.

4.6 Faulty Parallelism

Good writers try to present a series of ideas in similar grammatical structures so the ideas will read smoothly. If one element in a series is not parallel with the others, the result may be jarring or confusing.

Recognizing the Correct Use of Parallelism

To present a series of ideas of equal importance, you should use parallel grammatical structures.

> **Parallelism** involves presenting equal ideas in words, phrases, clauses, or sentences of similar types.

4.6.1 RULE

PARALLEL WORDS

The surfer looked **strong**, **fit**, and **agile**.

PARALLEL PHRASES

The greatest feeling I know is **to ride a giant wave flawlessly** and **to have all my friends watch me enviously**.

PARALLEL CLAUSES

The surfboard **that you recommended** and **that my brother wants** is on sale.

PARALLEL SENTENCES

It couldn't be, of course. **It could never, never be**. –Dorothy Parker

Correcting Faulty Parallelism

Faulty parallelism occurs when a writer uses unequal grammatical structures to express related ideas.

> Correct a sentence containing faulty parallelism by rewriting it so that each parallel idea is expressed in the same grammatical structure.

4.6.2 RULE

Faulty parallelism can involve words, phrases, and clauses in a series or in comparisons.

Nonparallel Words, Phrases, and Clauses in a Series

Always check for parallelism when your writing contains items in a series.

Correcting Faulty Parallelism in a Series

NONPARALLEL STRUCTURES

Planning, drafting, and revision are three
gerund gerund noun
steps in the writing process.

CORRECTION

Planning, drafting, and revising are three
gerund gerund gerund
steps in the writing process.

NONPARALLEL STRUCTURES

I could not wait to try my new surfboard,
infinitive phrase
to catch some waves, and visiting the
infinitive phrase   participial phrase
beach.

CORRECTION

I could not wait to try my new surfboard, to
infinitive phrase
catch some waves, and to visit the beach.
infinitive phrase   infinitive phrase

NONPARALLEL STRUCTURE

Some experts feel that surfing is not a
noun clause
sport, but it requires athleticism.
independent clause

CORRECTION

Some experts feel that surfing is not a
noun clause
sport but that it requires athleticism.
noun clause

Another potential problem involves correlative conjunctions, such as *both ... and* or *not only ... but also*. Though these conjunctions connect two related items, writers sometimes misplace or split the first part of the conjunction. The result is faulty parallelism.

NONPARALLEL	Pia **not only** won the local surfing championship **but also** the state title.
PARALLEL	Pia won **not only** the local surfing championship **but also** the state title.

Nonparallel Words, Phrases, and Clauses in Comparisons

As the saying goes, you cannot compare apples with oranges. In writing comparisons, you generally should compare a phrase with the same type of phrase and a clause with the same type of clause.

Correcting Faulty Parallelism in Comparisons

NONPARALLEL
STRUCTURES

Most people prefer **corn** to **eating beets**.
noun — gerund phrase

CORRECTION

Most people prefer **corn** to **beets**.
noun — noun

NONPARALLEL
STRUCTURES

I left my job **at 7:00 P.M.** rather than
prepositional phrase
stopping work at 5:00 P.M.
participial phrase

CORRECTION

I left my job **at 7:00 P.M.** rather than
prepositional phrase
at the usual 5:00 P.M.
prepositional phrase

NONPARALLEL
STRUCTURES

Jaime delights **in foggy days** as much as
subject — prepositional phrase
sunny **days** delight other **people**.
subject — direct object

CORRECTION

Jaime delights **in foggy days** as much as
subject — prepositional phrase
other **people** delight **in sunny days**.
subject — prepositional phrase

See Practice 4.6A

4.7 Faulty Coordination

When two or more independent clauses of unequal importance are joined by *and*, the result can be faulty **coordination**.

Recognizing Faulty Coordination

To *coordinate* means to "place side by side in equal rank." Two independent clauses that are joined by the coordinating conjunction *and*, therefore, should have equal rank.

> **Use *and* or other coordinating conjunctions only to connect ideas of equal importance.**

CORRECT COORDINATION
Otis designed an airplane, **and** Oliver built it.

Sometimes, however, writers carelessly use *and* to join main clauses that either should not be joined or should be joined in another way so that the real relationship between the clauses is clear. Faulty coordination puts all the ideas on the same level of importance, even though logically they should not be.

FAULTY COORDINATION
Production of aircraft accelerated in World War II, **and** aircraft became a decisive factor in the war.

I didn't do well, **and** the race was very easy.

The dog looked ferocious, **and** it was snarling and snapping at me.

Occasionally, writers will also string together so many ideas with *and's* that the reader is left breathless.

STRINGY SENTENCE
The plane that flew over the field did a few dips and turns, **and** the people on the ground craned their necks to watch, **and** everyone laughed and cheered.

Correcting Faulty Coordination

Faulty coordination can be corrected in several ways.

> **One way to correct faulty coordination is to put unrelated ideas into separate sentences.**

RULE 4.7.2

When faulty coordination occurs in a sentence in which the main clauses are not closely related, separate the clauses and omit the coordinating conjunction.

FAULTY COORDINATION	Production of aircraft accelerated in World War II, **and** aircraft became a decisive factor in the war.
CORRECTION	Production of aircraft accelerated in World War II. Aircraft became a decisive factor in the war.

> **You can correct faulty coordination by putting less important ideas into subordinate clauses or phrases.**

RULE 4.7.3

If one main clause is less important than, or subordinate to, the other, turn it into a subordinate clause. You can also reduce a less important idea to a phrase.

FAULTY COORDINATION	I didn't do well, **and** the race was easy.
CORRECTION	I didn't do well, **even though** the race was easy.
FAULTY COORDINATION	The dog looked angry, **and** it was snarling at me.
CORRECTION	Snarling at me, the dog looked angry.

Stringy sentences should be broken up and revised using any of the three methods just described. Following is one way that the stringy sentence on the previous page can be revised.

REVISION OF A STRINGY SENTENCE	The plane that flew over the field did a few dips and turns. Craning their necks to watch, the people on the ground laughed and cheered.

See Practice 4.6B

PRACTICE 4.6A Revising to Eliminate Faulty Parallelism

Read each sentence. Then, rewrite the sentence to correct any nonparallel structures.

EXAMPLE   I was wet, cold, and needing sleep.

ANSWER   *I was wet, cold, and tired.*

1. This weekend we have a paper to write, a cake to bake, and a birthday party.

2. I like my school because the teachers are good, the students are nice, and I play on the football team.

3. Tell me about the students in your classes and your soccer team.

4. I did a poor job painting more because I was rushed than that I did not know how to do it.

5. If my parents give permission and I can get a ride with my cousin, I'll go.

6. I did not buy the car because it needs brakes, and I would have to get new tires.

7. The book was funny, fast-paced, and kept us interested.

8. I had a hamburger, Kim had a salad, but coffee was all that Jon ordered.

9. The mayor proposed cutting library hours, recycling pickup, and to cut other services.

10. Mom both washed the car and the windows.

PRACTICE 4.6B Revising to Eliminate Faulty Coordination

Read each sentence. Then, rewrite the sentence to correct the faulty coordination.

EXAMPLE   I chose our new pet, and it's a puppy.

ANSWER   *I chose our new pet, a puppy.*

11. The rose is one of the most popular flowers, and it has a lovely scent.

12. We drove to the stadium, and crowds filled the stands.

13. The Canadian forests stretch for miles, and they provide a home for many kinds of wildlife.

14. There's a tree house, and it has running water!

15. The picnic basket was stuffed with food, and they headed for the park.

16. I was so tired that I went to bed at 7:00, and it was still light.

17. Jay is having his car fixed, and he was in a fender bender last week.

18. We were going to practice on Saturday, but some players couldn't make it, so we switched to Sunday, but that didn't work either, so now we have practice on Monday.

19. Kristen's favorite book is *Huckleberry Finn*, and she reads it over and over.

20. The bus arrived ten minutes late, and it arrived at its next stop on time.

SPEAKING APPLICATION

Take turns with a partner. Tell about something unusual that has happened to you or to someone you know. Your partner should point out and correct any faulty parallelism in your description.

WRITING APPLICATION

Write three sentences with faulty coordination. Exchange papers with a partner and correct each other's work.

CHAPTER 5

VERB USAGE

Using the correct verb tenses will help you present the timing of actions accurately in your writing.

WRITE GUY *Jeff Anderson, M.Ed.*

WHAT DO YOU NOTICE?

Spot the verbs as you zoom in on these sentences from the story "The Interlopers" by Saki.

MENTOR TEXT

> "I'm caught in my own forest land," retorted Ulrich. "When my men come to release us you will wish, perhaps, that you were in a better plight than caught poaching on a neighbor's land, shame on you."

Now, ask yourself the following questions:

- Which verb tense did the author use in the clause *I'm caught* in the first sentence? (Remember that the word *I'm* in the first sentence is the shortened form of *I am*.)
- Which verb tense did the author use in the phrase *will wish* in the second sentence?

The author used present tense in *I'm caught*. The clause shows what is happening now to the subject of the sentence. In *will wish*, the author uses *will* before *wish* to create the future tense form. The narrator follows the phrase *will wish* with *perhaps*, showing that this might happen.

Grammar for Writers Verbs are tools that writers use to show action and to link important ideas within sentences. To help your readers follow the action in your writing, use verb tenses that accurately describe the timing of events.

Using this verb will put my action in the future.

How about using some action on this assignment in the present?

5.1 Verb Tenses

Besides expressing actions or conditions, verbs have different **tenses** to indicate when the action or condition occurred.

A tense is the form of a verb that shows the time of an action or a condition.

The Six Verb Tenses

There are six tenses that indicate when an action or a condition of a verb is, was, or will be in effect. Each of these six tenses has at least two forms.

Each tense has a basic and a progressive form.

The chart that follows shows examples of the six tenses.

THE BASIC FORMS OF THE SIX TENSES	
Present	I visit the Statue of Liberty.
Past	I visited Ellis Island last Sunday.
Future	I will visit Washington, D.C.
Present Perfect	I have visited children at the hospital for almost a year now.
Past Perfect	I had visited my grandmother every weekend until this past month.
Future Perfect	I will have visited Dallas three times a week by the end of May.
Present	Tim runs for fun.
Past	Tim ran every day during the summer.
Future	Tim will run a race next week.
Present Perfect	Tim has run in many races.
Past Perfect	Tim had run his first race by age five.
Future Perfect	Tim will have run in ten races by June.

See Practice 5.1A

Basic Verb Forms or Tenses

Verb tenses are identified simply by their tense names. The **progressive tenses,** however, are identified by their tense names plus the word *progressive*. Progressive tenses show that an action is or was happening for a period of time.

The chart below shows examples of the six tenses in their progressive form or tense. Note that all of these progressive tenses end in -*ing*. (See the section on verb conjugation later in this chapter for more about the progressive tense.)

THE PROGRESSIVE TENSES	
Present Progressive	I am drawing right now.
Past Progressive	I was drawing when you called.
Future Progressive	I will be drawing all weekend.
Present Perfect Progressive	I have been drawing more than usual lately.
Past Perfect Progressive	I had been drawing apples until the art teacher suggested that I draw boats.
Future Perfect Progressive	I will have been drawing for two years by the end of March.

The Emphatic Form

There is also a third form or tense, the **emphatic,** which exists only for the present and past tenses. The **present emphatic** is formed with the helping verbs *do* or *does,* depending on the subject. The **past emphatic** is formed with *did.* The purpose of the emphatic tense is to put more emphasis on, or to stress, the action of the verb.

THE EMPHATIC TENSES OF THE PRESENT AND THE PAST	
Present Emphatic	I do exercise more frequently than you. Sally does practice piano more often than I do.
Past Emphatic	I did exercise last night to work on my form. Jerome did work later than Alia did.

See Practice 5.1B

PRACTICE 5.1A > Identifying Verb Tenses

Read each sentence. Write the tense (*present, past, future, present perfect, past perfect,* or *future perfect*) of the underlined verb or verbs in each sentence.

EXAMPLE   The runner <u>sprinted</u> across the finish line and <u>smiled</u>.

ANSWER   *past, past*

1. After he <u>had taken</u> a nap, the pilot <u>felt</u> much more awake.

2. My family <u>will drive</u> to the beach on Saturday.

3. The circus <u>will have traveled</u> 3,000 miles by the time it <u>ends</u> its tour.

4. This play <u>has interested</u> many drama students.

5. Joe <u>enjoys</u> playing basketball outdoors.

6. After she <u>passed</u> her test, Lisa <u>worked</u> even harder.

7. People of all ages <u>have participated</u> in fund-raising events.

8. The girl <u>answered</u> when her mother <u>called</u> her.

9. Once he <u>had received</u> his allowance, the boy <u>bought</u> a baseball mitt.

10. When I <u>am</u> older, I <u>will go</u> to college.

PRACTICE 5.1B > Recognizing Tenses or Forms of Verbs

Read each sentence. Rewrite each sentence and the underlined verb, using the verb tense or form shown in parentheses.

EXAMPLE   I <u>finished</u> my homework after school. (past emphatic)

ANSWER   *I did finish my homework after school.*

11. The home team <u>won</u> the game by the tenth inning. (future perfect)

12. The violin instructor <u>plays</u> beautifully. (present emphatic)

13. The baby <u>sucked</u> his thumb until today. (past perfect progressive)

14. The athlete <u>planned</u> to run a marathon. (past emphatic)

15. The zookeeper <u>attends</u> a month-long conference. (future progressive)

16. The appetizers <u>taste</u> delicious! (present emphatic)

17. My friend <u>saw</u> the play. (future perfect)

18. I <u>tried</u> to win the game. (past progressive)

19. The traffic <u>gets</u> worse every day. (present perfect progressive)

20. The family <u>will have lived</u> here for ten years. (past perfect progressive)

SPEAKING APPLICATION

Take turns with a partner. Tell about your favorite after-school activity. Say a sentence with each of the six verb tenses in your description.

WRITING APPLICATION

Write a paragraph about a good friend. Use at least eight different verb forms or tenses in your paragraph.

The Four Principal Parts of Verbs

Every verb in the English language has four **principal parts** from which all of the tenses are formed.

> A verb has four principal parts: the **present**, the **present participle**, the **past**, and the **past participle**.

The chart below shows the principal parts of the verbs *talk*, *draw*, and *run*.

THE FOUR PRINCIPAL PARTS			
PRESENT	PRESENT PARTICIPLE	PAST	PAST PARTICIPLE
talk	talking	talked	(have) talked
draw	drawing	drew	(have) drawn
run	running	ran	(have) run

The first principal part, the present, is used for the basic forms of the present and future tenses, as well as for the emphatic forms or tenses. The present tense is formed by adding an -s or -es when the subject is *he, she, it,* or a singular noun. The future tense is formed with the helping verb *will. (I will talk. Mary will draw. Carl will run.)* The present emphatic is formed with the helping verb *do* or *does. (I do talk. Mary does draw. Carl does run.)* The past emphatic is formed with the helping verb *did. (I did talk. Mary did draw. Carl did run.)*

EL6

The second principal part, the present participle, is used with helping verbs for all of the progressive forms. *(I am talking. Mary is drawing. Carl is running.)*

The third principal part, the past, is used to form the past tense. *(I talked. Mary drew. Carl ran.)* As in the example *ran*, the past tense of a verb can change its spelling. (See the next section for more information.)

The fourth principal part, the past participle, is used with helping verbs to create the perfect tenses. *(I have talked. Mary had drawn. Carl had run.)*

See Practice 5.1C
See Practice 5.1D

PRACTICE 5.1C > **Recognizing the Four Principal Parts of Verbs**

Read each set of words. Find the verb that is in the form indicated in parentheses. Write the word and its present tense.

EXAMPLE   jumping, fly, swoop (present participle)

ANSWER   *jumping, jump*

1. shrinking, like, said (past)

2. worked, trying, listen (past)

3. smile, (have) grinned, winking (past participle)

4. scribble, typed, studying (present participle)

5. coloring, sketch, (have) painted (present participle)

6. whistle, (have) played, strumming (past participle)

7. close, shutting, slammed (past)

8. (have) cried, leap, laughing (past participle)

9. bowed, surprise, sighing (past)

10. dancing, performed, trip (present participle)

PRACTICE 5.1D > **Identifying the Four Principal Parts of Verbs**

Read each sentence. Rewrite each sentence by replacing the underlined verb with the verb form indicated in parentheses.

EXAMPLE   The actress <u>wishes</u> for a quieter life. (present participle)

ANSWER   *The actress is wishing for a quieter life.*

11. The doctor <u>was explaining</u> why the patient's arm hurt. (past participle)

12. On her birthday, the girl <u>had wanted</u> a horse. (present)

13. I <u>have liked</u> picking apples off of trees. (past)

14. The students <u>were singing</u> well. (present)

15. After the dam broke, the water <u>was flowing</u> through the street. (past)

16. The boy <u>pedals</u> his bike quickly through the park. (past participle)

17. My father <u>has driven</u> past the house. (present participle)

18. Uncle Berto <u>raked</u> the leaves. (present)

19. The dog <u>was barking</u> loudly in the kennel. (present participle)

20. I <u>went fishing</u> down by the lake. (past)

SPEAKING APPLICATION

Take turns with a partner. Tell a fictional story, using many verbs in your story. Your partner should listen for and identify the principal parts of the verbs that you use.

WRITING APPLICATION

Write a paragraph that uses sentence 19 as the beginning of an interesting story, and underline all of the past participles.

Regular and Irregular Verbs

The way the past and past participle forms of a verb are formed determines whether the verb is **regular** or **irregular.**

Regular Verbs The majority of verbs are regular. Regular verbs form their past and past participles according to a predictable pattern.

> A **regular verb** is one for which the past and past participle are formed by adding *-ed* or *-d* to the present form.

In the chart below, notice that a final consonant is sometimes doubled to form the present participle, the past, and the past participle. A final *e* may also be dropped to form the participle.

PRINCIPAL PARTS OF REGULAR VERBS			
PRESENT	PRESENT PARTICIPLE	PAST	PAST PARTICIPLE
contend	contending	contended	(have) contended
manage	managing	managed	(have) managed
stop	stopping	stopped	(have) stopped

See Practice 5.1E
See Practice 5.1F

Irregular Verbs Although most verbs are regular, many of the most common verbs are irregular. Irregular verbs do not use a predictable pattern to form their past and past participles.

> An **irregular verb** is one whose past and past participle are *not* formed by adding *-ed* or *-d* to the present form.

Usage Problems Remembering the principal parts of irregular verbs can help you avoid usage problems. One common usage problem is using a principal part that is not standard.

INCORRECT   They **knowed** about the Jefferson Memorial.

CORRECT   They **knew** about the Jefferson Memorial.

A second usage problem is confusing the past and past participle when they have different forms.

INCORRECT She **done** the right thing.

CORRECT She **did** the right thing.

Some common irregular verbs are shown in the charts that follow. Use a dictionary if you are not sure how to form the principal parts of an irregular verb.

IRREGULAR VERBS WITH THE SAME PRESENT, PAST, AND PAST PARTICIPLE			
PRESENT	PRESENT PARTICIPLE	PAST	PAST PARTICIPLE
burst	bursting	burst	(have) burst
cost	costing	cost	(have) cost
cut	cutting	cut	(have) cut
hit	hitting	hit	(have) hit
hurt	hurting	hurt	(have) hurt
let	letting	let	(have) let
put	putting	put	(have) put
set	setting	set	(have) set
shut	shutting	shut	(have) shut
split	splitting	split	(have) split
spread	spreading	spread	(have) spread

Note About *Be*: *Be* is one of the most irregular of all of the verbs. The present participle of *be* is *being*. The past participle is *been*. The present and the past depend on the subject and tense of the verb.

EL6

CONJUGATION OF *BE*		
	SINGULAR	PLURAL
Present	I am .	We are .
	You are .	You are .
	He, she, or it is .	They are .
Past	I was .	We were .
	You were .	You were .
	He, she, or it was .	They were .
Future	I will be .	We will be .
	You will be .	You will be .
	He, she, or it will be .	They will be .

IRREGULAR VERBS WITH THE SAME PAST AND PAST PARTICIPLE			
PRESENT	**PRESENT PARTICIPLE**	**PAST**	**PAST PARTICIPLE**
bring	bringing	brought	(have) brought
build	building	built	(have) built
buy	buying	bought	(have) bought
catch	catching	caught	(have) caught
fight	fighting	fought	(have) fought
find	finding	found	(have) found
get	getting	got	(have) got or (have) gotten
hold	holding	held	(have) held
keep	keeping	kept	(have) kept
lay	laying	laid	(have) laid
lead	leading	led	(have) led
leave	leaving	left	(have) left
lose	losing	lost	(have) lost
pay	paying	paid	(have) paid
say	saying	said	(have) said
sell	selling	sold	(have) sold
send	sending	sent	(have) sent
shine	shining	shone or shined	(have) shone or (have) shined
sit	sitting	sat	(have) sat
sleep	sleeping	slept	(have) slept
spend	spending	spent	(have) spent
stand	standing	stood	(have) stood
stick	sticking	stuck	(have) stuck
sting	stinging	stung	(have) stung
strike	striking	struck	(have) struck
swing	swinging	swung	(have) swung
teach	teaching	taught	(have) taught
win	winning	won	(have) won
wind	winding	wound	(have) wound

IRREGULAR VERBS THAT CHANGE IN OTHER WAYS			
PRESENT	**PRESENT PARTICIPLE**	**PAST**	**PAST PARTICIPLE**
arise	arising	arose	(have) arisen
become	becoming	became	(have) become
begin	beginning	began	(have) begun
bite	biting	bit	(have) bitten
break	breaking	broke	(have) broken
choose	choosing	chose	(have) chosen
come	coming	came	(have) come
do	doing	did	(have) done
draw	drawing	drew	(have) drawn
drink	drinking	drank	(have) drunk
drive	driving	drove	(have) driven
eat	eating	ate	(have) eaten
fall	falling	fell	(have) fallen
fly	flying	flew	(have) flown
give	giving	gave	(have) given
go	going	went	(have) gone
grow	growing	grew	(have) grown
know	knowing	knew	(have) known
lie	lying	lay	(have) lain
ride	riding	rode	(have) ridden
ring	ringing	rang	(have) rung
rise	rising	rose	(have) risen
run	running	ran	(have) run
see	seeing	saw	(have) seen
sing	singing	sang	(have) sung
sink	sinking	sank	(have) sunk
speak	speaking	spoke	(have) spoken
swim	swimming	swam	(have) swum
take	taking	took	(have) taken
tear	tearing	tore	(have) torn
throw	throwing	threw	(have) thrown
wear	wearing	wore	(have) worn
write	writing	wrote	(have) written

See Practice 5.1G
See Practice 5.1H

PRACTICE 5.1E > Recognizing Principal Parts of Regular Verbs

Read each set of verbs. Write the missing principal part of the verb indicated in parentheses.

EXAMPLE   slump, slumping, slumped (past participle)

ANSWER   *(have) slumped*

1. peering, peered, (have) peered (present)

2. cough, coughed, (have) coughed (present participle)

3. fear, fearing, (have) feared (past)

4. discuss, discussing, discussed (past participle)

5. pretend, pretending, (have) pretended (past)

6. need, needed, (have) needed (present participle)

7. polishing, polished, (have) polished (present)

8. restore, restoring, restored (past participle)

9. grab, grabbed, (have) grabbed (present participle)

10. train, training, (have) trained (past)

PRACTICE 5.1F > Using the Correct Form of Regular Verbs

Read each sentence. Then, write a correct form of the verb in parentheses to complete each sentence, and write the principal part of the verb.

EXAMPLE   The mouse is (run) quickly through the maze.

ANSWER   *running* — present participle

11. Students who graduated from high school (receive) a diploma.

12. The water (flow) down the hill.

13. I (pause) for a break.

14. If you had hurried, you could (reach) the bus on time.

15. Classical music (help) me feel relaxed.

16. I (hope) that I could learn to waltz easily.

17. The jury members (prepare) for the trial.

18. After losing the game, the players (vow) to practice more.

19. The moon looks as though it (float) in the sky.

20. John joined me as I (travel) through Timbuktu.

SPEAKING APPLICATION

Take turns with a partner. Tell about your last summer vacation. Use as many principal parts of verbs as you can in your description.

WRITING APPLICATION

Write a letter to a friend that describes a day in your life, using principal verb forms from Practice 5.1F.

PRACTICE 5.1G ▷ **Recognizing Principal Parts of Irregular Verbs**

Read each group of words. Write the two words in each group that are correct forms of the same verb.

EXAMPLE   set, setted, setting

ANSWER   *set, setting*

1. sit, sitted, sat

2. ground, grinded, grinding

3. crepted, creep, crept

4. lending, lended, lent

5. sing, sang, singed

6. fell, falled, fallen

7. written, writed, wrote

8. flying, flied, flew

9. swung, swinged, swing

10. shut, shutted, shutting

PRACTICE 5.1H ▷ **Supplying the Correct Form of Irregular Verbs**

Read each sentence. The underlined verb has been written incorrectly in each sentence. Write the correct form of the verb and its present form.

EXAMPLE   The chef <u>will spreaded</u> jam on the cake.

ANSWER   *will spread, spread*

11. The woman <u>has drawed</u> a beautiful portrait.

12. After a long time, he <u>swimming</u> across the English Channel.

13. My grandfather was happy that he <u>has finded</u> his missing hat.

14. The corn <u>grown</u> until it was eight feet tall!

15. Tracy <u>hitted</u> a home run!

16. The plane <u>has flew</u> high into the sky.

17. I <u>am slept</u> on the top bunk bed.

18. The *Titanic* <u>sunk</u> after it hit an iceberg.

19. After school, a group of students <u>seen</u> their teacher at the library.

20. Each student <u>has chose</u> a different research topic.

SPEAKING APPLICATION

Take turns with a partner. Say sentences with irregular verbs. Your partner should listen for and identify the form of the verbs that you use.

WRITING APPLICATION

Use irregular verbs to write a short story about an animal that goes on an adventure. Be sure to use correct verb forms.

Verb Conjugation

The **conjugation** of a verb displays all of its different forms.

> A **conjugation** is a complete list of the singular and plural forms of a verb in a particular tense.

The singular forms of a verb correspond to the singular personal pronouns (*I, you, he, she, it*), and the plural forms correspond to the plural personal pronouns (*we, you, they*).

To conjugate a verb, you need the four principal parts: the present (*go*), the present participle (*going*), the past (*went*), and the past participle (*gone*). You also need various helping verbs, such as *has, have,* or *will.*

Notice that only three principal parts—the present, the past, and the past participle—are used to conjugate all six of the basic forms.

CONJUGATION OF THE BASIC FORMS OF *GO*			
		SINGULAR	PLURAL
Present	First Person Second Person Third Person	I go. You go. He, she, or it goes.	We go. You go. They go.
Past	First Person Second Person Third Person	I went. You went. He, she, or it went.	We went. You went. They went.
Future	First Person Second Person Third Person	I will go. You will go. He, she, or it will go.	We will go. You will go. They will go.
Present Perfect	First Person Second Person Third Person	I have gone. You have gone. He, she, or it has gone.	We have gone. You have gone. They have gone.
Past Perfect	First Person Second Person Third Person	I had gone. You had gone. He, she, or it had gone.	We had gone. You had gone. They had gone.
Future Perfect	First Person Second Person Third Person	I will have gone. You will have gone. He, she, or it will have gone.	We will have gone. You will have gone. They will have gone.

See Practice 5.1I

Conjugating the Progressive Tense With *Be*

As you learned earlier, the **progressive tense** shows an ongoing action or condition. To form the progressive tense, use the present participle form of the verb (the *-ing* form) with a form of the verb *be*.

CONJUGATION OF THE PROGRESSIVE FORMS OF *GO*			
		SINGULAR	PLURAL
Present Progressive	First Person Second Person Third Person	I am going. You are going. He, she, or it is going.	We are going. You are going. They are going.
Past Progressive	First Person Second Person Third Person	I was going. You were going. He, she, or it was going.	We were going. You were going. They were going.
Future Progressive	First Person Second Person Third Person	I will be going. You will be going. He, she, or it will be going.	We will be going. You will be going. They will be going.
Present Perfect Progressive	First Person Second Person Third Person	I have been going. You have been going. He, she, or it has been going.	We have been going. You have been going. They have been going.
Past Perfect Progressive	First Person Second Person Third Person	I had been going. You had been going. He, she, or it had been going.	We had been going. You had been going. They had been going.
Future Perfect Progressive	First Person Second Person Third Person	I will have been going. You will have been going. He, she, or it will have been going.	We will have been going. You will have been going. They will have been going.

See Practice 5.1J

PRACTICE 5.1I > **Conjugating the Basic Forms of Verbs**

Read each group of words. Then, write the words in each group that are missing from the verb conjugation. Use the verb and tense shown in parentheses.

EXAMPLE   I _____, you _____, he _____ (buy; present perfect)

ANSWER   *have bought, have bought, has bought*

1. we _____, you _____, it _____ (care; future)
2. I _____, she _____, they _____ (give; past perfect)
3. he _____, we _____, you _____ (think; past)
4. you _____, we _____, she _____ (work; future perfect)
5. I _____, we _____, you _____ (begin; present perfect)
6. I _____, you _____, it _____ (bat; future)
7. we _____, you _____, they _____ (test; past perfect)
8. I _____, she _____, they _____ (run; past)
9. it _____, we _____, you _____ (kick; present)
10. you _____, we _____, she _____ (see; present perfect)

PRACTICE 5.1J > **Conjugating the Progressive Forms of Verbs**

Read each sentence. Rewrite each sentence, using the form of the verb that is indicated in parentheses.

EXAMPLE   I bake. (present perfect progressive)

ANSWER   *I have been baking.*

11. He throws. (future progressive)
12. They train. (past perfect progressive)
13. We laugh. (present progressive)
14. It cries. (past progressive)
15. You see. (present perfect progressive)
16. I jog. (present progressive)
17. You make. (future progressive)
18. We cook. (past progressive)
19. They speak. (present progressive)
20. She looks. (past perfect progressive)

SPEAKING APPLICATION

Challenge a partner. Give your partner a verb, such as *write*. Your partner should conjugate the verb in all the singular and plural forms for all six tenses.

WRITING APPLICATION

Use the conjugated verb forms from at least two of the items in Practice 5.1J to write a humorous paragraph.

5.2 The Correct Use of Tenses

The basic, progressive, and emphatic forms of the six tenses show time within one of three general categories: **present, past,** and **future.** This section will explain how each verb form has a specific use that distinguishes it from the other forms.

Present, Past, and Future Tense

Good usage depends on an understanding of how each form works within its general category of time to express meaning.

Uses of Tense in Present Time
Three different forms can be used to express present time.

RULE 5.2.1

> The three forms of the **present tense** show present actions or conditions as well as various continuing actions or conditions.

EXPRESSING PRESENT TENSE	
Present	I paint .
Present Progressive	I am painting .
Present Emphatic	I do paint .

The main uses of the basic form of the present tense are shown in the chart below.

EXPRESSING PRESENT TENSE	
Present Action	The shopper strolls down the aisle.
Present Condition	My head is aching .
Regularly Occurring Action	They frequently drive to Maine.
Regularly Occurring Condition	This road is slippery in winter.
Constant Action	Fish breathe through gills.
Constant Condition	Human beings are primates.

See Practice 5.2A

Historical Present The present tense may also be used to express historical events. This use of the present, called the **historical present tense,** is occasionally used in narration to make past actions or conditions sound more lively.

THE HISTORICAL PRESENT TENSE	
Past Actions Expressed in Historical Present Tense	In the late 1800s, thousands of immigrants are passing through Ellis Island.
Past Condition Expressed in Historical Present Tense	The exodus of middle-class people from the cities in the 1960s is one of the factors in the decline of urban areas.

The **critical present tense** is most often used to discuss deceased authors and their literary achievements.

THE CRITICAL PRESENT TENSE	
Action Expressed in Critical Present	Dame Agatha Christie writes with a skill that makes her stories classics.
Condition Expressed in Critical Present	In addition to his novels, Thomas Hardy is the author of several volumes of poetry.

The **present progressive tense** is used to show a continuing action or condition of a long or short duration.

USES OF THE PRESENT PROGRESSIVE TENSE	
Long Continuing Action	I am working at the park this summer.
Short Continuing Action	I am watering the plants this week.
Continuing Condition	Julio is being very helpful.

USES OF THE PRESENT EMPHATIC TENSE	
Emphasizing a Statement	I do intend to meet her at the airport.
Denying a Contrary Assertion	No, he does not have the answer.
Asking a Question	Do you guide tours of the parks?
Making a Sentence Negative	She does not have our blessing.

See Practice 5.2B

PRACTICE 5.2A > **Identifying Tense in Present Time**

Read each sentence. For the underlined verb in each sentence, write the form of the present tense that is used.

EXAMPLE   All living things <u>digest</u> food.

ANSWER   *present*

1. The crickets <u>do chirp</u>, but not very loudly.
2. Robots <u>are making</u> life easier for some people.
3. My friend <u>is traveling</u> to Italy with her parents.
4. I <u>do attend</u> dance classes.
5. The bridge <u>freezes</u> before the road freezes.
6. Piers Anthony <u>writes</u> fantasy novels to entertain readers.
7. The hockey team <u>is hoping</u> for a victory this weekend.
8. Labrador retrievers <u>are</u> good family pets.
9. I <u>am eating</u> dinner.
10. The manager <u>asks</u> employees to arrive on time.

PRACTICE 5.2B > **Supplying Verbs in Present Time**

Read each sentence. Rewrite each sentence, changing the underlined verb according to the verb tense indicated in parentheses.

EXAMPLE   The seamstress <u>makes</u> hats. (present progressive)

ANSWER   *The seamstress is making hats.*

11. The family <u>will travel</u> to Asia. (present progressive)
12. The girl <u>is wearing</u> a jacket. (present)
13. People in the early 1900s <u>had</u> electricity. (historical present)
14. Mozart <u>composed</u> piano and symphonic music. (historical present)
15. With a glass of milk, the sandwich <u>tastes</u> wonderful. (present emphatic)
16. Students often <u>wrote</u> with quills and ink in a one-room schoolhouse. (historical present)
17. Students at the school <u>support</u> their student government. (present emphatic)
18. Joblessness <u>was</u> a common problem during the 1930s. (historical present)
19. After the play closes, I <u>will move</u> to New York. (present progressive)
20. The main characters in Jane Austen's books <u>were</u> often women. (critical present)

SPEAKING APPLICATION

Take turns with a partner. Describe a normal day in your life. Use the present progressive, present emphatic, and present tenses in your description. Your partner should listen for and identify each present tense form.

WRITING APPLICATION

Write about your favorite day of the year. Using the present progressive tense, describe what you will do on that day the next time it comes around. Using the present emphatic tense, tell the best features of the day.

Uses of the Past Tense

There are seven verb forms that express past actions or conditions.

> **The seven forms that express past tense show actions and conditions that began at some time in the past.**

FORMS EXPRESSING PAST TENSE	
Past	I drew .
Present Perfect	I have drawn .
Past Perfect	I had drawn .
Past Progressive	I was drawing .
Present Perfect Progressive	I have been drawing .
Past Perfect Progressive	I had been drawing .
Past Emphatic	I did draw .

The uses of the most common form, the past, are shown below.

USES OF THE PAST TENSE	
Completed Action	They halted work on the bridge.
Completed Condition	Several apartments were empty.

Notice in the chart above that the time of the action or the condition could be changed from indefinite to definite if such words as *last week* or *yesterday* were added to the sentences.

Present Perfect The **present perfect tense** always expresses indefinite time. Use it to show actions or conditions continuing from the past to the present.

See Practice 5.2C

USES OF THE PRESENT PERFECT TENSE	
Completed Action (Indefinite Time)	They have invited us to the party.
Completed Condition (Indefinite Time)	I have been here before.
Action Continuing to Present	It has rained intermittently for days.
Condition Continuing to Present	I have felt sluggish all day.

Past Perfect The **past perfect tense** expresses an action that took place before another action.

USES OF THE PAST PERFECT TENSE	
Action Completed Before Another Action	Perhaps the nomadic hunters had drawn on the ground before they drew on the cave walls.
Condition Completed Before Another Condition	Rhoda had been a photographer until she became ill.

These charts show the **past progressive** and **emphatic tenses.**

USES OF THE PROGRESSIVE TENSE TO EXPRESS PAST TIME	
Past Progressive	**LONG CONTINUING ACTION** She was going to China that year. **SHORT CONTINUING ACTION** I was talking to Mary when you tried to call. **CONTINUOUS CONDITION** I was being honest when I said I was sorry about the incident.
Present Perfect Progressive	**CONTINUING ACTION** Edith has been touring the Southwest all summer.
Past Perfect Progressive	**CONTINUING ACTION INTERRUPTED** He had been dreaming of victory until reality interrupted that dream.

USES OF THE PAST EMPHATIC TENSE	
Emphasizing a Statement	The cactus did grow without any water.
Denying a Contrary Assertion	But I did hike to the ancient ruins!
Asking a Question	When did the United States add Alaska as a state?
Making a Sentence Negative	He did not appreciate her hard work.

See Practice 5.2D

PRACTICE 5.2C ▷ Identifying Tense in Past Time

Read each sentence. Then, write the tense of the underlined verb in each sentence.

EXAMPLE   The captain <u>had pulled</u> up the anchor.

ANSWER   *past perfect*

1. After writing his paper, the boy <u>gave</u> himself a break.

2. The couples <u>were dancing</u> until the music stopped.

3. Although she <u>had been planning</u> to leave, she stayed.

4. I got overly tired, but I <u>did enjoy</u> the hike.

5. The tourist <u>had wanted</u> to see Rome, but she changed her mind.

6. After school, the students <u>rode</u> the bus home.

7. Sometimes it <u>had been</u> too hot to sleep.

8. The barber <u>was thinking</u> about becoming a butcher.

9. The stars <u>have been twinkling</u> for many nights.

10. Asking lots of questions <u>did not get</u> him into trouble.

PRACTICE 5.2D ▷ Supplying Verbs in Past Time

Read each sentence. For the underlined verb in each sentence, write the past tense indicated in parentheses.

EXAMPLE   Long ago, people <u>drew</u> on stones. (past emphatic)

ANSWER   *did draw*

11. The boy <u>gave</u> his friend a drink of water. (past perfect progressive)

12. I <u>had</u> a flu vaccination seven years in a row. (past emphatic)

13. The girl <u>had left</u> her purse on the coffee table. (past perfect progressive)

14. I accidentally <u>ground</u> dirt into the carpet. (past progressive)

15. The teacher <u>shut</u> the door when it became too noisy outside. (past perfect)

16. The poster <u>stuck</u> to the wall. (past perfect progressive)

17. Nancy <u>slept</u> late yesterday. (past progressive)

18. He <u>tasted</u> each type of cheese. (past perfect progressive)

19. The objects <u>cast</u> strange shadows on the wall. (past progressive)

20. After dinner, the young couple <u>paid</u> the bill. (past perfect progressive)

SPEAKING APPLICATION

Take turns with a partner. Tell about something interesting you did after school last week. Use as many different forms of the past tense as possible. Your partner should listen for and identify the tenses you use.

WRITING APPLICATION

Write a paragraph about a time when you forgot to do something. Use four different forms of the past tense in your paragraph.

Uses of the Future Tense

The **future tense** shows actions or conditions that will happen at a later date.

> The future tense expresses actions or conditions that have not yet occurred.

FORMS EXPRESSING FUTURE TENSE	
Future	I will walk.
Future Perfect	I will have walked.
Future Progressive	I will be walking.
Future Perfect Progressive	I will have been walking.

USES OF THE FUTURE AND THE FUTURE PERFECT TENSE	
Future	I will jog in the morning. I will be late for the meeting.
Future Perfect	I will have run a mile by the time you arrive. The orchestra will have toured for a month before the new concert season begins.

Notice in the next chart that the **future progressive** and the **future perfect progressive tenses** express only future actions.

USES OF THE PROGRESSIVE TENSE TO EXPRESS FUTURE TIME	
Future Progressive	Rita will be studying all weekend.
Future Perfect Progressive	Sharon will have been preparing for ten years before she embarks on her trip around the world.

The basic forms of the present and the present progressive tense are often used with other words to express future time.

EXAMPLES The new store **opens** next weekend.

My family **is leaving** next month for Hawaii.

See Practice 5.2E
See Practice 5.2F

PRACTICE 5.2E **Identifying Tense in Future Time**

Read each sentence. Then, write the future-tense verbs in each sentence and identify the form of the tense.

EXAMPLE   Mary will be working on Friday night.

ANSWER   *will be working* — *future progressive*

1. In January, Mom will have been playing piano for twenty years.

2. Grandpa will visit us next month.

3. The bus will have left without us.

4. I will be cleaning the garage all day.

5. Crista will help us prepare for the recital.

6. You will have gone home by then.

7. New islands will have been forming by volcanic eruptions.

8. Tomorrow, our class will take a trip to the park.

9. After you arrive, we will discuss our plans.

10. The reporter will have written four articles by next week.

PRACTICE 5.2F **Supplying Verbs in Future Time**

Read each sentence. Then, rewrite each sentence, filling in the blank with the future tense form of the verb indicated in parentheses.

EXAMPLE   The train _____ soon. (arrive, future)

ANSWER   *The train will arrive soon.*

11. Aunt Elaine _____ us next week. (visit, future progressive)

12. I _____ decorations for the party by tomorrow. (make, future perfect progressive)

13. On June 1, the event _____. (occur, future)

14. When you receive your money, the bank _____. (call, future progressive)

15. Next year, my parents _____ their 25th wedding anniversary. (celebrate, future progressive)

16. By tonight, we _____ at baby pictures. (look, future perfect progressive)

17. The glass _____ if dropped. (break, future)

18. If the wind blows too hard, the leaves _____ off the trees. (fall, future progressive)

19. By Saturday, the teacher _____ all the essays. (grade, future perfect)

20. At the end of the race, I _____ over ten miles. (run, future perfect progressive)

SPEAKING APPLICATION

Take turns with a partner. Tell about what you hope to be doing in five years. Use future-tense verbs in your sentences. Your partner should listen for and identify the future-tense verbs that you use.

WRITING APPLICATION

Rewrite your corrections of sentences 11, 12, and 13, changing the verbs to include other future-tense verbs. Make sure your sentences still make sense.

Sequence of Tenses

A sentence with more than one verb must be consistent in its time sequence.

RULE 5.2.4

> **When showing a sequence of events, do not shift tenses unnecessarily.**

EXAMPLES   Joe **will go** to school, then he **will go** to practice.

Maria **has walked** her dog, and she **has fed** her three cats.

Liz **skied** all day and **danced** all night.

Sometimes, however, it is necessary to shift tenses, especially when a sentence is complex or compound-complex. The tense of the main verb often determines the tense of the verb in the subordinate clause. Moreover, the form of the participle or infinitive often depends on the tense of the verb in the main clause.

Verbs in Subordinate Clauses It is frequently necessary to look at the tense of the main verb in a sentence before choosing the tense of the verb in the subordinate clause.

RULE 5.2.5

> **The tense of a verb in a subordinate clause should follow logically from the tense of the main verb.**

INCORRECT I **will understand** that Paul **wrote** a play.

CORRECT I **understand** that Paul **wrote** a play.

As you study the combinations of tenses in the charts on the next pages, notice that the choice of tenses affects the logical relationship between the events being expressed. Some combinations indicate that the events are **simultaneous**—meaning that they occur at the same time. Other combinations indicate that the events are **sequential**—meaning that one event occurs before or after the other.

SEQUENCE OF EVENTS		
MAIN VERB	**SUBORDINATE VERB**	**MEANING**
	MAIN VERB IN PRESENT TENSE	
I understand…	**PRESENT** that he writes novels. **PRESENT PROGRESSIVE** that he is writing a novel. **PRESENT EMPHATIC** that he does write novels.	Simultaneous events: All events occur in present time.
I understand…	**PAST** that he wrote a novel. **PRESENT PERFECT** that he has written a novel. **PAST PERFECT** that he had written a novel. **PAST PROGRESSIVE** that he was writing a novel. **PRESENT PERFECT PROGRESSIVE** that he has been writing a novel. **PAST PERFECT PROGRESSIVE** that he had been writing a novel. **PAST EMPHATIC** that he did write a novel.	Sequential events: The writing comes before the understanding.
I understand…	**FUTURE** that he will write a novel. **FUTURE PERFECT** that he will have written a novel. **FUTURE PROGRESSIVE** that he will be writing a novel. **FUTURE PERFECT PROGRESSIVE** that he will have been writing a novel.	Sequential events: The understanding comes before the writing.

SEQUENCE OF EVENTS		
MAIN VERB	**SUBORDINATE VERB**	**MEANING**
MAIN VERB IN PAST TENSE		
I understood...	**PAST** that he wrote a novel. **PAST PROGRESSIVE** that he was writing a novel. **PAST EMPHATIC** that he did write a novel.	Simultaneous events: All events take place in the past.
I understood...	**PAST PERFECT** that he had written a novel. **PAST PERFECT PROGRESSIVE** that he had been writing a novel.	Sequential events: The writing came before the understanding.
MAIN VERB IN FUTURE TENSE		
I will understand...	**PRESENT** if he writes a novel. **PRESENT PROGRESSIVE** if he is writing a novel. **PRESENT EMPHATIC** if he does write a novel.	Simultaneous events: All events take place in future time.
I will understand...	**PAST** if he wrote a novel. **PRESENT PERFECT** if he has written a novel. **PRESENT PERFECT PROGRESSIVE** if he has been writing a novel. **PAST EMPHATIC** if he did write a novel.	Sequential events: The writing comes before the understanding.

Time Sequence With Participles and Infinitives Frequently, the form of a participle or infinitive determines whether the events are simultaneous or sequential. Participles can be present (*seeing*), past (*seen*), or perfect (*having seen*). Infinitives can be present (*to see*) or perfect (*to have seen*).

> **The form of a participle or an infinitive should logically relate to the verb in the same clause or sentence.**

5.2.6 RULE

To show simultaneous events, you will generally need to use the present participle or the present infinitive, whether the main verb is present, past, or future.

Simultaneous Events

IN PRESENT TIME

Seeing the results, she **laughs**.
present   present

IN PAST TIME

Seeing the results, she **laughed**.
present   past

IN FUTURE TIME

Seeing the results, she **will laugh**.
present   future

To show sequential events, use the perfect form of the participle and infinitive, regardless of the tense of the main verb.

Sequential Events

IN PRESENT TIME

Having seen the results, she **is laughing**.
perfect   present progressive
(She saw *before* she laughed.)

IN PAST TIME

Having seen the results, she **laughed**.
perfect   past
(She saw *before* she laughed.)

SPANNING PAST AND FUTURE TIME

Having seen her work, I **will recommend** her.
perfect   future
(Someone recommended her *after* seeing her work.)

See Practice 5.2G
See Practice 5.2H

PRACTICE 5.2G > Identifying the Time Sequence in Sentences With More Than One Verb

Read each sentence. Then, write the verb of the event that happens second in each sentence.

EXAMPLE   Having read the viewers' letters, the network will cancel the program.

ANSWER   *will cancel*

1. I am lucky that I will be studying French this year.

2. Worried about missing her flight, Carol left an hour early.

3. Having failed to hail a cab, I rode a bus instead.

4. I was happy that Janelle had been gracious.

5. He was told that the team will be practicing every Saturday afternoon.

6. I was thrilled that my sister arrived.

7. Having survived the long winter, our trees have been growing at an amazing rate.

8. Having taken a new job, my aunt will be traveling in Brazil for a month.

9. After milking the cows, the farmer's wife began to feed the chickens.

10. I was told that the Bergers will be traveling to Texas this summer.

PRACTICE 5.2H > Recognizing and Correcting Errors in Tense Sequence

Read each sentence. Then, if a sentence has an error in tense sequence, rewrite it to correct the error. If a sentence is correct, write *correct*.

EXAMPLE   Lea knocks and waited patiently at the door.

ANSWER   *Lea knocked and waited patiently at the door.*

11. I picked up the telephone receiver quickly, but the line is still dead.

12. When we go shopping, we bought shoes.

13. My uncle comes back to visit us, and he drives his vintage sports car.

14. Ava finished her assignment, but she forgets to include a title page.

15. The stages of the rocket dropped away as the space shuttle climbed into the sky.

16. Aunt Maureen jumped to her feet and cheers when Mia makes the winning basket.

17. When George presents his science fair project, all the judges were very impressed.

18. Every time Roger comes to visit me, he brought his dog with him.

19. Randy has played drums before, but now he plays the guitar.

20. After the bell rang, we left the building.

SPEAKING APPLICATION

Take turns with a partner. Tell about something fun that you like to do. Use two verbs in your sentences. Your partner should listen for and identify the sequence of events in your sentences.

WRITING APPLICATION

Use sentences 16, 17, and 18 as models to write your own sentences with incorrect tense sequence. Then, exchange papers with a partner. Your partner should rewrite your sentences, using the correct sequence in tense.

Modifiers That Help Clarify Tense

The time expressed by a verb can often be clarified by adverbs such as *often*, *sometimes*, *always*, or *frequently* and phrases such as *once in a while*, *within a week*, *last week*, or *now and then*.

> **Use modifiers when they can help clarify tense.**

In the examples below, the modifiers that help clarify the tense of the verb are highlighted in orange. Think about how the sentences would read without the modifiers. Modifiers help to make your writing more precise and interesting.

EXAMPLES

We **read** the sports scores **every weekend**.

My brother **practices** his saxophone **once a day**.

My brother **practices** his saxophone **now and then**.
(These two sentences have very different meanings.)

Occasionally, I **enjoy** playing volleyball at the beach.

Susan **always swims** with her goggles on.

By next year, Walter **will have fished** in every river in Colorado.

I **swim** 40 laps **once a week**.

Water-skiing **is now** one of my favorite water sports.

Sometimes, people **attempt** to swim across large bodies of water.

I **always visit** my grandfather on weekends.

See Practice 5.2I
See Practice 5.2J

PRACTICE 5.2I Identifying Modifiers That Help Clarify Tense

Read each sentence. Then, write the modifier in each sentence that helps clarify the verb tense.

EXAMPLE   Suddenly, the balloon burst.

ANSWER   *Suddenly*

1. The clothes sometimes shrink in the dryer.
2. All at once, the computers and printers shut down.
3. He always brings all of his books to class.
4. One at a time, the pitcher threw the balls high and outside.
5. Steve drives me home once a week.
6. He never wants to walk home in the rain.
7. Frequently, we pay our bills early.
8. Quickly, I laid the dishes on the table.
9. I always see the same television commercials.
10. We sometimes see the sunrise over the mountains.

PRACTICE 5.2J Supplying Modifiers to Clarify Meaning

Read each sentence. Then, fill in the blank in each sentence with a modifier that will clarify the meaning of the sentence.

EXAMPLE   _____, the writer worked on the revisions.

ANSWER   *Recently, the writer worked on the revisions.*

11. The musicians will _____ perform for an audience.
12. _____, our flight from Chicago arrived.
13. My grandfather _____ works on the Sunday crossword puzzle.
14. _____, a news station crew arrived.
15. Our neighbors will be moving away _____.
16. I returned the call _____.
17. He is _____ polite.
18. The guests arrived _____.
19. _____, we finished our work.
20. Eliana can _____ answer the teacher's questions.

SPEAKING APPLICATION

Take turns with a partner. Tell about a trip that you have taken. Use modifiers that help clarify tense in your sentences. Your partner should listen for and identify the modifiers in your sentences.

WRITING APPLICATION

Use your corrections of sentences 13, 16, and 19 as models to write your own sentences. Rewrite the sentences to include different modifiers that clarify the meaning of each sentence.

5.3 The Subjunctive Mood

There are three **moods,** or ways in which a verb can express an action or condition: **indicative, imperative,** and **subjunctive.** The **indicative** mood, which is the most common, is used to make factual statements (*Karl is helpful.*) and to ask questions (*Is Karl helpful?*). The **imperative** mood is used to give orders or directions (*Be helpful.*).

Using the Subjunctive Mood

There are two important differences between verbs in the **subjunctive** mood and those in the indicative mood. First, in the present tense, third-person singular verbs in the subjunctive mood do not have the usual *-s* or *-es* ending. Second, the subjunctive mood of *be* in the present tense is *be;* in the past tense, it is *were,* regardless of the subject.

INDICATIVE MOOD	SUBJUNCTIVE MOOD
He listens to me.	I suggest that he listen to me.
They are ready.	He insists that they be ready.
She was impatient.	If she were impatient, she could not do this work.

> **Use the subjunctive mood (1) in clauses beginning with *if* or *that* to express an idea that is contrary to fact or (2) in clauses beginning with *that* to express a request, a demand, or a proposal.**

RULE 5.3.1

Expressing Ideas Contrary to Fact Ideas that are contrary to fact are commonly expressed as wishes or conditions. Using the subjunctive mood in these situations shows that the idea expressed is not true now and may never be true.

EXAMPLES   He wishes that the climate **were** milder.

Brett wished that he **were** a better driver.

She could have reached the top shelf if she **were** taller.

RULE 5.3.2

Some *if* clauses do not take a subjunctive verb. If the idea expressed may be true, an indicative form is used.

EXAMPLES   I said that **if** the weather **was** bad, we'd leave early, so let's go.

If I **want** to ski, I'll have to get up early.

Expressing Requests, Demands, and Proposals Verbs that request, demand, or propose are often followed by a *that* clause containing a verb in the subjunctive mood.

REQUEST   She requests that we **be** on time for the trip.

DEMAND   It is required that each student **wear** a uniform.

PROPOSAL   He proposed that a motion **be** made to adjourn.   See Practice 5.3A

Auxiliary Verbs That Express the Subjunctive Mood

EL7

Because certain helping verbs suggest conditions contrary to fact, they can often be used in place of the subjunctive mood.

RULE 5.3.3

Could, would, or *should* can be used with a verb to express the subjunctive mood.

The sentences on the left in the chart below have the usual subjunctive form of the verb *be: were.* The sentences on the right have been reworded with *could, would,* and *should.*

THE SUBJUNCTIVE MOOD WITH AUXILIARY VERBS	
WITH FORMS OF *BE*	WITH *COULD, WOULD,* OR *SHOULD*
If the future **were** clear, we'd act.	If the future **could** be clear, we'd act.
If someone **were** to escort her, she would go.	If someone **would** escort her, she would go.
If you **were** to move, would you write to me?	If you **should** move, would you write to me?

See Practice 5.3B

PRACTICE 5.3A Identifying Mood (Indicative, Imperative, Subjunctive)

Read each sentence. Then, identify whether the sentence expresses doubts, wishes and possibilities in the *indicative, imperative,* or *subjunctive* mood.

EXAMPLE   The principal asked that Hal drop by the office.

ANSWER   *subjunctive*

1. It is urgent that he take the next plane.

2. Get your homework done before you go to rehearsal.

3. If it were possible, I would do it myself.

4. Mr. Jimenez treats me as if I were one of his students.

5. The writer sat at the computer all day.

6. Include a cash payment with your order form.

7. I wish that I were back in my warm, comfortable bed.

8. Please leave!

9. The judge ordered that the defendant pay a fine.

10. Did the dog bark nonstop in the yard?

PRACTICE 5.3B Supplying Auxiliary Verbs to Express the Subjunctive Mood

Read each sentence. Then, rewrite each sentence, and complete it by supplying an auxiliary verb.

EXAMPLE   I _____ prefer that you leave tomorrow.

ANSWER   *I would prefer that you leave tomorrow.*

11. I _____ insist that he finish his homework.

12. It _____ be better if she went with us.

13. We _____ demand that they listen to what we have to say.

14. I _____ be glad if he _____ give me the paper.

15. You _____ clean your room before it gets any messier.

16. It _____ be necessary that we work together.

17. If Mary wants good advice, she _____ listen to her mother.

18. I recommended that he _____ be more generous with his time.

19. It _____ be best if you helped us this weekend.

20. He _____ show that he cared by offering to accompany you.

SPEAKING APPLICATION

Take turns with a partner. Say sentences that express doubts, wishes, and possibilities. Use the subjunctive mood in your sentences. Your partner should identify the subjunctive mood that identifies wishes, doubts, and possibilities in your sentences.

WRITING APPLICATION

Write your own sentences using auxiliary verbs to express the subjunctive mood. Then, exchange papers with a partner. Your partner should underline all the auxiliary verbs in your sentences.

5.4 Voice

This section discusses a characteristic of verbs called **voice.**

5.4.1

> **Voice** or tense is the form of a verb that shows whether the subject is performing the action or is being acted upon.

In English, there are two voices: **active** and **passive.** Only action verbs can indicate the active voice; linking verbs cannot.

Active and Passive Voice or Tense

If the subject of a verb performs the action, the verb is active; if the subject receives the action, the verb is passive.

Active Voice Any action verb can be used in the active voice. The action verb may be transitive (that is, it may have a direct object) or intransitive (without a direct object).

5.4.2

> A verb is active if its subject performs the action.

In the examples below, the subject performs the action. In the first example, the verb *telephoned* is transitive; *team* is the direct object, which receives the action. In the second example, the verb *developed* is transitive; *pictures* is the direct object. In the third example, the verb *gathered* is intransitive; it has no direct object. In the last example, the verb *worked* is intransitive and has no direct object.

ACTIVE
VOICE

The captain **telephoned** the **team** .
transitive verb direct object

Bill **developed** twenty-five **pictures** of the ocean.
transitive verb direct object

Telephone messages **gathered** on the desk while
intransitive verb
she was away.

Bill **worked** quickly.
intransitive verb

See Practice 5.4A
See Practice 5.4B

EL6

Passive Voice Most action verbs can also be used in the passive voice.

> **A verb is passive if its action is performed upon the subject.**

RULE 5.4.3

In the following examples, the subjects are the receivers of the action. The first example names the performer, the captain, as the object of the preposition *by* instead of the subject. In the second example, no performer of the action is mentioned.

PASSIVE
VOICE

The **team** **was telephoned** by the captain.
receiver of action   verb

The **messages** **were gathered** into neat piles.
receiver of action   verb

> **A passive verb is always a verb phrase made from a form of *be* plus the past participle of a verb. The tense of the helping verb *be* determines the tense of the passive verb.**

RULE 5.2.4

The chart below provides a conjugation in the passive voice of the verb *believe* in the three moods. Notice that there are only two progressive forms and no emphatic form.

THE VERB *BELIEVE* IN THE PASSIVE VOICE	
Present Indicative	He is believed.
Past Indicative	He was believed.
Future Indicative	He will be believed.
Present Perfect Indicative	He has been believed.
Past Perfect Indicative	He had been believed.
Future Perfect Indicative	He will have been believed.
Present Progressive Indicative	He is being believed.
Past Progressive Indicative	He was being believed.
Present Imperative	(You) be believed.
Present Subjunctive	(if) he be believed
Past Subjunctive	(if) he were believed

See Practice 5.2C

Using Active and Passive Voice

Writing that uses the active voice tends to be much more lively than writing that uses the passive voice. The active voice is usually more direct and economical. That is because active voice shows someone doing something.

RULE 5.4.5

Use the active voice whenever possible.

ACTIVE VOICE   Finally, Debbie **repaired** the telephone.

PASSIVE VOICE   Finally, the telephone **was repaired** by Debbie.

The passive voice has two uses in English.

RULE 5.4.6

Use the passive voice when you want to emphasize the receiver of an action rather than the performer of an action.

EXAMPLE   My best friend **was awarded** a medal.

RULE 5.4.7

Use the passive voice to point out the receiver of an action whenever the performer is not important or not easily identified.

EXAMPLE   At noon, the doors to the tomb **were unlocked**, and the archaeologists entered it.

The active voice lends more excitement to writing, making it more interesting to readers. In the example below, notice how the sentence you just read has been revised to show someone doing something, rather than something just happening.

EXAMPLE   At noon, the archaeologists **unlocked** the doors to the tomb and entered it.
(*Who* unlocked the doors and entered the tomb?)

See Practice 5.4D

Recognizing Active Voice (Active Tense)

Read each sentence. Write the active verb in each sentence.

EXAMPLE   Sally added fresh cucumbers to the salad.

ANSWER   *added*

1. The team selected a new member.
2. Linda talked with us this week.
3. Robert picked his tennis partner.
4. We each bought several notebooks.
5. Later, the student wrote an essay.
6. Many wild animals live in the forest.
7. Amy grew her own vegetables this summer.
8. In the winter, snow covers the ground.
9. The train reached Baton Rouge in three hours.
10. He always reads the morning paper before breakfast.

PRACTICE 5.4B   **Using Active Verbs**

Read each item. Then, write different sentences, using each item as an active verb.

EXAMPLE   signed

ANSWER   *The author signed the book.*

11. identifies
12. played
13. ask
14. nest
15. elect
16. performed
17. eaten
18. skips
19. cooked
20. slept

SPEAKING APPLICATION

Take turns with a partner. Give directions on how to do something, such as how to perform a search using the Internet. Your partner should listen for and identify the active verbs in your directions.

WRITING APPLICATION

Write a paragraph about yourself and the activities that you enjoy doing. Underline all the active verbs in your paragraph.

PRACTICE 5.4C > Forming the Tenses of Passive Verbs

Read each verb. Then, using the subject indicated in parentheses, conjugate each verb in the passive voice for the present indicative, past indicative, future indicative, present perfect indicative, past perfect indicative, and future perfect indicative.

EXAMPLE   say (it)

ANSWER   *it is said, it was said, it will be said, it has been said, it had been said, it will have been said*

1. drive (they)
2. tell (you)
3. ask (we)
4. mow (it)
5. forgive (we)
6. move (it)
7. alert (they)
8. instruct (we)
9. play (it)
10. create (it)

PRACTICE 5.4D > Supplying Verbs in the Active Voice (Active Tense)

Read each sentence. Then, complete each sentence by supplying a verb a in the active voice.

EXAMPLE   A little boy _____ the door.

ANSWER   *opened*

11. Reporters _____ the president.
12. Thomas _____ the podium on the stage.
13. Miss Van Patten _____ the bird calls.
14. That college _____ advanced algebra to undergraduate students.
15. Renoir _____ the portrait.
16. They _____ the posters.
17. The lost dog _____ us home.
18. The magazine _____ my first story.
19. Eduardo _____ the phone.
20. Rachel _____ the new computer system.

SPEAKING APPLICATION

Take turns with a partner. Exchange a list of five verbs. Your partner should say the conjugation of each verb in the passive voice for the present indicative, past indicative, and future indicative.

WRITING APPLICATION

Show that you understand active and passive tenses by writing four sentences, using active tenses twice and passive tenses twice. Read your sentences to a partner who should tell if the sentence is active tense or passive tense as you speak.

CHAPTER 6

PRONOUN USAGE

Knowing how to use pronouns correctly will help you write clear sentences that flow.

WRITE GUY *Jeff Anderson, M.Ed.*

WHAT DO YOU NOTICE?

Stay on the lookout for pronouns as you zoom in on this sentence from "My English," an excerpt from *Something to Declare* by Julia Alvarez.

MENTOR TEXT

> Mami and Papi used to speak it when they had a secret they wanted to keep from us children.

Now, ask yourself the following questions:

- Which words do the pronouns *it* and *they* refer to?
- Why does the author use the pronoun *us* instead of *we* in the phrase *us children*?

The pronoun *it* is the object of the verb *speak*, so *it* refers to the language used by the subjects of the sentence. The pronoun *they* renames the subjects *Mami* and *Papi* both times it appears. The author uses the pronoun *us* instead of *we* because *us* is the object of the preposition in the prepositional phrase *from us children*.

Grammar for Writers Understanding the uses of pronouns helps writers to craft sentences that convey the meaning that is intended. As you edit your writing, check that your readers will be able to tell to whom or what your pronouns refer.

I need to give it to him from all of us.

Wow! You're a pronoun pro this morning.

6.1 Case

Nouns and pronouns are the only parts of speech that have **case**.

Case is the form of a noun or a pronoun that shows how it is used in a sentence.

The Three Cases

Nouns and pronouns have three cases, each of which has its own distinctive uses.

The three cases of nouns and pronouns are the **nominative,** the **objective,** and the **possessive.**

CASE	USE IN SENTENCE
Nominative	As the Subject of a Verb, Predicate Nominative, or Nominative Absolute
Objective	As the Direct Object, Indirect Object, Object of a Preposition, Object of a Verbal, or Subject of an Infinitive
Possessive	To Show Ownership

Case in Nouns

The case, or form, of a noun changes only to show possession.

NOMINATIVE The **map** had been hidden for years.

(*Map* is the subject of the verb *had been hidden*.)

OBJECTIVE We tried to find the **map** .

(*Map* is the object of the infinitive *to find*.)

POSSESSIVE The **map's** location could not be determined.

(The form changes when *'s* is added to show possession.)

Case in Pronouns

Personal pronouns often have different forms for all three cases. The pronoun that you use depends on its function in a sentence.

NOMINATIVE	OBJECTIVE	POSSESSIVE
I	me	my, mine
you	you	your, yours
he, she, it	him, her, it	his, her, hers, its
we, they	us, them	our, ours
		their, theirs

EXAMPLES **I** read the book about space.

Jerome sent the book to **me**.

See Practice 6.1A

The book about space is **mine**.

The Nominative Case in Pronouns

The **nominative case** is used when a personal pronoun acts in one of three ways.

> **Use the nominative case** when a pronoun is the subject of a verb, the subject of a predicate nominative, or the subject of a pronoun in a nominative absolute.

6.1.3 RULE

A **nominative absolute** consists of a noun or nominative pronoun followed by a participial phrase. It functions independently from the rest of the sentence.

EXAMPLE **We having opened our textbooks,** the geography teacher pointed out the map on page 435.

NOMINATIVE PRONOUNS	
As the Subject of a Verb	**I** will consult the map while **she** asks for directions.
As a Predicate Nominative	The finalists were **he** and **she**.
In a Nominative Absolute	**We** having finished the meal, the waiter cleared our table.

Nominative Pronouns in Compounds

When you use a pronoun in a compound subject or predicate nominative, check the case either by mentally crossing out the other part of the compound or by inverting the sentence.

COMPOUND SUBJECT	The teacher and **I** inspected the map. (**I** inspected the map.)
	She and her father sailed the boat. (**She** sailed the boat.)
COMPOUND PREDICATE NOMINATIVE	The fastest sailors were Jody and **he**. (Jody and **he** were the fastest sailors.)
	The surveyors were Lin and **I**. (Lin and **I** were the surveyors.)

Nominative Pronouns With Appositives

When an appositive follows a pronoun that is being used as a subject or predicate nominative, the pronoun should stay in the nominative case. To check that you have used the correct case, either mentally cross out the appositive or isolate the subject and verb.

SUBJECT	**We** mapmakers use technology. (**We** use technology.)
PREDICATE NOMINATIVE	The winners were **we** seniors. (**We** were the winners.)
APPOSITIVE AFTER NOUN	The nominees, who were **she** and **I**, ran for class president. (**She** and **I** ran for class president.)

See Practice 6.1B

PRACTICE 6.1A > **Identifying Case**

Read each sentence. Then, label the underlined pronoun in each sentence *nominative, objective,* or *possessive.*

EXAMPLE   Within an hour of leaving, <u>we</u> had a flat tire.

ANSWER   *nominative*

1. The realtor will not meet with <u>you</u> until next Tuesday.

2. Amanda has lost <u>her</u> sunglasses.

3. Choi dropped <u>his</u> glove in the snow.

4. The Foresters brought their cat with <u>them</u> to their summer house.

5. There is no doubt that this scarf is <u>yours</u>.

6. <u>I</u> appreciate a helping hand.

7. Stella mentioned that someone requested <u>her</u> presence at the meeting.

8. The car showed dents and scratches on <u>its</u> roof.

9. <u>You</u> asked us for the homework assignment.

10. <u>It</u> was a moment of complete tranquility.

PRACTICE 6.1B > **Supplying Pronouns in the Nominative Case**

Read each sentence. Then, supply a nominative pronoun to complete each sentence.

EXAMPLE   Sophia and _____ worked overtime.

ANSWER   *she*

11. Marica and _____ are looking for him at the library.

12. _____ is a warm and beautiful evening.

13. Are _____ sincere in your apology?

14. _____ are longing for a phone call from Jill.

15. The solution to the problem is that she and _____ need to deposit money into the account.

16. _____ is the teacher that I highly respect.

17. You understand that _____ is absent today.

18. My closest friend is _____.

19. I know that _____ will travel with me.

20. The leaders of the band are he and _____.

SPEAKING APPLICATION

Take turns with a partner. Describe a class that you have really enjoyed. Use at least one example of a pronoun in each of the three cases. Your partner should listen for and identify your use of pronouns as nominative, objective, and possessive.

WRITING APPLICATION

Write a paragraph describing an event you have attended. Use at least three nominative pronouns in your paragraph.

The Objective Case

Objective pronouns are used for any kind of object in a sentence as well as for the subject of an infinitive.

RULE 6.1.4

> Use the **objective case** for the object of any verb, preposition, or verbal or for the subject of an infinitive.

OBJECTIVE PRONOUNS	
Direct Object	A basketball hit him in the head.
Indirect Object	My uncle sent me a lace fan from Hong Kong.
Object of Preposition	Three very tall men sat in front of us in the movie theater.
Object of Participle	The sharks following them were very hungry.
Object of Gerund	Meeting them will be a great pleasure.
Object of Infinitive	I am obligated to help her move this Saturday.
Subject of Infinitive	The firm wanted her to work the night shift.

Objective Pronouns in Compounds

As with the nominative case, errors with objective pronouns most often occur in compounds. To find the correct case, mentally cross out the other part of the compound.

EXAMPLES

Cracking ice floes alarmed Burt and **him**.
(Cracking ice floes alarmed **him**.)

Sally drew Laurie and **me** a map to her house.
(Sally drew **me** a map.)

Note About *Between:* Be sure to use the objective case after the preposition *between*.

INCORRECT   This argument is between you and **I**.

CORRECT   This argument is between you and **me**.

Objective Pronouns With Appositives

Use the objective case when a pronoun that is used as an object or as the subject of an infinitive is followed by an appositive.

EXAMPLES   The mapmaking quiz intimidated **us** students.

My aunt brought **us** nieces an iguana.

See Practice 6.1C   The guide asked **us** stragglers to hurry.

The Possessive Case

One use for the **possessive case** is before gerunds. A **gerund** is a verbal form ending in *-ing* that is used as a noun.

> Use the **possessive case** before gerunds.

6.1.5 RULE

EXAMPLES   **Your** tracing of the map was sloppy.

We objected to **his** insinuating that we were lazy.

Sarah insists on **our** attending the dance.

Common Errors in the Possessive Case

Be sure not to use an apostrophe with a possessive pronoun because possessives already show ownership. Spellings such as *her's, our's, their's,* and *your's* are incorrect.

In addition, be sure not to confuse possessive pronouns and contractions that sound alike. *It's* (with an apostrophe) is the contraction for *it is* or *it has*. *Its* (without the apostrophe) is a possessive pronoun that means "belonging to it." *You're* is a contraction of *you are*; the possessive form of *you* is *your*.

POSSESSIVE PRONOUNS   The map had served **its** purpose.

Don't forget **your** map.

CONTRACTIONS   **It's** not likely you will become lost.

You're the only ones who wouldn't use the map.

See Practice 6.1D

PRACTICE 6.1C	Supplying Pronouns in the Objective Case

Read each sentence. Then, supply an objective pronoun to complete each sentence.

EXAMPLE   I applauded _____ and the other cast members.

ANSWER   *them*

1. Emily offered _____ her prom dress.

2. Abigail gave Jessie and _____ lots of unwanted attention.

3. The children waved at _____ mothers.

4. My boss advanced _____ a week's pay.

5. Our coaches bought _____ brand new basketballs after our trip to the finals.

6. The secret is between you and _____ .

7. The incident gave _____ a new perspective.

8. Ask for Wai and _____ when you arrive.

9. I gave _____ new books to read.

10. The teacher asked _____ to answer the question.

PRACTICE 6.1D	Recognizing Pronouns in the Possessive Case

Read each sentence. Then, select the correct pronoun from the choices in parentheses to complete each sentence.

EXAMPLE   That pig has (it's, its) own pen to play in.

ANSWER   *its*

11. (Him, His) endless kindness is extremely thoughtful.

12. None of the books on this shelf are (mine, my).

13. I'm positive Mrs. Landry appreciated (our, us) assisting her.

14. These are Christopher's pencils, but where are (your's, yours)?

15. Jhanna remembered (her, hers) appointment.

16. Did you confront Joshua about (him, his) playing his radio too loudly?

17. The Thompsons told us that these garden supplies are (their's, theirs).

18. (Me, My) teaching piano lessons helped pay my tuition.

19. After you have looked through it, put the comic book back into (it's, its) original plastic sleeve.

20. No one appreciated (them, their) cheerful attitude.

SPEAKING APPLICATION

Take turns with a partner. Describe a kind act that you have witnessed. Include at least three objective pronouns in your description.

WRITING APPLICATION

Write a paragraph about the type of person who inspires you, and explain why. Use at least three pronouns in the possessive case in your paragraph.

6.2 Special Problems With Pronouns

Choosing the correct case is not always a matter of choosing the form that "sounds correct," because writing is usually more formal than speech. For example, it would be incorrect to say, "John is smarter than *me*." because the verb is understood in the sentence: "John is smarter than *I [am]*."

Using *Who* and *Whom* Correctly

In order to decide when to use *who* or *whom* and the related forms *whoever* and *whomever*, you need to know how the pronoun is used in a sentence and what case is appropriate.

> ***Who*** is used for the nominative case. ***Whom*** is used for the objective case.

6.2.1 RULE

CASE	PRONOUNS	USE IN SENTENCES
Nominative	who whoever	As the Subject of a Verb or Predicate Nominative
Objective	whom whomever	As the Direct Object, Object of a Verbal, Object of a Preposition, or Subject of an Infinitive
Possessive	whose whosever	To Show Ownership

EXAMPLES   I know **who** has a new car.

Tippy brought **whoever** was sitting down her chew toy.

Jake did not know **whom** Tim chose.

Whose car is in front of the store?

The nominative and objective cases are the source of certain problems. Pronoun problems can appear in two kinds of sentences: direct questions and complex sentences.

In Direct Questions

Who is the correct form when the pronoun is the subject of a simple question. *Whom* is the correct form when the pronoun is the direct object, object of a verbal, or object of a preposition.

Questions in subject–verb word order always begin with *who*. However, questions in inverted order never correctly begin with *who*. To see if you should use *who* or *whom*, reword the question as a statement in subject–verb word order.

EXAMPLES

Who wants a free ticket to the movies?

Whom did you take with you?

(You did take **whom** with you.)

In Complex Sentences

Follow these steps to see if the case of a pronoun in a subordinate clause is correct. First, find the subordinate clause. If the complex sentence is a question, rearrange it in subject–verb order. Second, if the subordinate clause is inverted, rearrange the words in subject–verb word order. Finally, determine how the pronoun is used in the subordinate clause.

EXAMPLE

Who , may I ask, has seen a whale?

REARRANGED

I may ask **who** has seen a whale.

USE OF PRONOUN

(subject of the verb *has seen*)

EXAMPLE

Is Jake the one **whom** they chose to leave?

REARRANGED

They chose **whom** to leave.

USE OF PRONOUN

(object of the verb *chose*)

Note About *Whose*: The word *whose* is a possessive pronoun; the contraction *who's* means "who is" or "who has."

POSSESSIVE PRONOUN

Whose umbrella is this?

CONTRACTION

Who's [who has] taken my umbrella?

See Practice 6.2A

Pronouns in Elliptical Clauses

An **elliptical clause** is one in which some words are omitted but still understood. Errors in pronoun usage can easily be made when an elliptical clause that begins with *than* or *as* is used to make a comparison.

> In **elliptical clauses** beginning with *than* or *as*, use the form of the pronoun that you would use if the clause were fully stated.

6.2.2 RULE

The case of the pronoun is determined by whether the omitted words fall before or after the pronoun. The omitted words in the examples below are shown in brackets.

WORDS OMITTED BEFORE PRONOUN
You gave Lewis more than **me**.

(You gave Lewis more than [you gave] **me**.)

WORDS OMITTED AFTER PRONOUN
Ray is as dedicated as **he**.

(Ray is as dedicated as **he** [is].)

Mentally add the missing words. If they come *before* the pronoun, choose the objective case. If they come *after* the pronoun, choose the nominative case.

CHOOSING A PRONOUN IN ELLIPTICAL CLAUSES
1. Consider the choices of pronouns: nominative or objective.
2. Mentally complete the elliptical clause.
3. Base your choice on what you find.

The case of the pronoun can sometimes change the entire meaning of the sentence.

NOMINATIVE PRONOUN
He liked whales more than **I**.

He liked whales more than **I** [did].

OBJECTIVE PRONOUN
He liked whales more than **me**.

See Practice 6.2B

He liked whales more than [he liked] **me**.

PRACTICE 6.2A ⟩ **Choosing *Who* or *Whom*
Correctly**

Read each sentence. Then, write *who* or *whom* to complete the sentence.

EXAMPLE _____ will start for the Houston Astros tomorrow?

ANSWER *Who*

1. _____ is the best student in the class?

2. For _____ did you vote?

3. He is a talented singer _____ is destined for great things.

4. The woman on the phone was not _____ he had anticipated.

5. To _____ did you speak about the charity event?

6. _____ was at the dance last weekend?

7. Ada knows _____ made the mistake.

8. Do you know _____ wrote that song?

9. With _____ did you drive?

10. _____ should I ask about the return policy?

PRACTICE 6.2B ⟩ **Identifying the Correct
Pronoun in Elliptical Clauses**

Read each sentence. Then, select the correct pronoun from the choices in parentheses to complete each elliptical clause.

EXAMPLE Grant is much stronger than _____. (me, I)

ANSWER *I*

11. He is taller than _____. (her, she)

12. Penny sends e-mails to others more often than to _____. (I, me)

13. Tim and Ronan speak better Spanish than _____. (he, him)

14. I am not as well prepared as _____. (her, she)

15. Edith is a lot funnier than _____. (I, me)

16. Mr. Qin does not visit a doctor as often as _____. (I, me)

17. She can write faster than _____. (I, me)

18. Harold always thought he was more outgoing than _____. (her, she)

19. You offered more of your advice to Gia than _____. (mine, me)

20. Abdel is as misunderstood as _____. (him, he)

SPEAKING APPLICATION

Take turns with a partner. Ask questions using both *who* and *whom*. Your partner should respond by also using *who* and *whom* correctly in his or her response.

WRITING APPLICATION

Write a paragraph describing a funny scene from a movie. Use two elliptical clauses in your paragraph.

CHAPTER 7

AGREEMENT

Making subjects agree with verbs and pronouns agree with their antecedents, or the words they refer to, will help you write clear, meaningful sentences.

WRITE GUY *Jeff Anderson, M.Ed.*

WHAT DO YOU NOTICE?

Look out for examples of agreement as you zoom in on these sentences from "My English," an excerpt from *Something to Declare* by Julia Alvarez.

MENTOR TEXT

> One Sunday at our extended family dinner, my grandfather sat down at the children's table to chat with us. He was famous, in fact, for the way he could carry on adult conversations with his grandchildren.

Now, ask yourself the following questions:

- In the context of both sentences, whom does the pronoun *us* refer to?
- In the second sentence, how do the pronouns *he* and *his* relate to their antecedent?

When using the plural pronoun *us*, the author is referring to herself and other children. In the second sentence, *grandchildren* clarifies to whom *us* refers. Both *he* and *his* are third-person pronouns that are singular in number and masculine in gender; they relate to the singular, masculine antecedent, *grandfather*.

Grammar for Writers Writers can avoid repetition of nouns by using pronouns. By checking that pronouns agree in number, person, and gender with their antecedents, you can craft sentences that are clear in meaning.

Check with the nouns.

Whom does this pronoun belong to?

7.1 Subject–Verb Agreement

For a subject and a verb to agree, both must be singular, or both must be plural. In this section, you will learn how to make sure singular and plural subjects and verbs agree.

Number in Nouns, Pronouns, and Verbs

In grammar, **number** indicates whether a word is singular or plural. Only three parts of speech have different forms that indicate number: nouns, pronouns, and verbs.

7.1.1

> **Number** shows whether a noun, pronoun, or verb is singular or plural.

Recognizing the number of most nouns is seldom a problem because most form their plurals by adding -*s* or -*es*. Some, such as *mouse* or *ox,* form their plurals irregularly: *mice, oxen.*

Pronouns, however, have different forms to indicate their number. The chart below shows the different forms of personal pronouns in the nominative case, the case that is used for subjects.

PERSONAL PRONOUNS		
SINGULAR	**PLURAL**	**SINGULAR OR PLURAL**
I	*we*	*you*
he, she, it	*they*	

The grammatical number of verbs is sometimes difficult to determine. That is because the form of many verbs can be either singular or plural, and they may form plurals in different ways.

SINGULAR   She **sees** .

She **has seen** .

PLURAL   We **see** .

We **have seen** .

Some verb forms can be only singular. The personal pronouns *he, she,* and *it* and all singular nouns call for singular verbs in the present and the present perfect tense.

ALWAYS SINGULAR

He **sees** .

He **has seen** .

Pat **runs** .

Chris **has run** .

She **jumps** .

She **has jumped** .

The verb *be* in the present tense has special forms to agree with singular subjects. The pronoun *I* has its own singular form of *be;* so do *he, she, it,* and singular nouns.

ALWAYS SINGULAR

I **am** hungry.

He **is** tall.

Jody **is** late.

She **is** ready.

All singular subjects except *you* share the same past tense verb form of *be.*

ALWAYS SINGULAR

I **was** going home.

He **was** team captain.

Carolyn **was** early to practice.

See Practice 7.1A

She **was** getting on the bus.

A verb form will always be singular if it has had an *-s* or *-es* added to it or if it includes the words *has, am, is,* or *was.* The number of any other verb depends on its subject.

The chart on the next page shows verb forms that are always singular and those that can be singular or plural.

VERBS THAT ARE ALWAYS SINGULAR	VERBS THAT CAN BE SINGULAR OR PLURAL
(he, she, Jane) sees	(I, you, we, they) see
(he, she, Jane) has seen	(I, you, we, they) have seen
(I) am	(you, we, they) are
(he, she, Jane) is	(you, we, they) were
(I, he, she, Jane) was	

Singular and Plural Subjects

When making a verb agree with its subject, be sure to identify the subject and determine its number.

RULE 7.1.2

> A singular subject must have a singular verb. A plural subject must have a plural verb.

SINGULAR SUBJECT AND VERB	PLURAL SUBJECT AND VERB
The archaeologist works in Egypt.	These archaeologists work in Egypt.
She was being mysterious about the dig's location.	They were being mysterious about the dig's location.
Roni looks through an encyclopedia for information about China.	Mike and Sam look through an encyclopedia for information about China.
China is a large country in Asia.	China and India are large countries in Asia.
Chris takes organic chemistry.	Annie and Kelly take organic chemistry.
Rhonda is planning a vacation to Yellowstone National Park.	Our neighbors are planning a vacation to Yellowstone National Park.
Sasha plays forward on the basketball team.	Julio and Jim play on the soccer team.
He looks through the telescope.	They look through the telescope.
Elizabeth has been studying the solar system.	We have been studying the solar system.

See Practice 7.1B

PRACTICE 7.1A Identifying Number in Nouns, Pronouns, and Verbs

Read each word or group of words. Then, write whether the word or words are *singular, plural,* or *both.*

EXAMPLE   toes

ANSWER   *plural*

1. men

2. listens

3. you

4. musical note

5. sneakers

6. should

7. we

8. is

9. he

10. have seen

PRACTICE 7.1B Identifying Singular and Plural Subjects and Verbs

Read each sentence. Write the correct verb form from the choices in parentheses. Then, label the verb *singular* or *plural.*

EXAMPLE   That song (has, have) become a classic.

ANSWER   *has become*— singular

11. Vacations (is, are) often very expensive.

12. In the morning, the ships (sails, sail) out to sea.

13. The twins (wash, washes) the dishes.

14. Meshaun's brother (likes, like) to play baseball.

15. The chairs (is, are) made of pine.

16. The people on the talk show sometimes (disagrees, disagree).

17. The students (listens, listen) to the speech.

18. (Does, Do) lions live in this area?

19. She told us that English literature (was, were) her best class.

20. (There's, There are) the leaders of both groups.

Intervening Phrases and Clauses

When you check for agreement, mentally cross out any words that separate the subject and verb.

> **A phrase or clause that interrupts a subject and its verb does not affect subject–verb agreement.**

In the first example below, the singular subject *discovery* agrees with the singular verb *interests* despite the intervening prepositional phrase *of mummies*, which contains a plural noun.

EXAMPLES The **discovery** of mummies **interests** many people.

The **archaeologists**, whose work is nearly complete, **require** more funding.

Intervening parenthetical expressions—such as those beginning with *as well as, in addition to, in spite of,* or *including*—also have no effect on the agreement of the subject and verb.

EXAMPLES Your **information**, in addition to the data gathered by those working at the site, **is helping** to solve the mystery.

Jonathan's **trip**, including visits to Germany and France, **is lasting** four months.

See Practice 7.1C

Relative Pronouns as Subjects

When *who, which,* or *that* acts as a subject of a subordinate clause, its verb will be singular or plural depending on the number of the antecedent.

> **The antecedent of a relative pronoun determines its agreement with a verb.**

EXAMPLES He is the only **one** of the students **who has** prior experience working in a chemistry lab.

(The antecedent of *who* is *one*.)

He is the only one of several **students who have** prior experience working in chemistry labs.

(The antecedent of *who* is *students*.)

Compound Subjects

A **compound subject** has two or more simple subjects, which are usually joined by *or* or *and*. Use the following rules when making compound subjects agree with verbs.

Subjects Joined by *And*

Only one rule applies to compound subjects connected by *and*: The verb is usually plural, whether the parts of the compound subject are all singular, all plural, or mixed.

> **A compound subject joined by *and* is generally plural and must have a plural verb.**

7.1.5 RULE

TWO SINGULAR SUBJECTS	A **thunderstorm** and a **tornado hit** the town.
TWO PLURAL SUBJECTS	**Thunderstorms** and **tornadoes appear** on the radar screen.
A SINGULAR SUBJECT AND A PLURAL SUBJECT	Luckily, a **tornado** and the **winds** it brings often **miss** our area.

There are two exceptions to this rule. The verb is singular if the parts of a compound subject are thought of as one item or if the word *every* or *each* precedes the compound subject.

EXAMPLES **Bread and butter was** all they served

for snack.

Every weather center and emergency

network issues warnings for severe weather.

Singular Subjects Joined by *Or* or *Nor*

When both parts of a compound subject connected by *or* or *nor* are singular, a singular verb is required.

Two or more singular subjects joined by *or* or *nor* must have a singular verb.

EXAMPLE A **tornado** or **windstorm causes** damage.

Plural Subjects Joined by *Or* or *Nor*

When both parts of a compound subject connected by *or* or *nor* are plural, a plural verb is required.

Two or more plural subjects joined by *or* or *nor* must have a plural verb.

EXAMPLE Either **grapes** or **raisins make** a nice dessert for lunch.

Subjects of Mixed Number Joined by *Or* or *Nor*

If one part of a compound subject is singular and the other is plural, the verb agrees with the subject that is closer to it.

If one or more singular subjects are joined to one or more plural subjects by *or* or *nor*, the subject closest to the verb determines agreement.

EXAMPLES Neither **David** nor my **parents are frightened**.

Neither my **parents** nor **David is frightened**. See Practice 7.1D

PRACTICE 7.1C	Identifying Intervening Phrases and Clauses

Read each sentence. Then, underline the intervening phrase or clause between the subject and verb in each sentence.

EXAMPLE   My painting for the art show was not quite finished.

ANSWER   *My painting <u>for the art show</u> was not quite finished.*

1. The planting of the new trees took place yesterday.

2. The singers as well as the dancers worked very hard on the show.

3. Math, like history, is an interesting subject.

4. The neighbor across the street grows roses.

5. Two students in my school wrote a play.

6. New York, despite its crowded streets, is fun to visit.

7. Her team, including the coaches, had pizza after the game.

8. My sisters, who live all over the country, get together once a year.

9. The rehearsals for the concert began at eight o'clock.

10. The picnic feast that we brought tasted delicious.

PRACTICE 7.1D	Making Verbs Agree With Singular and Compound Subjects

Read each sentence. Then, fill in the blank with the form of a verb that agrees with the singular or compound subject in each sentence.

EXAMPLE   Amy and Sarah _____ next door to each other.

ANSWER   *live*

11. Either chicken or fish _____ good.

12. Neither hats nor phones _____ allowed in school.

13. My mom _____ me run at the track meet.

14. Mary, Casey, and I _____ to the music.

15. Aunts, uncles, cousins, and grandparents _____ all at the reunion.

16. After the game, Melinda and Juanita _____ shopping.

17. Swimming _____ fun to do in the summer.

18. Seagulls _____ around the beach in search of food.

19. Both Jim and Dasai _____ mountain climbing.

20. Neither Ken nor his brother _____ home.

SPEAKING APPLICATION

Take turns with a partner. Say sentences with intervening clauses to tell about a trip you once took. Your partner should listen for and identify the intervening clauses in your sentences.

WRITING APPLICATION

Use sentences 13, 14, 19, and 20 as models to write similar sentences. Exchange papers with a partner. Your partner should complete the sentences with the correct form of a verb that agrees with the subject.

Confusing Subjects

Some kinds of subjects have special agreement problems.

Hard-to-Find Subjects and Inverted Sentences
Subjects that appear after verbs are said to be **inverted.**
Subject–verb order is usually inverted in questions. To find out
whether to use a singular or plural verb, mentally rearrange the
sentence into subject–verb order.

> A verb must still agree in number with a subject that comes
> after it.

EXAMPLE

On the roof **are** two lightning **rods** .

REARRANGED IN
SUBJECT–VERB ORDER

Two lightning **rods are** on the roof.

The words *there* and *here* often signal an inverted sentence.
These words never function as the subject of a sentence.

EXAMPLES

There **are** the satellite **photos** .

Here **is** the revised **information** .

Note About *There's* and *Here's*: Both of these contractions
contain the singular verb *is: there is* and *here is.* They should be
used only with singular subjects.

CORRECT

There's only one **class** expected.

Here's a blue **dress** to try on.   See Practice 7.1E

Subjects With Linking Verbs
Subjects with linking verbs may also cause agreement problems.

> A linking verb must agree with its subject, regardless of the
> number of its predicate nominative.

EXAMPLES **Tulips are** my favorite flower.

One **reason** we expect a tornado **is** that strong winds are forecast.

In the first example, the plural verb *are* agrees with the plural subject *tulips*. In the next example, the singular subject *reason* takes the singular verb *is*.

Collective Nouns

Collective nouns name groups of people or things. Examples include *audience, class, club,* and *committee*.

> **A collective noun takes a singular verb when the group it names acts as a single unit. A collective noun takes a plural verb when the group acts as individuals.**

SINGULAR The senior **class graduates** on Wednesday.

(The members act as a unit.)

PLURAL The senior **class were going** on separate trips.

(The members act individually.)

Nouns That Look Like Plurals

Some nouns that end in *-s* are actually singular. For example, nouns that name branches of knowledge, such as *civics,* and those that name single units, such as *mumps,* take singular verbs.

> **Use singular verbs to agree with nouns that are plural in form but singular in meaning.**

SINGULAR **Physics is** a lot of fun.

When words such as *ethics* and *politics* do not name branches of knowledge but indicate characteristics, their meanings are plural. Similarly, such words as *eyeglasses, pants,* and *scissors* generally take plural verbs.

PLURAL   Only my green **pants are** in the laundry.

Indefinite Pronouns

Some indefinite pronouns are always singular, some are always plural, and some may be either singular or plural. Prepositional phrases do not affect subject–verb agreement.

Singular indefinite pronouns take singular verbs. Plural indefinite pronouns take plural verbs.

SINGULAR   *anybody, anyone, anything, each, either, everybody, everyone, everything, neither, nobody, no one, nothing, somebody, someone, something*

PLURAL   *both, few, many, others, several*

SINGULAR   **Everyone** on the rescue squad **has left**.

PLURAL   **Many** of the houses **were repaired**.

The pronouns *all, any, more, most, none,* and *some* usually take a singular verb if the antecedent is singular, and a plural verb if it is plural.

SINGULAR   **Some** of the area **was ruined** by the hurricane.

PLURAL   **Some** of the damaged cars **are** beyond repair.

Titles of Creative Works and Names of Organizations

Plural words in the title of a creative work or in the name of an organization do not affect subject–verb agreement.

A title of a creative work or name of an organization is singular and must have a singular verb.

EXAMPLES **The National Institutes of Health is**

a helpful agency.
(organization)

Sunflowers by Vincent Van Gogh **is** a famous

painting.
(creative work)

Amounts and Measurements
Although they appear to be plural, most amounts and
measurements actually express single units or ideas.

> **A noun expressing an amount or measurement is usually
> singular and requires a singular verb.**

7.1.16 RULE

EXAMPLES **Two hundred million dollars is** the cost in

property damage from the snowstorm.

(*Two hundred million dollars* is one sum of money.)

Two miles was our distance from the nearest

food store.

(*Two miles* is a single distance.)

Three quarters of the class **attends**

the big game.

(*Three quarters* is one part of the class.)

Half of the trees **were uprooted**.

(*Half* refers to a number of individual trees, and not part of an
individual tree, so it is plural.)

See Practice 7.1F

PRACTICE 7.1E Identifying Subjects and Verbs in Inverted Sentences

Read each sentence. Then, identify the subject and verb in each sentence.

EXAMPLE   Outside our kitchen window blooms a beautiful rosebush.

ANSWER   *subject:* **rosebush**; *verb:* **blooms**

1. Between the street and our house is a small creek.
2. Here is your copy of the rehearsal schedule.
3. Into the mall file the many eager shoppers.
4. All around the teacher sit the quiet students.
5. Here comes the marching band.
6. Ahead of Efrem runs his dog.
7. Next to the school was a new playground.
8. Here are the best movies of the year.
9. There is no doubt about who will win.
10. To the south stretches a shimmering lake.

PRACTICE 7.1F Making Verbs Agree With Confusing Subjects

Read each sentence. Then, write the correct subject or verb from the choices in parentheses to complete each sentence.

EXAMPLE   One half of the students (was, were) late.

ANSWER   *were*

11. Economics (is, are) one of my hardest classes.
12. (Each, Both) of the students have completed their tests.
13. No one (has, have) seen her all day.
14. Many people (was, were) at the first game of the season.
15. Her glasses (help, helps) her to see the board better.
16. High winds usually (causes, cause) lots of damage.
17. The audience (watches, watch) the play.
18. *Eliminating Carbon Emissions* (was, were) the name of the documentary film.
19. Three hundred dollars (is, are) the cost of the bike.
20. Few of the dogs at the park (were, was) on a leash.

SPEAKING APPLICATION

Take turns with a partner. Tell about your summer plans, using four inverted sentences. Your partner should listen for and identify the subject and verb in each of your sentences.

WRITING APPLICATION

Write three sentences that include confusing subjects. Underline the subject in each sentence, and make sure that the verb agrees with the subject.

7.2 Pronoun–Antecedent Agreement

Like a subject and its verb, a pronoun and its antecedent must agree. An **antecedent** is the word or group of words for which the pronoun stands.

Agreement Between Personal Pronouns and Antecedents

While a subject and verb must agree only in number, a personal pronoun and its antecedent must agree in three ways.

> **A personal pronoun must agree with its antecedent in number, person, and gender.**

7.2.1 RULE

The **number** of a pronoun indicates whether it is singular or plural. **Person** refers to a pronoun's ability to indicate either the person speaking (first person), the person spoken to (second person), or the person, place, or thing spoken about (third person). **Gender** is the characteristic of nouns and pronouns that indicates whether the word is *masculine* (referring to males), *feminine* (referring to females), or *neuter* (referring to neither males nor females).

The only pronouns that indicate gender are third-person singular personal pronouns.

GENDER OF THIRD-PERSON SINGULAR PRONOUNS	
Masculine	*he, him, his*
Feminine	*she, her, hers*
Neuter	*it, its*

In the example below, the pronoun *her* agrees with the antecedent *actress* in number (both are singular), in person (both are third person), and in gender (both are feminine).

EXAMPLE   The actress has opened **her** home to the public.

Agreement in Number

There are three rules to keep in mind to determine the number of compound antecedents.

RULE 7.2.2 | Use a singular personal pronoun when two or more singular antecedents are joined by *or* or *nor.*

EXAMPLES   Either Craig **or** Todd will bring **his** model of a castle to class.

Neither Charlie **nor** Pepper will eat **his** new dog food.

RULE 7.2.3 | Use a plural personal pronoun when two or more antecedents are joined by *and.*

EXAMPLE   Melissa **and** I are studying for **our** exams.

An exception occurs when a distinction must be made between individual and joint ownership. If individual ownership is intended, use a singular pronoun to refer to a compound antecedent. If joint ownership is intended, use a plural pronoun.

SINGULAR   **Thomas and Cecily** played **her** guitar.

PLURAL   **Thomas and Cecily** paid for **their** guitar.

SINGULAR   Neither **Tim nor Kevin** let me ride **his** horse.

PLURAL   Neither **Tim nor Kevin** let me ride **their** horse.

The third rule applies to compound antecedents whose parts are mixed in number.

RULE 7.2.4 | Use a plural personal pronoun if any part of a compound antecedent joined by *or* or *nor* is plural.

See Practice 7.2A

EXAMPLE　If either the **teacher** or the **students** arrive, take **them** to the cafeteria.

Agreement in Person and Gender　Avoid shifts in person or gender of pronouns.

> As part of pronoun–antecedent agreement, take care not to shift either person or gender.

7.2.5 RULE

SHIFT IN PERSON　**Mike** is planning to visit Windsor Castle because **you** can see how royalty lives.

CORRECT　**Mike** is planning to visit Windsor Castle because **he** wants to see how royalty lives.

SHIFT IN GENDER　The **horse** threw **its** head back and stood on **his** hind legs.

CORRECT　The **horse** threw **its** head back and stood on **its** hind legs.

Generic Masculine Pronouns　Traditionally, a masculine pronoun has been used to refer to a singular antecedent whose gender is unknown. Such use is called *generic* because it applies to both masculine and feminine genders. Many writers now prefer to use *his or her, he or she, him or her,* or to rephrase a sentence to eliminate the situation.

> When gender is not specified, either use *his or her* or rewrite the sentence.

7.2.6 RULE

EXAMPLES　Each **student** found a useful Web site on which to research **his or her report** on castles.

Students found useful Web sites on which to research **their reports** on castles.

See Practice 7.2B

PRACTICE 7.2A Making Personal Pronouns Agree With Their Antecedents

Read each sentence. Then, rewrite each sentence to include the correct personal pronoun.

EXAMPLE   My sister and I visited _____ aunt and uncle.

ANSWER   *My sister and I visited our aunt and uncle.*

1. Jim and Doreen called loudly from the cave, but nobody heard _____.

2. Annie will read _____ report to the class.

3. The president and the Congress announced _____ new ideas.

4. Either Ryan or Cal will drive _____ truck.

5. Neither Heather nor Celia had a pencil with _____.

6. Antonio said he had done _____ homework.

7. One of the girls has lost _____ backpack.

8. When my brothers or my sister celebrates a birthday, _____ always request cupcakes.

9. Either the boy or his brothers spoke to _____ parents.

10. Neither puppy will thrive if _____ is not well cared for.

PRACTICE 7.2B Revising for Agreement in Person and Gender

Read each sentence. Then, revise each sentence so that the personal pronoun agrees with the antecedent.

EXAMPLE   All of the boys lost his money.

ANSWER   *All of the boys lost their money.*

11. One of the managers gave his approval.

12. Every one of the girls has their assignments.

13. The hiker realized that you can't explore the Grand Canyon in just one day.

14. Neither of the students agreed to ask their parents.

15. One of the men will have to volunteer their time.

16. One of the monkeys had her tail wrapped around a tree limb.

17. Each of the women was given their award.

18. All of the parents refused to give her consent.

19. Both of my relatives sent her congratulations.

20. None of the men had lost their maps.

SPEAKING APPLICATION

Take turns with a partner. Tell about members of your family. Use several different personal pronouns in your sentences. Your partner should listen for and name the personal pronouns you use and tell whether they agree with their antecedents.

WRITING APPLICATION

Use sentences 14, 15, and 16 as models to write similar sentences. Then, exchange papers with a partner. Your partner should revise each sentence to make the personal pronoun agree with the antecedent.

Agreement With Indefinite Pronouns

When an indefinite pronoun, such as *each, all,* or *most,* is used with a personal pronoun, the pronouns must agree.

> **Use a plural personal pronoun when the antecedent is a plural indefinite pronoun.**

RULE 7.2.7

EXAMPLES **Many** of the children were excited about **their** music lessons.

All of the boys forgot to bring **their** books.

When both pronouns are singular, a similar rule applies.

> **Use a singular personal pronoun when the antecedent is a singular indefinite pronoun.**

RULE 7.2.8

In the first example, the personal pronoun *his* agrees in number with the singular indefinite pronoun *one.* The gender (masculine) is determined by the word *boys.*

EXAMPLES Only **one** of the boys practiced **his** trumpet.

One of the girls remembered to bring **her** music.

If other words in the sentence do not indicate a gender, you may use *him or her, he or she, his or her,* or rephrase the sentence.

EXAMPLES **Each** of the musicians wore **his or her** new band uniform.

The **musicians** wore **their** new band uniforms.

For indefinite pronouns that can be either singular or plural, such as *all, any, more, most, none,* and *some,* agreement depends on the antecedent of the indefinite pronoun.

Most of the music had lost **its** appeal.
(The antecedent of *most* is *music,* which is singular.)

Most of the listeners wanted **their** money back.
(The antecedent of *most* is *listeners,* which is plural.)

Some of the food **was** cold.
(The antecedent of *some* is *food,* which is singular.)

All of the documents **were** on the table.
(The antecedent of *all* is *documents,* which is plural.)

In some situations, strict grammatical agreement may be illogical. In these situations, either let the meaning of the sentence determine the number of the personal pronoun, or reword the sentence.

ILLOGICAL When **each of the telephones** rang,
I answered **it** as quickly as possible.

MORE LOGICAL When **each of the telephones** rang,
I answered **them** as quickly as possible.

MORE LOGICAL When **all of the telephones** rang,
I answered **them** as quickly as possible. See Practice 7.2C

Agreement With Reflexive Pronouns

Reflexive pronouns, which end in *-self* or *-selves,* should only refer to a word earlier in the same sentence.

A reflexive pronoun must agree with an antecedent that is clearly stated.

EXAMPLES **Frank** made dinner for **himself**.

You should consider **yourself** lucky.

Class **clowns** enjoy making fools of **themselves**. See Practice 7.2D

PRACTICE 7.2C **Making Personal and Indefinite Pronouns Agree**

Read each sentence. Then, rewrite each sentence, filling in the blank with an appropriate personal pronoun that agrees with the indefinite pronoun.

EXAMPLE   Each of the students presented _____ project.

ANSWER   *Each of the students presented his or her project.*

1. Each of the women wanted _____ turn to speak.

2. Every student in our class finished _____ paper on time.

3. Many students in the class already paid _____ share of the party expenses.

4. All of the artists displayed _____ paintings at the art show.

5. One of the tigers in the zoo hurt _____ paw.

6. A few of the dancers brought _____ shoes.

7. Each of the male leads remembered _____ lines.

8. Anyone who needs help with a particular scene may review _____ script.

9. Several of the cats had _____ claws clipped.

10. Most of the girls softball team members brought _____ rule book.

PRACTICE 7.2D **Supplying Reflexive Pronouns**

Read each sentence. Then, write the correct reflexive pronoun that agrees with the antecedent in each sentence.

EXAMPLE   We told _____ to keep working.

ANSWER   *ourselves*

11. Gina, please help _____ to some pizza.

12. The musicians amused _____ by playing different musical selections.

13. Louie and I will take the dogs to the park by _____.

14. Amanda and Wilson kept _____ busy by playing a board game.

15. She found _____ reading another chapter before she went to sleep.

16. Jason wrote the entire play by _____.

17. I made _____ a salad for lunch.

18. Sal was worried that he might hurt _____ while running the obstacle course.

19. All of you should be proud of _____ for the improvements you have made in your writing.

20. Deb gave _____ a manicure before her sister's wedding.

SPEAKING APPLICATION

Take turns with a partner. Choose three indefinite pronouns. Your partner should say sentences, using a personal pronoun that agrees with each indefinite pronoun.

WRITING APPLICATION

Use sentences 11, 12, and 15 as models to write similar sentences. Then, exchange papers with a partner. Your partner should rewrite each sentence, using the correct reflexive pronoun that agrees with the antecedent.

7.3 Special Problems With Pronoun Agreement

This section will show you how to avoid some common errors that can obscure the meaning of your sentences.

Vague Pronoun References

One basic rule governs all of the rules for pronoun reference.

> To avoid confusion, a pronoun requires an antecedent that is either stated or clearly understood.

The pronouns *which*, *this*, *that*, and *these* should not be used to refer to a vague or overly general idea.

In the following example, it is impossible to determine exactly what the pronoun *these* stands for because it may refer to three different groups of words.

VAGUE REFERENCE   Jay was carsick, the dog was restless, and the air conditioner was broken. **These** made our trip to the aquarium unpleasant.

This vague reference can be corrected in two ways. One way is to change the pronoun to an adjective that modifies a specific noun. The second way is to revise the sentence so that the pronoun *these* is eliminated.

CORRECT   Jay was carsick, the dog was restless, and the air conditioner was broken. **These misfortunes** made our trip to the aquarium unpleasant.

CORRECT   Jay's carsickness, the dog's restlessness, and the air conditioner's breakdown made our trip to the aquarium unpleasant.

> **The personal pronouns *it, they,* and *you* should always have a clear antecedent.**

In the next example, the pronoun *it* has no clearly stated antecedent.

VAGUE REFERENCE | Marge is studying marine mammals next year. **It** should be very educational.

Again, there are two methods of correction. The first method is to replace the personal pronoun with a specific noun. The second method is to revise the sentence entirely in order to make the whole idea clear.

CORRECT | Marge is studying marine mammals next year. **The experience** should be very educational.

CORRECT | **Marge's study** of marine mammals next year should be very educational.

In the next example, the pronoun *they* is used without an accurate antecedent.

VAGUE REFERENCE | I enjoyed reading *Moby-Dick*, but **they** never explained what the whale symbolized.

CORRECT | I enjoyed reading *Moby-Dick*, but **the author** never explained what the whale symbolized.

VAGUE REFERENCE | When we arrived at the aquarium, **they** told us that the whale show was about to start.

CORRECT | When we arrived at the aquarium, **the ticket taker** told us that the whale show was about to start.

Use *you* only when the reference is truly to the reader or listener.

VAGUE REFERENCE **You** couldn't understand a word Jim said.

CORRECT **We** couldn't understand a word Jim said.

VAGUE REFERENCE In the school my great-aunt attended, **you** were expected to stand up when addressed.

CORRECT In the school my great-aunt attended, **students** were expected to stand up when addressed.

Note About *It*: In many idiomatic expressions, the personal pronoun *it* has no specific antecedent. In statements such as "It is late," *it* is an idiom that is accepted as standard English.

See Practice 7.3A

Ambiguous Pronoun References

A pronoun is **ambiguous** if it can refer to more than one antecedent.

A pronoun should never refer to more than one antecedent.

In the following sentence, *he* is confusing because it can refer to either *Joe* or *Walt*. Revise such a sentence by changing the pronoun to a noun or rephrasing the sentence entirely.

AMBIGUOUS REFERENCE Joe told Walt about the whales **he** observed.

CORRECT Joe told Walt about the whales **Walt** observed.

(Joe knew about the whales.)

Do not repeat a personal pronoun in a sentence if it can refer to a different antecedent each time.

AMBIGUOUS REPETITION	When Jon asked his father if **he** could borrow the car, **he** said that **he** needed it.
CLEAR	When Jon asked his father if **he** could borrow the car, **Jon** said that **he** needed it.
CLEAR	When Jon asked his father if **he** could borrow the car, his **father** said that **he** needed it **himself**.

Notice that in the first sentence above, it is unclear whether *he* is referring to Jon or to his father. To eliminate the confusion, Jon's name was used in the second sentence. In the third sentence, the reflexive pronoun *himself* helps to clarify the meaning.

Avoiding Distant Pronoun References

A pronoun should be placed close to its antecedent.

> **A personal pronoun should always be close enough to its antecedent to prevent confusion.**

7.3.6 RULE

A distant pronoun reference can be corrected by moving the pronoun closer to its antecedent or by changing the pronoun to a noun. In the example below, *it* is too far from the antecedent *leg*.

DISTANT REFERENCE	Molly shifted her weight from her injured leg. Two days ago she had fallen, cutting herself on the glass in the street. Now **it** was swathed in bandages.
CORRECT	Molly shifted her weight from her injured leg. Two days ago she had fallen, cutting herself on the glass in the street. Now her **leg** was swathed in bandages.

See Practice 7.3B

(*Leg* replaces the pronoun *it*.)

PRACTICE 7.3A > Correcting Vague Pronouns

Read each sentence. Then, rewrite each sentence to avoid the use of vague pronouns.

EXAMPLE   At the end of the play, they bow to the audience.

ANSWER   *At the end of the play, the actors bow to the audience.*

1. They predict that this summer will be very hot.

2. On the news, it mentioned that people are saving more money.

3. The road was dangerous because they had not yet cleared the snow.

4. The flyer says that you must be eighteen to enter.

5. To learn to play an instrument, you must practice often.

6. After forgetting her lines in the play, my sister did not want to try it again.

7. This is the movie that they have raved about in all the papers.

8. You have to pass a swimming test in order to become a lifeguard.

9. During the basketball game, they called a lot of fouls on both teams.

10. In the club, you have to pay dues every six months.

PRACTICE 7.3B > Recognizing Ambiguous Pronouns

Read each sentence. Then, rewrite each sentence to avoid the use of ambiguous pronouns.

EXAMPLE   Tasha told Annie that she must not be late for the party.

ANSWER   *Tasha told Annie that Annie must not be late for the party.*

11. Sammie left the car in the garage without locking it.

12. Mike told Ethan that his bicycle had a flat tire.

13. When Mother shops for my sister, she is usually distracted.

14. Take the shoes out of the bags and throw them away.

15. Whenever Andrea talks to Evita, she enjoys the conversation.

16. Aunt Mary fed Kirsten before she took a nap.

17. Take the curtain off the window and wash it.

18. The polls said that our choices for city council would lose, but they are often wrong.

19. Whenever Serena calls Karen, she never gets a chance to say much.

20. When Andrew invites Omar to go to the movies, he is always late.

SPEAKING APPLICATION

Take turns with a partner. Use sentences from Practice 7.3A as models to say similar sentences that contain vague pronoun references. Your partner should reword each sentence to make it clearer.

WRITING APPLICATION

Use sentences 11, 12, and 15 as models to write similar sentences. Then, exchange papers with a partner. Your partner should rewrite each sentence, correcting the ambiguous pronoun references.

USING MODIFIERS

Understanding how to use different degrees of adjectives and adverbs as modifiers will help you to write logical comparisons.

CHAPTER 8

WRITE GUY *Jeff Anderson, M.Ed.*

WHAT DO YOU NOTICE?

Hunt for degrees of comparison as you zoom in on this sentence from the first inaugural address by President Franklin Delano Roosevelt.

MENTOR TEXT

> That is why our constitutional system has proved itself the most superbly enduring political mechanism the modern world has produced.

Now, ask yourself the following questions:

- What modifier does the speaker use to make a comparison in this sentence?
- What is being compared in the sentence?

The speaker uses the modifier *most* to form the superlative degree of the adverb *superbly*. The superlative degree is used to compare three or more things. The speaker uses the adverbial phrase *most superbly* to describe *enduring*. He is comparing our constitutional system to *all* other political mechanisms in the modern world by saying that no other can match its endurance.

Grammar for Writers Using modifiers is an effective way for writers to demonstrate their viewpoints. Check your modifiers to be sure you have used the appropriate degrees of comparison.

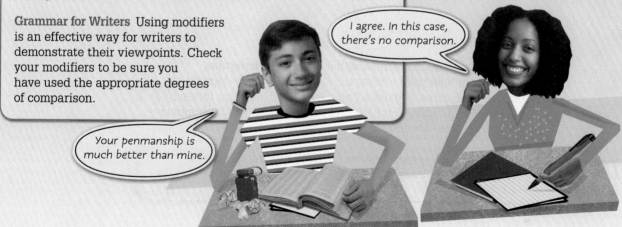

I agree. In this case, there's no comparison.

Your penmanship is much better than mine.

8.1 Degrees of Comparison

In the English language, there are three degrees, or forms, of most adjectives and adverbs that are used in comparisons.

Recognizing Degrees of Comparison

In order to write effective comparisons, you first need to know the three degrees.

The three degrees of comparison are the positive, the comparative, and the superlative.

The following chart shows adjectives and adverbs in each of the three degrees. Notice the three different ways that modifiers are changed to show degree: (1) by adding -er or -est, (2) by adding *more* or *most*, and (3) by using entirely different words.

DEGREES OF ADJECTIVES		
POSITIVE	COMPARATIVE	SUPERLATIVE
slow	slower	slowest
disagreeable	more disagreeable	most disagreeable
good	better	best
DEGREES OF ADVERBS		
slowly	more slowly	most slowly
disagreeably	more disagreeably	most disagreeably
well	better	best

See Practice 8.1A

Regular Forms

Adjectives and adverbs can be either **regular** or **irregular,** depending on how their comparative and superlative degrees are formed. The degrees of most adjectives and adverbs are formed regularly. The number of syllables in regular modifiers determines how their degrees are formed.

Use -er or *more* to form the comparative degree and -est or *most* to form the superlative degree of most one- and two-syllable modifiers.

EXAMPLES

smart	smarter	smartest
harmful	more harmful	most harmful

> **All adverbs that end in *-ly* form their comparative and superlative degrees with *more* and *most*.**

8.1.3 RULE

EXAMPLES

curtly	more curtly	most curtly
shrewdly	more shrewdly	most shrewdly

> **Use *more* and *most* to form the comparative and superlative degrees of all modifiers with three or more syllables.**

8.1.4 RULE

EXAMPLES

beautiful	more beautiful	most beautiful
generous	more generous	most generous

Note About Comparisons With *Less* and *Least*: *Less* and *least* can be used to form another version of the comparative and superlative degrees of most modifiers.

EXAMPLES

soft	less soft	least soft
appetizing	less appetizing	least appetizing

See Practice 8.1B

Irregular Forms

The comparative and superlative degrees of a few commonly used adjectives and adverbs are formed in unpredictable ways.

> **The irregular comparative and superlative forms of certain adjectives and adverbs must be memorized.**

8.1.5 RULE

In the chart on the following page, the form of some irregular modifiers differs only in the positive degree. The modifiers *bad*, *badly*, and *ill*, for example, all have the same comparative and superlative degrees *(worse, worst)*.

IRREGULAR MODIFIERS		
POSITIVE	COMPARATIVE	SUPERLATIVE
bad, badly, ill	worse	worst
far (distance)	farther	farthest
far (extent)	further	furthest
good, well	better	best
late	later	last or latest
little (amount)	less	least
many, much	more	most

Bad is an adjective. Do not use it to modify an action verb. **Badly** is an adverb. Use it after an action verb but not after a linking verb.

INCORRECT Keith plays the bassoon **bad**.

CORRECT Keith plays the bassoon **badly**.

INCORRECT Keith feels **badly**.

CORRECT Keith feels **bad**.

Note About *Good* and *Well:* *Good* is always an adjective and cannot be used as an adverb after an action verb. It can, however, be used as a predicate adjective after a linking verb.

INCORRECT Jennifer plays the oboe **good**.

CORRECT This oboe sounds **good**.

Well is generally an adverb. However, when *well* means "healthy," it is an adjective and can be used after a linking verb.

CORRECT Jennifer plays the oboe **well**.

CORRECT Jennifer should be **well** soon.

See Practice 8.1C
See Practice 8.1D

PRACTICE 8.1A > Recognizing Positive, Comparative, and Superlative Degrees of Comparison

Read each sentence. Then, identify the degree of comparison of the underlined word or words as *positive*, *comparative*, or *superlative*.

EXAMPLE   Andy sleeps in the <u>lower</u> bunk.

ANSWER   *comparative*

1. We are hoping for <u>better</u> weather today.
2. Landry spoke to a <u>famous</u> movie star.
3. Jessie is the <u>strongest</u> pitcher on the team.
4. This is the <u>juiciest</u> mango I ever ate.
5. Garlic is the <u>most strongly</u> flavored spice.
6. Cheetahs run <u>more swiftly</u> than any other animal.
7. The dancers moved <u>gracefully</u> across the stage.
8. This is the <u>hardest</u> puzzle I have ever worked on.
9. That performer has a <u>loyal</u> fan club.
10. Today's exam was <u>easier</u> than last week's.

PRACTICE 8.1B > Forming Regular Comparative and Superlative Degrees of Comparison

Read each sentence. Then, rewrite each sentence with the correct comparative or superlative degree of the modifier indicated in parentheses.

EXAMPLE   You will feel _____ by the fire than by the window. (warm)

ANSWER   *You will feel warmer by the fire than by the window.*

11. We ran _____ than usual. (slow)
12. The _____ day all week was Saturday. (beautiful)
13. That tree is _____ than the one in the park. (tall)
14. The _____ car sold for the most money. (fast)
15. The boring movie is _____ than the action drama. (exciting)
16. His mother is _____ with him than mine is with me. (strict)
17. Tim is the _____ player on the soccer team. (short)
18. Of the three houses, our house is the one _____ to the corner. (close)
19. This is the _____ room in the house. (large)
20. That is the _____ thing to happen. (likely)

SPEAKING APPLICATION

Take turns with a partner. Compare the size of objects in your classroom. Use comparative, superlative, and positive degrees of comparison. Your partner should listen for and identify which degree of comparison you are using in each of your descriptions.

WRITING APPLICATION

Rewrite sentences 14, 15, and 19, changing the modifiers in parentheses. Then, exchange papers with a partner. Your partner should write the correct degree of the modifiers you provided.

PRACTICE 8.1C ▷ **Supplying Irregular Comparative and Superlative Forms**

Read each modifier. Then, write its irregular comparative and superlative forms.

EXAMPLE   good

ANSWER   *better, best*

1. little (amount)
2. much
3. bad
4. many
5. far (distance)
6. far (extent)
7. well
8. badly
9. late
10. ill

PRACTICE 8.1D ▷ **Supplying Irregular Modifiers**

Read each sentence. Then, fill in the blank with the form of the modifier indicated in parentheses that best completes each sentence.

EXAMPLE   I performed the clarinet solo _____ than I ever had before. (good)

ANSWER   *better*

11. During the track meet, I threw the javelin the _____. (far)
12. _____ students ride the bus to school than walk. (many)
13. Because I practiced every day, I was able to perform at my _____. (good)
14. Before I begin writing my paper, I plan to research the topic _____. (far)
15. Because my alarm didn't go off, I was the _____ student on the bus. (late)
16. To help control blood pressure, patients should try to use _____ salt in their cooking. (little)
17. I sometimes hum off-key, but I sing _____. (badly)
18. The _____ I can do is buy her lunch. (little)
19. When I sprained my ankle, the pain was always the _____ at night. (bad)
20. According to our records, the _____ people attended the fair on Saturday. (many)

SPEAKING APPLICATION

Take turns with a partner. Say sentences with irregular comparative and superlative forms. Your partner should indicate if incorrect comparisons have been used and suggest corrections.

WRITING APPLICATION

Write pairs of sentences in which you use *farther* and *further*, *worse* and *worst*, and *more* and *most* correctly.

8.2 Making Clear Comparisons

The comparative and superlative degrees help you make comparisons that are clear and logical.

Using Comparative and Superlative Degrees

One basic rule that has two parts covers the correct use of comparative and superlative forms.

> Use the **comparative degree** to compare two persons, places, or things. Use the **superlative degree** to compare three or more persons, places, or things.

8.2.1 RULE

The context of a sentence should indicate whether two items or more than two items are being compared.

COMPARATIVE   My calculator is **more dependable** than Troy's.

My dog is **larger** than his.

He requires **less money** than she does.

SUPERLATIVE   Emily is the **most dependable** friend I have.

This is the **largest** gym I have ever seen.

He is the **least materialistic** person I know.

In informal writing, the superlative degree is sometimes used just for emphasis, without any specific comparison.

EXAMPLE   He is the **greatest**!

Note About Double Comparisons: A double comparison is caused by using both -er and *more* or both -est and *most* to form a regular modifier or by adding an extra comparison form to an irregular modifier.

INCORRECT   Your workload is **more heavier** than mine.

See Practice 8.2A
See Practice 8.2B   CORRECT   Your workload is **heavier** than mine.

PRACTICE 8.2A Supplying the Comparative and Superlative Degrees of Modifiers

Read each sentence. Then, fill in the blank with the correct form of the underlined modifier.

EXAMPLE   I may have <u>little</u> money, but he has _____ than I do.

ANSWER   *less*

1. Salmon tastes <u>good</u>, but trout tastes _____.

2. Tanya is <u>late</u>, but Nellie is usually _____.

3. James danced <u>better</u> than Kerri did, but Sam danced the _____.

4. Brian is <u>funny</u>, but of all the students, Steve is the _____.

5. Many of the books are <u>suspenseful</u>, but this one is _____.

6. Today, the weather is <u>warm</u>, but the weather will be _____ tomorrow.

7. Kara is <u>sad</u> that the class trip is over, but Paula is the _____ in the group.

8. Eduardo's house is <u>far</u> from town, but Hannah's house is even _____.

9. All of my friends are <u>fun</u>, but Mandy is _____. (fun)

10. Dallas is farther from Houston than Austin is, but Amarillo is the _____ from Houston.

PRACTICE 8.2B Revising Sentences to Correct Errors in Modifier Usage

Read each sentence. Then, rewrite each sentence, correcting any errors in the usage of modifiers to make comparisons. If a sentence contains no errors, write *correct*.

EXAMPLE   The patient seems somewhat best today.

ANSWER   *The patient seems somewhat better today.*

11. Mom's health is most robust than it was last year.

12. Your memory is more best than mine.

13. The tractor moved more slower across the field than on the road.

14. This sculpture is the better artwork I have ever created.

15. I thought the movie was more interesting than the book.

16. She is best in biology than she is in reading.

17. We arrived more earlier than Tiffany.

18. The young tiger roared most ferociously.

19. Didn't the juggler in the red cape perform more better than the other juggler?

20. Of those three dancers, the third one dances the most skillfully.

SPEAKING APPLICATION

Take turns with a partner comparing two movies. Your partner should listen for and identify the comparisons in your sentences.

WRITING APPLICATION

Write three sentences with errors in modifier usage. Then, exchange papers with a partner. Your partner should correct your sentences.

Using Logical Comparisons

Two common usage problems are the comparison of unrelated items and the comparison of something with itself.

Balanced Comparisons
Be certain that things being compared in a sentence are similar.

> Your sentences should only compare items of a similar kind.

The following unbalanced sentences illogically compare dissimilar things.

UNBALANCED   **Jim's play** is better written than **Ray**.

CORRECT   **Jim's play** is better written than **Ray's**.

UNBALANCED   The **height of the bookcase** is greater than the **wall**.

CORRECT   The **height of the bookcase** is greater than the **height of the wall**.

Note About *Other* and *Else* in Comparisons
Another illogical comparison results when something is inadvertently compared with itself.

> When comparing one of a group with the rest of the group, make sure that your sentence contains the word *other* or the word *else*.

8.2.3 RULE

Adding *other* or *else* when comparing one person or thing with a group will make the comparison clear and logical.

ILLOGICAL   John was busier than any clerk on the floor.
              (John cannot be busier than himself.)

LOGICAL   John was busier than any **other** clerk on the floor.

See Practice 8.2C
See Practice 8.2D

PRACTICE 8.2C > Revising to Make
Comparisons Balanced
and Logical

Read each sentence. Then, rewrite each
sentence, correcting the unbalanced or illogical
comparison.

EXAMPLE   Jana's skating ability is better than
Sara.

ANSWER   *Jana's skating ability is better
than Sara's.*

1. Carol's watch is smaller than Shaun.

2. Anna travels more than anyone in her family.

3. Steve's suitcase is newer than Molly.

4. Mark's parrot talks more cheerfully than
Albert.

5. The Panthers have won more state
championships than any football team.

6. Rob's skateboard is in better condition than
Mike.

7. The student who answered the question
speaks French better than anyone in our
class.

8. Carolyn runs faster than any athlete on the
track team.

9. Kevin's backpack is larger than Dan.

10. The length of Madison's desk is shorter than
Jill's.

PRACTICE 8.2D > Writing Clear Comparisons

Read each sentence. Then, rewrite each sentence,
filling in the blanks to make a comparison that is
clear and logical.

EXAMPLE   Joe's painting is better than _____.

ANSWER   *Joe's painting is better than
Rose's painting.*

11. Caroline is more talented than _____ in her
class.

12. The size of Jupiter is larger than _____.

13. Felix's cat is more playful than _____.

14. That flower is brighter than _____ flower in
the yard.

15. Margarita's guitar is better tuned than _____.

16. The smell of a rose is stronger than _____.

17. My foot is bigger than _____.

18. Sherilyn's photographs of mountains are more
impressive than _____.

19. I prefer the color blue more than _____ color.

20. Thomas Edison is more famous than _____
scientist.

SPEAKING APPLICATION

**Take turns with a partner. Say sentences that
have unbalanced or illogical comparisons. Your
partner should restate the sentences, using
balanced and logical comparisons.**

WRITING APPLICATION

**Use sentences 12, 13, and 20 as models to write
similar sentences. Then, exchange papers with
a partner. Your partner should fill in the blanks
to make the comparison in each sentence clear
and logical.**

Avoiding Comparisons With Absolute Modifiers

Some modifiers cannot be used logically to make comparisons because their meanings are *absolute*—that is, their meanings are entirely contained in the positive degree. For example, if a line is *vertical*, another line cannot be *more* vertical. Some other common absolute modifiers are *dead, entirely, fatal, final, identical, infinite, opposite, perfect, right, straight,* and *unique*.

> **Avoid using absolute modifiers illogically in comparisons.**

8.2.4 RULE

| INCORRECT | The color pattern he chose was **most unique**. |
| CORRECT | The color pattern he chose was **unique**. |

Often, it is not only the word *more* or *most* that makes an absolute modifier illogical; sometimes it is best to replace the absolute modifier with one that expresses the intended meaning more precisely.

| ILLOGICAL | The color pattern he chose was **more unique** than Sandor's choice. |
| CORRECT | The color pattern he chose was **more distinctive** than Sandor's choice. |

Sometimes an absolute modifier may overstate the meaning that you want.

| ILLOGICAL | This hockey loss was the **most fatal**. |
| CORRECT | This hockey loss was the **most severe**. |

See Practice 8.2E
See Practice 8.2F

In the preceding example, *most fatal* is illogical because something is either fatal or it is not. However, even *fatal* is an overstatement. *Most severe* better conveys the intended meaning.

PRACTICE 8.2E	Revising Sentences to Correct Comparisons Using Absolute Modifiers

Read each sentence. Then, correct each illogical comparison by replacing the absolute modifier with more precise words.

EXAMPLE   The new painting she chose was most unique.

ANSWER   *The new painting she chose was unique.*

1. The story he told was most entirely untrue.

2. The accident yesterday was more fatal.

3. The competition results were most final.

4. Her two brothers are more identical.

5. Scientists think that the realm of space is most infinite.

6. My two best friends are the most opposite in personality.

7. The color of the house is more perfect.

8. Sandy drew two most right angles in geometry.

9. Highway 81 is more straight.

10. My mom's rosebush is more dead.

PRACTICE 8.2F	Revising Overstated Absolute Modifiers

Read each sentence. Then, rewrite each sentence, revising the overstated absolute modifier.

EXAMPLE   The plastic flowers are not quite real.

ANSWER   *The plastic flowers are not real.*

11. The plan to build a new stadium is completely dead.

12. Maya's hypothesis was very wrong.

13. The dancer performed a very perfect leap into her partner's arms.

14. Maria was committed to singing her very absolute best in the musical.

15. Derrick treated all his friends more equally.

16. My decision to run in the marathon is extremely final.

17. The testimony of the witness was most entirely true.

18. Eva created a most unique design for a wedding gown.

19. The party last year was the most supremely fun event.

20. People and all other living things are most mortal.

SPEAKING APPLICATION

Take turns with a partner. Say sentences that incorrectly use absolute modifiers. Your partner should restate your sentences correctly.

WRITING APPLICATION

Write three sentences with overstated absolute modifiers. Then, exchange papers with a partner. Your partner should revise the overstated absolute modifiers in your sentences.

CHAPTER 9

MISCELLANEOUS PROBLEMS *in* USAGE

Knowing the rules of correct usage will help you construct sentences that read well.

WRITE GUY *Jeff Anderson, M.Ed.*

WHAT DO YOU NOTICE?

Note how prepositions are used as you zoom in on lines from the poem "Dream Deferred" by Langston Hughes.

MENTOR TEXT

> What happens to a dream deferred?
>
> Does it dry up
> Like a raisin in the sun?
> Or fester like a sore . . . ?

Now, ask yourself the following questions:

- How is the preposition *like* used in these lines?
- Could you use the preposition *as* in the same way? Why or why not?

Prepositions show the relationship of a noun or a pronoun to another word in a sentence. In the poem, *like* is used to mean "similar to" or "such as." While the phrase *as if* is similar in meaning to *like*, the preposition *as* cannot be used alone as a substitute for *like*.

Grammar for Writers Writers use prepositions to show relationships. Check how you use prepositions in order to clearly express what you mean in your writing.

I want to make fewer mistakes in usage.

Fewer is all right with me!

9.1 Negative Sentences

In English, only one *no* is needed in a sentence to deny or refuse something. You can express a negative idea with words such as *not* or *never* or with contractions such as *can't, couldn't,* and *wasn't.* (The ending *-n't* in a contraction is an abbreviation of *not.*)

Recognizing Double Negatives

Using two negative words in a sentence when one is sufficient is called a **double negative.** While double negatives may sometimes be used in informal speech, they should be avoided in formal English speech and writing.

RULE 9.1.1

> Do not use **double negatives** in formal writing.

The following chart provides examples of double negatives and two ways each can be corrected.

DOUBLE NEGATIVE	CORRECTIONS
Starfish don't bother no one.	Starfish don't bother anyone. Starfish bother no one.
I haven't seen no whales.	I haven't seen any whales. I have seen no whales.
Tom never said nothing.	Tom never said anything. Tom said nothing.

Sentences that contain more than one clause can correctly contain more than one negative word. Each clause, however, should contain only one negative word.

EXAMPLES   The fish **did not** survive because the tank **was not** properly aerated.

Even if you **don't** know an answer, you **shouldn't** leave a space blank.

208   Miscellaneous Problems in Usage

208   **Miscellaneous Problems in Usage**

Forming Negative Sentences Correctly

There are three common ways to form negative sentences.

Using One Negative Word The most common ways to make a statement negative are to use one **negative word,** such as *never, no,* or *none,* or to add the contraction *-n't* to a helping verb.

> Use only one **negative word** in each clause.

9.1.2 RULE

DOUBLE NEGATIVE   We **don't** want **no** help from you.

PREFERRED   We **don't** want **any** help from you.

We want **no** help from you.

Using *But* in a Negative Sense When *but* means "only," it usually acts as a negative. Do not use it with another negative word.

DOUBLE NEGATIVE   There **wasn't but** one whale in the inlet.

PREFERRED   There was **but** one whale in the inlet.

There was **only** one whale in the inlet.

Using *Barely, Hardly,* and *Scarcely* Each of these words is negative. If you use one of these words with another negative word, you create a double negative.

> Do not use *barely, hardly,* or *scarcely* with another negative word.

9.1.3 RULE

DOUBLE NEGATIVE   The tree **wasn't barely** visible in the dim light.

PREFERRED   The tree was **barely** visible in the dim light.

DOUBLE NEGATIVE   We **didn't scarcely** recognize you.

PREFERRED   We **scarcely** recognized you.

DOUBLE NEGATIVE   I **couldn't hardly** stop laughing.

See Practice 9.1A   PREFERRED   I could **hardly** stop laughing.

Using Negatives to Create Understatement

Sometimes a writer wants to express an idea indirectly, either to minimize the importance of the idea or to draw attention to it. One such technique is called **understatement.**

> **Understatement can be achieved by using a negative word and a word with a negative prefix, such as *un-*, *in-*, *im-*, *dis-*, and *under-*.**

EXAMPLES   Keisha was **hardly inexperienced** at baking.

The home team did **not underestimate** its opponent.

The moon's light **isn't** completely **unromantic**.

These examples show that the writer is praising the people or things he or she is discussing. In the first example, the writer states that Keisha is actually quite experienced at baking. In the second example, the writer states that the home team understood the challenge they would face when they played the opposing team. In the third example, the writer states that the moon's light is romantic.

If you choose to use understatement, be sure to use it carefully so that you do not sound critical when you wish to praise.

EXAMPLES   Malia does **not dislike** Sara's fruit pies and muffins.

Even though they were on sale, the jeans were **not inexpensive**.

In both examples above, the writer is actually making a negative statement. In the first example, although the writer "does not dislike" Sara's pies and muffins, he or she clearly doesn't like them very much, either. In the second example, the writer seems to think that, although the jeans were on sale, they were still expensive.

See Practice 9.1B

PRACTICE 9.1A > Revising Sentences to Avoid Double Negatives

Read each sentence. Then, rewrite each sentence to correct the double negative.

EXAMPLE   The stranded explorers hadn't had no food for days.

ANSWER   *The stranded explorers hadn't had any food for days.*

1. You shouldn't have said nothing about our trip.

2. We couldn't hardly stand the suspense toward the end of the movie.

3. Are you sure I can't bring no book?

4. The missing cat wasn't nowhere in sight.

5. You can be sure Sam won't eat none of those desserts.

6. Mrs. Fernandes didn't say nothing about her vacation.

7. We don't need but two other players.

8. They can't never get cellphone reception there.

9. There wasn't barely an inch of snow by morning.

10. He couldn't find none of the lost jewelry.

PRACTICE 9.1B > Using Negatives to Create Understatement

Read each item. Then, use each item to create understatement.

EXAMPLE   unsure

ANSWER   *She was not unsure of her way in the dark.*

11. invisible

12. disapprove

13. undernourished

14. uninterested

15. impenetrable

16. dislike

17. impossible

18. undervalue

19. unaware

20. unfavorable

SPEAKING APPLICATION

Take turns with a partner. Say sentences that contain double negatives. Your partner should listen to and correct your sentences to avoid the double negatives.

WRITING APPLICATION

Use items 13, 16, and 19 to write other sentences that contain double negatives. Then, exchange papers with a partner. Your partner should correct your sentences.

9.2 Common Usage Problems

(1) a, an   The use of the article *a* or *an* is determined by the sound of the word that follows it. *A* is used before consonant sounds, while *an* is used before vowel sounds. Words beginning with *hon-, o-,* or *u-* may have either a consonant or a vowel sound.

EXAMPLES

a honeybee (*h* sound)

a one-day excursion (*w* sound)

an honest merchant (no *h* sound)

an omen (*o* sound)

an urgent message (*u* sound)

(2) accept, except   *Accept,* a verb, means "to receive." *Except,* a preposition, means "to leave out" or "other than."

VERB   We must all **accept** responsibility for pollution.

PREPOSITION   Everyone joined in the cleanup **except** Jermaine.

(3) adapt, adopt   *Adapt* means "to change." *Adopt* means "to take as one's own."

EXAMPLES   The Puritans had to **adapt** to the harsh weather.

Newcomers often **adopt** new customs.

(4) affect, effect   *Affect* is almost always a verb meaning "to influence." *Effect,* usually a noun, means "a result." Sometimes, *effect* is a verb meaning "to bring about" or "to cause."

VERB   An increase in prices **affects** everyone.

NOUN   Economists study the **effect** of increased prices.

VERB   The council **effected** many changes in tax policies.

(5) aggravate   *Aggravate* means "to make worse." Avoid using this word to mean "annoy."

INCORRECT   The chirping of the birds at 6:00 A.M. **aggravated** me.

PREFERRED   The drought is **aggravating** the risk of forest fires.

(6) ain't *Ain't,* which was originally a contraction for
am not, is no longer considered acceptable in standard English.
Always use *am not,* and never use *ain't.* The exception is in
certain instances of dialogue.

(7) all ready, already *All ready,* which consists of two separate
words used as an adjective, means "ready." *Already,* which is an
adverb, means "by or before this time" or "even now."

ADJECTIVE   The cowboys were **all ready** for the cattle drive.

ADVERB   My brother had **already** eaten breakfast.

(8) all right, alright *Alright* is a nonstandard spelling. Make
sure you use the two-word form.

INCORRECT   The coach said it was **alright** for me to come to
practice late.

PREFERRED   The coach said it was **all right** for me to come to
practice late.

(9) all together, altogether *All together* means "together as a
single group." *Altogether* means "completely" or "in all."

EXAMPLES   The birds flew **all together** in a chevron pattern.

The old television set finally broke **altogether**.

(10) among, between Both of these words are prepositions.
Among shows a connection between three or more items.
Between generally shows a connection between two items.

EXAMPLES   The teacher divided the tasks **among** all the
members of the class.

It was difficult for voters to choose **between** Sammi
and Len.

See Practice 9.2A

(11) anxious This adjective implies uneasiness, worry, or fear.
Do not use it as a substitute for *eager.*

INCORRECT   The ranchers were **anxious** to start the cattle drive.

PREFERRED   The ranchers were **anxious** about cattle thieves.

(12) anyone, any one, everyone, every one   *Anyone* and *everyone* mean "any person" or "every person." *Any one* means "any single person (or thing)"; *every one* means "every single person (or thing)."

EXAMPLES   **Anyone** is eligible to try out for the chorus.

Any one of the singers may be chosen to perform a solo.

Everyone enjoys beautiful harmonies.

Every one of the singers can read music.

(13) anyway, anywhere, everywhere, nowhere, somewhere   These adverbs should never end in *-s*.

INCORRECT   There is a treasure hidden **somewheres** on this island.

PREFERRED   There is a treasure hidden **somewhere** on this island.

(14) as   Do not use the conjunction *as* to mean "because" or "since."

INCORRECT   There are few plants growing in this area **as** there is very little sunlight.

PREFERRED   There are few plants growing in this area **because** there is very little sunlight.

(15) as to   *As to* is awkward. Replace it with *about*.

INCORRECT   There is some doubt **as to** the effectiveness of this home remedy.

PREFERRED   There is some doubt **about** the effectiveness of this home remedy.

(16) at   Do not use *at* after *where*. Simply eliminate *at*.

INCORRECT   We weren't sure **where** the town was **at** on the map.

PREFERRED   We weren't sure **where** the town was on the map.

(17) at, about Avoid using *at* with *about*. Simply eliminate *at* or *about*.

| INCORRECT | The city is located **at about** sea level. |
| PREFERRED | The city is located **at** sea level. |

(18) awful, awfully *Awful* is used informally to mean that something is "extremely bad." *Awfully* is used informally to mean "very." Both words are overused and should be replaced with more descriptive words. In standard English speech and writing, *awful* should only be used to mean "inspiring fear or awe in someone."

OVERUSED	The heat is **awful**.
PREFERRED	The heat is **oppressive**.
OVERUSED	It can get **awfully** hot in equatorial countries.
PREFERRED	It can get **extremely** hot in equatorial countries.
OVERUSED	The weather report was **awful**.
PREFERRED	The weather report was **dreadful**.

(19) awhile, a while *Awhile* is an adverb that means "for a short time." *A while*, which is a noun, means "a period of time." It is usually used after the preposition *for* or *after*.

ADVERB	Let's wait **awhile** and play ball when it's cooler.
	Jake blew on his soup **awhile** so that it cooled more quickly.
NOUN	We remained in the meeting room for quite **a while**.
	It will take **a while** for me to learn the new guitar solo.

(20) beat, win When you *win*, you "achieve a victory in something." When you *beat* someone or something, you "overcome an opponent."

INCORRECT	Ellen **won** her sister playing checkers.
PREFERRED	Ellen **beat** her sister playing checkers.
	I hope I **win** the game.

See Practice 9.2B

> **PRACTICE 9.2A** Recognizing Usage
> Problems 1–10

Read each sentence. Then, choose the correct
item to complete each sentence.

EXAMPLE   The drawing has (already, all ready)
been held.

ANSWER   *already*

1. What is (a, an) honorary degree?

2. Air pollution (affects, effects) bodies of water,
monuments, statues, and buildings.

3. My cousins and I had only three dollars
(among, between) us.

4. Amusement parks (ain't, aren't) my favorite
places to visit.

5. Adding more lanes to the highways is
(annoying, aggravating) the delays at the toll
booths.

6. Are you (all ready, already) to go?

7. Everyone visited the museum (accept, except)
my father.

8. Is everything (all right, alright) in the office?

9. The horses were standing (all together,
altogether).

10. Carmen (adapted, adopted) the customs of
each country that she lived in.

> **PRACTICE 9.2B** Recognizing Usage
> Problems 11–20

Read each sentence. Then, choose the correct
item to complete each sentence.

EXAMPLE   Will (anyone, any one) of these toys
appeal to a four-year-old?

ANSWER   *any one*

11. They had plenty of suggestions (as to, about)
how to spend the prize money.

12. Todd was so (anxious, eager) about the play
that he couldn't sleep last night.

13. Our new kitten is (awfully, extremely) playful.

14. My new sweater is hanging (somewhere,
somewheres) in the closet.

15. We need directions to determine where the
new store (is at, is located).

16. The students are well prepared (as, because)
they have studied hard.

17. (Everyone, Every one) in the class wants to
participate in the science fair.

18. We hiked for (a while, awhile).

19. We will start the cleanup (at about, at)
2:00 P.M.

20. Tanisha (won, beat) all of her opponents in
the chess tournament.

SPEAKING APPLICATION

Take turns with a partner. Choose any pair of
words from Practice 9.2A (except from #4 or
#8), and tell your partner your choices. Your
partner should say two sentences, using both
words correctly.

WRITING APPLICATION

Write two sentences that include usage
problems. Exchange papers with a partner.
Your partner should correct your sentences.

(21) because   Do not use *because* after the phrase
the reason. Say "The reason is that" or reword the sentence.

INCORRECT   One **reason** to preserve the environment **is because**
              it will benefit humans.

PREFERRED   One **reason** to preserve the environment **is that**
              it will benefit humans.

(22) being as, being that   Avoid using either of these
expressions. Use *because* instead.

INCORRECT   **Being as** (or **that**) we were late, we decided to skip
              lunch.

PREFERRED   **Because** we were late, we decided to skip lunch.

(23) beside, besides   *Beside* means "at the side of" or "close to."
Besides means "in addition to."

EXAMPLES   Zebras often live **beside** gnus on the African plains.

              Other animals **besides** zebras can be found nearby.

(24) bring, take   *Bring* means "to carry from a distant place to
a nearer one." *Take* means "to carry from a near place to a far
one."

EXAMPLES   Please **bring** your gym clothes home today so
              I can wash them.

              You can **take** your clean clothes back tomorrow.

(25) can, may   Use *can* to mean "have the ability to." Use *may* to
mean "have permission to" or "to be likely to."

ABILITY   Helene **can** spell many difficult words.

PERMISSION   The teacher said we **may** use dictionaries to help
              correct our spelling.

POSSIBILITY   I **may** need to look up these words in the dictionary.

(26) clipped words   Avoid using clipped or shortened words,
such as *gym* and *photo* in formal writing.

INFORMAL   The basketball team posed for a **photo**.

FORMAL   The basketball team posed for a **photograph**.

(27) different from, different than *Different from* is preferred in standard English.

| INCORRECT | Monday's menu is **different than** Tuesday's. |
| PREFERRED | Monday's menu is **different from** Tuesday's. |

(28) doesn't, don't Do not use *don't* with third-person singular subjects. Instead, use *doesn't*.

| INCORRECT | This cactus **don't** need to be watered each week. |
| PREFERRED | This cactus **doesn't** need to be watered each week. |

(29) done *Done* is the past participle of the verb *do*. It should always take a helping verb.

| INCORRECT | We **done** what we could to help. |
| PREFERRED | We **have done** what we could to help. |

(30) due to *Due to* means "caused by" and should be used only when the words *caused by* can be logically substituted.

| INCORRECT | The plant didn't grow **due to** lack of sunlight. |
| PREFERRED | The plant's stunted growth was **due to** lack of sunlight. |

See Practice 9.2C

(31) each other, one another These expressions usually are interchangeable. At times, however, *each other* is more logically used in reference to only two and *one another* in reference to more than two.

| EXAMPLES | The relay team must rely on **one another's** motivation to win. |
| | The composer and lyricist appreciated **each other's** skills. |

(32) farther, further *Farther* refers to distance. *Further* means "additional" or "to a greater degree or extent."

| EXAMPLES | Our art teacher showed us how to make some objects appear **farther** away than others. |
| | Sharon's art skills are **further** developed than mine are. |

(33) fewer, less   Use *fewer* with things that can be counted. Use *less* with qualities and quantities that cannot be counted.

EXAMPLES   **fewer** resources, **less** space

(34) get, got, gotten   These forms of the verb *get* are acceptable in standard English, but a more specific word is preferable.

INCORRECT   **get** a new suit, **got** a job, **have gotten** awards

PREFERRED   **buy** a new suit, **found** a job, **have received** awards

(35) gone, went   *Gone* is the past participle of the verb *go* and is used only with a helping verb. *Went* is the past tense of *go* and is never used with a helping verb.

INCORRECT   Craig and Louise **gone** to the movies.

You really should **have went** to the game.

PREFERRED   Craig and Louise **went** to the movies.

You really should **have gone** to the game.

(36) good, lovely, nice   Replace these overused words with a more specific adjective.

WEAK   **good** example, **lovely** painting, **nice** aroma

BETTER   **fitting** example, **evocative** painting, **delicious** aroma

(37) in, into   *In* refers to position. *Into* suggests motion.

EXAMPLES   A wide variety of plants grew **in** the garden.

Plants absorb nutrients **into** their roots.

(38) irregardless   Avoid this word in formal speech and writing. Instead, use *regardless*.

(39) just   When you use *just* as an adverb to mean "no more than," place it immediately before the word it modifies.

INCORRECT   She **just** received one letter.

PREFERRED   She received **just** one letter.

(40) kind of, sort of   Do not use these phrases in formal speech. Instead, use *rather* or *somewhat*.

See Practice 9.2D

PRACTICE 9.2C ▷ Recognizing Usage Problems 21–30

Read each sentence. Then, choose the correct item to complete each sentence.

EXAMPLE   Did Timothy (bring, take) a book from the shelf?

ANSWER   *take*

1. The man with a beard stood (beside, besides) the oak tree.

2. This lawn mower (don't, doesn't) work very well.

3. Practice is canceled (being as, because) the coach is out of town.

4. This movie is very (different from, different than) the one we saw last week.

5. The trains are running today; therefore, we (may, can) take the subway.

6. (Because, Being as) I broke the eggs, I had to return to the store.

7. The games are scheduled to be played in the middle school (gym, gymnasium).

8. The reason we got lost is (because, that) Joey gave us the wrong directions.

9. Tyrone (done, has done) so much work for the senior class.

10. The lateness of the bus was (because of, due to) mechanical problems.

PRACTICE 9.2D ▷ Revising Sentences to Correct Usage Problems 31–40

Read each sentence. Then, rewrite each sentence, correcting the errors in usage.

EXAMPLE   The carnival will take place irregardless of the weather conditions.

ANSWER   *The carnival will take place regardless of the weather conditions.*

11. After farther consideration, we realized that changes needed to be made to the proposal.

12. Customers with less than ten items may use the express line.

13. Mr. Lee had went to visit his daughter.

14. Let's go in the lobby to wait for them.

15. He just brought a single change of clothing.

16. Cherise was acting kind of mysterious.

17. Jermaine has got all *A*'s on his report card.

18. How much further do we have to go before we get to the Grand Canyon?

19. That color looks nice on you.

20. I had just gotten home when the telephone rang.

SPEAKING APPLICATION

Take turns with a partner. Say sentences with usage problems. Your partner should correct each of your sentences.

WRITING APPLICATION

Write a paragraph about a topic of your choice. Include sentences that contain usage problems. Exchange papers with a partner. Your partner should correct the usage problems in your paragraph.

(41) lay, lie   The verb *lay* means "to put or set (something) down." Its principal parts—*lay, laying, laid, laid*—are followed by a direct object. The verb *lie* means "to recline." Its principal parts—*lie, lying, lay, lain*—are not followed by a direct object.

LAY
Please **lay** the basket on the counter.

Those turtles are **laying** their eggs on the beach.

When she arrived, she **laid** her keys on the table.

The masons **have laid** three layers of bricks.

LIE
If you are sick, you should **lie** down in bed.

The sunbathers **are lying** on lounges.

Last week, many of them **lay** in hammocks.

My brother **has lain** in bed all morning.

(42) learn, teach   *Learn* means "to receive knowledge." *Teach* means "to give knowledge."

EXAMPLES
Dolphins can **learn** to follow commands.

The trainer **taught** the killer whale a new trick.

(43) leave, let   *Leave* means "to allow to remain." *Let* means "to permit."

INCORRECT
Let the snake alone, and it won't bother you.

PREFERRED
Leave the snake alone, and it won't bother you.

(44) like, as   *Like* is a preposition meaning "similar to" or "such as." It should not be used in place of the conjunction *as*.

INCORRECT
She acted **like** she was nervous.

PREFERRED
She acted **as if** she was nervous.

She acted **like** a nervous person.

(45) loose, lose   *Loose* is usually an adjective or part of such idioms as *cut loose, turn loose,* or *break loose. Lose* is always a verb and usually means "to miss from one's possession."

EXAMPLES
The shelf is **loose**, and it may fall.

Take care, so you don't **lose** your place in line.

(46) maybe, may be   *Maybe* is an adverb meaning "perhaps." *May be* is a helping verb connected to a main verb.

ADVERB   **Maybe** we can preserve the marshland.

VERB   It **may be** too late to save the marshland.

(47) of   Do not use *of* after a helping verb such as *should, would, could,* or *must.* Use *have* instead. Do not use *of* after *outside, inside, off,* and *atop.* Simply eliminate *of.*

INCORRECT   If she had scored, Stella **would of** set a new record.

PREFERRED   If she had scored, Stella **would have** set a new record.

(48) OK, O.K., okay   In informal writing, *OK, O.K.,* and *okay* are acceptably used to mean "all right." Do not use them in standard English speech or writing, however.

INFORMAL   The mayor said the new ruling was **okay** .

PREFERRED   The mayor **approved** the new ruling.

(49) only   *Only* should be placed immediately before the word it modifies. Placing it elsewhere can lead to confusion.

EXAMPLES   **Only** Rita wanted to go bowling.
(No one else wanted to go bowling.)

Rita **only** wanted to go bowling.
(She didn't want to do anything else.)

(50) ought   Do not use *ought* with *have* or *had.*

INCORRECT   The settlers **hadn't ought** to have planted beans.

PREFERRED   The settlers **ought not** to have planted beans.

See Practice 9.2E

(51) outside of   Do not use this expression to mean "besides" or "except."

INCORRECT   We couldn't name any desert **outside of** the Mojave.

PREFERRED   We couldn't name any desert **except** the Mojave.

(52) plurals that do not end in -*s* The English plurals of certain nouns from Greek and Latin are formed as they were in their original language. Words such as *criteria, media,* and *phenomena* are plural. Their singular forms are *criterion, medium,* and *phenomenon.*

INCORRECT   The teacher explained the single most important
               criteria for the experiment.

PREFERRED   The teacher explained the single most important
               criterion for the experiment.

               The teacher explained the three most important
               criteria for the experiment.

(53) precede, proceed *Precede* means "to go before." *Proceed* means "to move or go forward."

EXAMPLES   Pasteur's research **preceded** Lister's by five years.

               Both men **proceeded** to investigate germ theory.

(54) principal, principle As an adjective, *principal* means "most important" or "chief." As a noun, it means "a person who has controlling authority," as in a school. *Principle* is always a noun that means "a fundamental law."

ADJECTIVE   The aorta is the **principal** artery in the body.

NOUN   Mr. Saunders is a **principal** in the new business.

NOUN   The company agreed to follow the **principles** of proper
               waste disposal.

(55) real *Real* means "authentic." In formal writing, avoid using *real* to mean "very" or "really."

INCORRECT   The crowd was **real** disappointed with the outcome.

PREFERRED   The crowd was **deeply** disappointed with the outcome.

(56) says *Says* should not be used as a substitute for *said.*

INCORRECT   Then the emperor **says**, "Let the games begin!"

PREFERRED   Then the emperor **said**, "Let the games begin!"

(57) seen   *Seen* is a past participle and must be used with a helping verb.

INCORRECT   Stephon **seen** his brother in the crowd.

PREFERRED   Stephon **had seen** his brother in the crowd.

(58) set, sit   *Set* means "to put (something) in a certain place." Its principal parts—*set, setting, set, set*—are usually followed by a direct object. *Sit* means "to be seated." Its principal parts—*sit, sitting, sat, sat*—are never followed by a direct object.

SET   She **set** the peaches carefully in the bowl.

Stanley **is setting** the basket in the corner.

They **set** the television on the new table.

I **have set** the alarm to ring at six.

SIT   I **will sit** in my dad's chair tonight.

You must **have been sitting** there for hours.

She **sat** quietly at her desk and daydreamed.

We **have sat** in these same seats at every game.

(59) so   When *so* is used as a coordinating conjunction, it means *and* or *but*. Avoid using *so* when you mean "so that."

INCORRECT   Sponges use filters **so** they can eat.

PREFERRED   Sponges use filters **so that** they can eat.

(60) than, then   Use *than* in comparisons. Use *then* as an adverb to refer to time.

EXAMPLES   Danielle is more graceful **than** her sister.

First, she studied ballet; **then** , she took jazz classes.

(61) that, which, who   Use these relative pronouns in the following ways: *that* and *which* refer to things; *who* refers only to people.

EXAMPLES   I went to the exhibit **that** you told me to see.

The walls, **which** were painted bright white, contrasted well with the paintings.

I admire the artist **who** painted the works.

(62) their, there, they're   *Their,* a possessive pronoun, always modifies a noun. *There* can be used either as an expletive at the beginning of a sentence or as an adverb showing place or direction. *They're* is a contraction of *they are.*

PRONOUN	Farmers spent all **their** time preparing **their** fields for the spring planting.
EXPLETIVE	**There** are so many problems for farmers to overcome to have a successful crop yield.
ADVERB	The fields over **there** will be planted with a different crop this year.
CONTRACTION	**They're** going to help us do the planting this year.

(63) them   Do not use *them* as a substitute for *those.*

INCORRECT	**Them** horses are extremely fast.
PREFERRED	**Those** horses are extremely fast.

(64) to, too, two   *To,* a preposition, begins a phrase or an infinitive. *Too,* an adverb, modifies adjectives and other adverbs and means "very" or "also." *Two* is a number.

PREPOSITION	**to** the ocean floor, **to** the shore
INFINITIVE	**to** swim, **to** fly
ADVERB	**too** tall, **too** quickly
NUMBER	**two** fins, **two** schools of fish

(65) when, where   Do not use *when* or *where* immediately after a linking verb. Do not use *where* in place of *that.*

INCORRECT	Night is **when** you can watch fish feed.
	On the beach is **where** turtles lay eggs.
PREFERRED	Night is **the time** you can watch fish feed.
	On the beach is **the place** turtles lay eggs.

See Practice 9.2F

Read each sentence. Then, choose the correct item to complete each sentence.

EXAMPLE   The dog loves (lying, laying) in the sun.

ANSWER   *lying*

1. (Let, Leave) your homework on top of your desk.

2. The (loose, lose) knot became untied.

3. Please (lie, lay) the bat on the ground.

4. Will the instructor (learn, teach) us the backstroke?

5. The girl (ought to have, should have) worn warmer clothes.

6. The cause of the leak (maybe, may be) a corroding pipe.

7. He ran (like, as if) he was being chased by wild animals.

8. The judge said that parking in front of the courthouse is (okay, permissible).

9. The flowers were placed (atop, atop of) the cake.

10. Of the group, (only Michelle, Michelle only) wanted to go fishing.

Read each sentence. Then, rewrite each sentence, correcting the errors in usage.

EXAMPLE   Them apples are ripening fast.

ANSWER   *Those apples are ripening fast.*

11. In the oak tree is where we will build the treehouse.

12. I'm afraid their not home right now.

13. Two see a meteor, the night sky has to be cloudless.

14. Noon is when the sun is highest in the sky.

15. The students voted for the candidate that gave the best speech.

16. After I seen who was at the door, I smoothed my hair.

17. I have spent more time training mynah birds then training parrots.

18. The speeches proceeded the fireworks display.

19. Only a few fans set in the bleachers, waiting for the game to begin.

20. I believe that keeping one's promises is an important principal to live by.

SPEAKING APPLICATION

Reread each sentence in Practice 9.2E. Discuss with a partner which usage errors you've made in past writing assignments.

WRITING APPLICATION

Write four sentences that include usage problems. Exchange papers with a partner. Your partner should correct your sentences.

PRACTICE 1 ▷ Combining and Varying Sentences

Read the sentences. Then, rewrite each sentence according to the instructions in parentheses.

1. The fire alarm went off in the middle of second period. (Start with a prepositional phrase.)

2. The squirrel hid in the basement. (Invert the subject-verb order.)

3. Mike played hockey. He also played basketball to prove his athleticism. (Create a compound direct object; start with an infinitive.)

4. Texas is the second largest state in the United States. It is also known as the Lone Star State. Austin is the capital of Texas. (Create a compound sentence; include an appositive.)

5. Some students become nervous around new technology. Other students seem to enjoy the challenges. (Create a compound sentence; include a semicolon.)

6. Nell had been nervous about her solo. She sang beautifully. (Create a compound sentence; include a conjunction.)

7. We've had record high winds this summer. We've also had record rainfalls. (Create a compound sentence; start with a phrase.)

8. Mrs. Johnson's missing cat was in the tree. (Invert the subject-verb order.)

9. Meghan wanted to surprise her sister. She bought a special gift. She bought a cake. (Create a compound direct object; start with an infinitive.)

10. Mr. Yen is a great teacher. He is my mathematics teacher. He has taught for ten years. (Create a compound sentence; include an appositive.)

PRACTICE 2 ▷ Revising Pronoun and Verb Usage

Read the sentences. Then, revise them to eliminate problems in pronoun and verb usage. You may need to reorder, add, or eliminate words in a sentence.

1. Only someone who likes heights will enjoy their trip to the top of the tower.

2. Whom is the best singer in the chorus?

3. Anna and Jen decides to join the club.

4. He and his sister returned them life jackets to the rack in the boathouse.

5. My dad left the car for him and I.

6. A student who commits to excellence should have no fears about their future.

7. To who did you give the key?

8. Neither Tom nor me are responsible for that.

9. Everybody on the team have new uniforms.

10. Aunt Jo gave gifts to my sister and I.

PRACTICE 3 ▷ Revising for Correct Use of Active and Passive Voice

Read the sentences. Then, revise each sentence to be in the active voice. You may reorder, add, or delete words.

1. People in the audience were blinded by the bright lights onstage.

2. The homework assignment will be finished by Jeannie before bedtime.

3. The bake sale will be organized by Sara.

4. A time-out was called by one of the coaches.

5. The employees were informed of the pay raise.

6. The rules were changed by the chairman.

Continued on next page ▶

7. Charlie was home-schooled by his mother.

8. Roller coasters were avoided by Angela because of her weak stomach.

9. Grapes are grown in the valley.

10. The door was opened by Mike.

PRACTICE 4 > **Correcting Errors in Pronoun and Verb Usage**

Read the sentences. Then, revise each sentence to correct errors in agreement, verb usage, and pronoun usage. Write *correct* if a sentence contains no errors.

1. Michael and his dad gave the dog a bath.

2. Neither Laura nor Lisa remembered their locker combination.

3. Pam noticed an old man who is sitting on a bench next to the post office.

4. Some of the flowers had lost its petals.

5. Neither of the boys brought their ticket.

PRACTICE 5 > **Using Comparative and Superlative Forms Correctly**

Read the sentences. Then, write the appropriate comparative or superlative degree of the modifier in parentheses.

1. This box is the (heavy) of the two.

2. Today is (cold) than yesterday.

3. I had a (good) time than I thought I would.

4. That was the (fancy) restaurant I have ever been to.

5. The Louvre has the (fine) art collection in Europe, in my opinion.

PRACTICE 6 > **Avoiding Double Negatives**

Read the sentences. Then, choose the word in parentheses that makes each sentence negative without forming a double negative.

1. I would not want to be (anywhere, nowhere) but here right now.

2. I am not going to buy (no, any) more DVDs.

3. Khadija hasn't met (no one, anyone) who can beat her at chess.

4. The accident wasn't (nobody's, anybody's) fault.

5. Maxine hasn't (never, ever) ridden in an airplane.

PRACTICE 7 > **Avoiding Usage Problems**

Read the sentences. Then, rewrite each sentence using the appropriate word in the parentheses.

1. The musicians were (all ready, already) for the concert.

2. (Lay, Lie) the papers on the table.

3. Flowers, (like, as if) roses, lilies, and tulips, are a popular gift on Valentine's Day.

4. The Sanchez family had to (adapt, adopt) to the cold weather when they moved from California to Alaska.

5. Mr. Carlos will not (accept, except) term papers written in pencil.

6. Volunteering at the animal shelter had a profound (affect, effect) on Miguel.

7. (Can, May) I help you find that book?

8. Ned found it difficult to (except, accept) the coach's decision to forfeit the game.

9. It's usually hotter (then, than) this in August.

10. (There, Their) are many possible answers to your question.

CAPITALIZATION

Knowing the rules of capitalization will help you identify and highlight names of people, places, and things in your writing.

WRITE GUY *Jeff Anderson, M.Ed.*

WHAT DO YOU NOTICE?

Look for the capitals as you zoom in on a sentence from "New Directions," an excerpt from *Wouldn't Take Nothing for My Journey Now* by Maya Angelou.

MENTOR TEXT

> In 1903 the late Mrs. Annie Johnson of Arkansas found herself with two toddling sons, very little money, a slight ability to read and add simple numbers.

Now, ask yourself the following questions:

- What do the capitalized words in the sentence indicate?
- Why is *Mrs.* capitalized?

The word *In* is capitalized to signal the start of the sentence. *Annie Johnson* and *Arkansas* indicate a person's name and a specific place, so they are capitalized as proper nouns. *Mrs.* is capitalized because it is the abbreviation of the title *Mistress*, which is used to show that a woman is married.

Grammar for Writers Writers use capitalization for many purposes, including starting sentences and quotations and identifying proper nouns and proper adjectives. Think of capital letters as signals that help readers navigate your writing.

What is the capital of our country?

It's W for Washington, as in Washington, D.C.

10.1 Capitalization in Sentences

Just as road signs help to guide people through a town, capital letters help to guide readers through sentences and paragraphs. Capitalization signals the start of a new sentence or points out certain words within a sentence to give readers visual clues that aid in their understanding.

Using Capitals for First Words

Always capitalize the first word in a sentence.

Capitalize the first word in declarative, interrogative, imperative, and exclamatory sentences.

DECLARATIVE   **K**atie visited the Grand Canyon.

INTERROGATIVE   **W**here will the dance be held?

IMPERATIVE   **W**atch out for icy sidewalks.

EXCLAMATORY   **W**hat an astounding turn of events!

Capitalize the first word in interjections and incomplete questions.

INTERJECTIONS   **O**h! Wonderful!

INCOMPLETE QUESTIONS   **W**here? **W**hat time?

The word *I* is always capitalized, whether it is the first word in a sentence or not.

Always capitalize the pronoun *I*.

EXAMPLE   Troy and **I** ran the race.

> Capitalize the first word after a colon only if the word begins a complete sentence. Do not capitalize the word if it begins a list of words or phrases.

RULE 10.1.4

SENTENCE
FOLLOWING
A COLON

He repeated his comment breathlessly: **H**e was unable to continue running.

LIST
FOLLOWING
A COLON

The campers packed the following equipment: **b**ackpacks, tents, and blankets.

> Capitalize the first word in each line of traditional poetry, even if the line does not start a new sentence.

RULE 10.1.5

EXAMPLE

I think that I shall never see
A poem lovely as a tree. – Joyce Kilmer

See Practice 10.1A

Using Capitals With Quotations

There are special rules for using capitalization with **quotations.**

> Capitalize the first word of a **quotation.** However, do not capitalize the first word of a continuing sentence when a quotation is interrupted by identifying words or when the first word of a quotation is the continuation of a speaker's sentence.

RULE 10.1.6

EXAMPLES

Joe said, "**T**he dog is loose on the ball field!"

"**A**s the ship came plowing through the water," he said, "**t**he crowd cheered."

Grant remarked that this was "**t**he noisiest concert I have ever attended."

See Practice 10.1B

PRACTICE 10.1A > Capitalizing Words

Read each sentence. Then, write the word or words that should be capitalized in each sentence.

EXAMPLE   will you be around after school today?

ANSWER   *Will*

1. how excited were we to get front-row tickets?

2. the teacher read the directions: fill in the blanks for each item.

3. doing too many things causes me to get confused.

4. i wondered if i prepared enough food for the party.

5. we packed the picnic basket for the trip: sandwiches, fruit, and drinks.

6. what? where did you say you were going?

7. wow! what a discovery!

8. they were very happy: their new house was a lot bigger than their old house.

9. will you be going to the town library this weekend?

10. roses are red
    violets are blue.

PRACTICE 10.1B > Using Capitals With Quotations

Read each sentence. Then, write the word or words in each sentence that should be capitalized.

EXAMPLE   monica asked, "are you going out to lunch today?"

ANSWER   *Monica, Are*

11. the coach said, "run ten laps and then take a break."

12. "ask what you can do for your country!" exclaimed President John F. Kennedy.

13. my mother cautioned, "don't answer too quickly."

14. "if i had wanted to go to the party," Christina said, "i would have asked for a ride."

15. "please talk quietly," the librarian requested.

16. "stop! don't move." Jacob continued, "you're standing on thin ice."

17. the director shouted, "places, everyone!"

18. my grandfather loved to say, "a quiet man can be heard better than anyone else."

19. one of my favorite sayings is "everywhere I go, there I am."

20. "as the car appeared around the corner," he said, "i could see the driver."

SPEAKING APPLICATION

Take turns with a partner. Say a variety of sentences, describing yourself in the first person. Your partner should indicate, with a nod of his or her head, each time you use a word that should be capitalized.

WRITING APPLICATION

Write a brief dialogue between you and a friend in which you discuss what you did last weekend. Be sure to use conventions of capitalization correctly in your quotations.

10.2 Proper Nouns

Capitalization make important words stand out in your writing, such as the names of people, places, countries, book titles, and other proper names. Sometimes proper names are used as nouns and sometimes as adjectives modifying nouns or pronouns.

Using Capitals for Proper Nouns

Nouns, as you may remember, are either **common** or **proper.**

Common nouns, such as *sailor*, *brother*, *city*, and *ocean*, identify classes of people, places, or things and are not capitalized.

Proper nouns name specific examples of people, places, or things and should be capitalized.

> **Capitalize all proper nouns.**

RULE 10.2.1

EXAMPLES   **J**ennifer   **P**rofessor **W**ilkens   **G**overnor **P**ercy

Chicago   **M**ain **S**treet   **H**alloran **H**ouse

The **R**ed **B**adge *of* **C**ourage   **U.S.S.** **M**onitor

Names

Each part of a person's name—the given name, the middle name or initial standing for that name, and the surname—should be capitalized. If a surname begins with *Mc* or *O'*, the letter following it is capitalized (McAdams, O'Reilly).

> **Capitalize each part of a person's name even when the full name is not used.**

RULE 10.2.2

EXAMPLES   **J**ean **G**rog   **R. R. B**rig   **E**rin **H. S**ands

Capitalize the proper names that are given to animals.

EXAMPLES   **F**lipper   **T**raveler   **R**in **T**in **T**in

Geographical and Place Names

If a place can be found on a map, it should generally be capitalized.

Capitalize geographical and place names.

Examples of different kinds of geographical and place names are listed in the following chart.

GEOGRAPHICAL AND PLACE NAMES	
Streets	Madison Avenue, First Street, Green Valley Road
Towns and Cities	Dallas, Oakdale, New York City
Counties, States, and Provinces	Champlain County, Texas, Quebec
Nations and Continents	Austria, Kenya, the United States of America, Asia, Mexico, Europe
Mountains	the Adirondack Mountains, Mount Washington
Valleys and Deserts	the San Fernando Valley, the Mojave Desert, the Gobi
Islands and Peninsulas	Aruba, the Faroe Islands, Cape York Peninsula
Sections of a Country	the Northeast, Siberia, the Great Plains
Scenic Spots	Gateway National Park, Carlsbad Caverns
Rivers and Falls	the Missouri River, Victoria Falls
Lakes and Bays	Lake Cayuga, Gulf of Mexico, the Bay of Biscayne
Seas and Oceans	the Sargasso Sea, the Indian Ocean
Celestial Bodies and Constellations	Mars, the Big Dipper, moon, Venus
Monuments and Memorials	the Tomb of the Unknown Soldier, Kennedy Memorial Library, the Washington Monument
Buildings	Madison Square Garden, Fort Hood, the Astrodome, the White House
School and Meeting Rooms	Room 6, Laboratory 3B, the Red Room, Conference Room C

Capitalizing Directions

Words indicating direction are capitalized only when they refer to a section of a country.

EXAMPLES   The courier made his way through the **S**outh.

The train stops two miles **e**ast of the city.

Capitalizing Names of Celestial Bodies

Capitalize the names of celestial bodies except *moon* and *sun*.

EXAMPLE   When the **m**oon passes between the **s**un

and **E**arth, a solar eclipse occurs.

Capitalizing Buildings and Places

Do not capitalize words such as *theater*, *hotel*, *university*, and *park*, unless the word is part of a proper name.

EXAMPLES   We visited Stone Mountain **P**ark.

I will meet you at the **p**ark.

Events and Times

Capitalize references to historic events, periods, and documents as well as dates and holidays. Use a dictionary to check capitalization.

> Capitalize the names of specific events and periods in history.

10.2.4 RULE

SPECIAL EVENTS AND TIMES	
Historic Events	the **B**attle of **W**aterloo, **W**orld **W**ar **I**
Historical Periods	the **M**anchu **D**ynasty, **R**econstruction
Documents	the **B**ill of **R**ights, the **M**agna **C**arta
Days and Months	**M**onday, **J**une 22, the third week in **M**ay
Holidays	**L**abor **D**ay, **M**emorial **D**ay, **V**eterans **D**ay
Religious Holidays	**R**osh **H**ashanah, **C**hristmas, **E**aster
Special Events	the **W**orld **S**eries, the **H**oliday **A**ntiques **S**how

Capitalizing Seasons

Do not capitalize seasons unless the name of the season is being used as a proper noun or adjective.

EXAMPLES   My cousins spent their **s**ummer vacation in Florida.

The **A**utumn Harvest Dance is next week.

Capitalize the names of organizations, government bodies, political parties, races, nationalities, languages, and religions.

VARIOUS GROUPS	
Clubs and Organizations	Rotary, Knights of Columbus, the Red Cross, National Organization for Women
Institutions	the Museum of Fine Arts, the Mayo Clinic
Schools	Kennedy High School, University of Texas
Businesses	General Motors, Prentice Hall
Government Bodies	Department of State, Federal Trade Commission, House of Representatives
Political Parties	Republicans, the Democratic party
Nationalities	American, Mexican, Chinese, Israeli, Canadian
Languages	English, Italian, Polish, Swahili
Religions and Religious References	Christianity: God, the Holy Spirit, the Bible Judaism: the Lord, the Prophets, the Torah Islam: Allah, the Prophets, the Qur'an, Mohammed Hinduism: Brahma, the Bhagavad Gita, the Vedas Buddhism: the Buddha, Mahayana, Hinayana

References to Mythological Gods When referring to mythology, do not capitalize the word *god* (the *gods* of Olympus).

Capitalize the names of awards; the names of specific types of air, sea, and spacecraft; and brand names.

EXAMPLES   the **P**ulitzer **P**rize   the **M**edal of **H**onor

Biska **T**reats   **A**pollo **V**

See Practice 10.2A
See Practice 10.2B

PRACTICE 10.2A **Identifying Proper Nouns**

Read each sentence. Then, write the proper noun or nouns in each sentence.

EXAMPLE   I went to Lake Michigan last winter.

ANSWER   *Lake Michigan*

1. I know that George Washington was the first president of the United States.

2. My friends and I always go to the same chain of movie theaters, MovieForU.

3. The Musicians for the Environment Board of Trustees meets twice a month.

4. After the moon rises, Mars can be seen in the east.

5. Both the Cherokee and Sioux live in the West.

6. Jonas Salk developed the polio vaccine.

7. The Daytona 500 takes place every year in Florida.

8. Clara Barton organized the American Red Cross.

9. The Oval Office is where the president works in the White House.

10. The Great Depression lasted for over a decade.

PRACTICE 10.2B **Capitalizing Proper Nouns**

Read each sentence. Then, write the word or words in each sentence that should be capitalized.

EXAMPLE   While in south america, we went to peru and argentina.

ANSWER   *South America, Peru, Argentina*

11. We have tickets to see the joffrey ballet.

12. The empire state building is in new york city.

13. abraham lincoln's birthday is on february 12.

14. The southwest is very hot and dry.

15. Every february, we celebrate african american history month.

16. The environmental protection agency helps reduce pollution in our world.

17. My best friend anna is european and asian.

18. The colorado river lies at the bottom of the grand canyon.

19. In greek mythology, zeus is the leader of the gods.

20. The uss *south dakota* was stationed in the pacific ocean during world war II.

SPEAKING APPLICATION

Take turns with a partner. Tell about an important period in history. Your partner should identify the proper nouns that you use.

WRITING APPLICATION

Use sentence 12 as a model to write three similar sentences. Replace the proper nouns in sentence 12 with other proper nouns.

Using Capitals for Proper Adjectives

A **proper adjective** is either an adjective formed from a proper noun or a proper noun used as an adjective.

> Capitalize most **proper adjectives.**

PROPER ADJECTIVES
FORMED FROM
PROPER NOUNS

Australian kangaroo   **S**hakespearean play

Afghan hound   **E**uropean settlers

Spanish ambassador   **I**talian food

PROPER NOUNS USED
AS ADJECTIVES

the **S**enate floor   the **R**iley speeches

Shakespeare festival   a **B**ible class

the **B**rowns' house   **C**hicago pizza

Some proper adjectives have become so commonly used that they are no longer capitalized.

EXAMPLES

herculean **e**ffort   **f**rench **f**ries

pasteurized **m**ilk   **q**uixotic **h**ope

venetian **b**linds   **t**eddy **b**ear

Brand names are often used as proper adjectives.

> Capitalize a **brand name** when it is used as an adjective, but do not capitalize the common noun it modifies.

EXAMPLES

Timo **w**atches   **S**witzles **c**hocolate

Super **C**ool **j**eans   **L**onglasting **r**efrigerator

Multiple Proper Adjectives

When you have two or more proper adjectives used together,
do not capitalize the associated common nouns.

> **Do not capitalize a common noun used with two proper
> adjectives.**

ONE PROPER ADJECTIVE	TWO PROPER ADJECTIVES
Mississippi River	Ohio and Mississippi rivers
Washington Street	Washington, Madison, and Lincoln streets
Suez Canal	Suez and Panama canals
Banking Act	Banking and Taxing acts
Atlantic Ocean	Atlantic and Pacific oceans
Bergen County	Bergen and Morris counties
Fiji Islands	Fiji and Canary islands

Prefixes and Hyphenated Adjectives

Prefixes and hyphenated adjectives cause special problems.
Prefixes used with proper adjectives should be capitalized only if
they refer to a nationality.

> **Do not capitalize prefixes attached to proper adjectives unless
> the prefix refers to a nationality. In a hyphenated adjective,
> capitalize only the proper adjective.**

EXAMPLES   all-American   Anglo-American

Spanish-speaking   pro-English

American Korean-language newspaper

pre-Renaissance   Sino-Russian

pre-Mayan architecture   Indo-European

See Practice 10.2C

See Practice 10.2D

PRACTICE 10.2C Capitalizing Proper Adjectives

Read each sentence. Then, write the word or words in each sentence that should be capitalized.

EXAMPLE   Terrance and Carol were late for english class.

ANSWER   *English*

1. I have never been to a spanish-speaking country.

2. Steamed dumplings is my favorite chinese dish.

3. We live near an indian grocery store.

4. My mother reads a hebrew-language newspaper every morning.

5. The florida panther is on the endangered species list.

6. Pro-american sentiments were felt during the president's african tour.

7. The excavated pottery is pre-colombian.

8. The russo-japanese war lasted one year.

9. In 1916, irish patriots proclaimed independence from England on o'connell street.

10. Marla has an english bulldog and a french poodle.

PRACTICE 10.2D Revising Sentences to Correct Capitalization Errors

Read each sentence. Then, rewrite each sentence using the conventions of capitalization.

EXAMPLE   Dov thinks our greek tragedy is fine, but I think it could be improved.

ANSWER   *Dov thinks our Greek tragedy is fine, but I think it could be improved.*

11. The national football league has many teams.

12. Many businesspeople have been lobbying in congress.

13. My ecuadorian sweater is very warm.

14. Sam Houston, a virginia-born statesman, was the governor of both tennessee and texas.

15. I cannot decide if I should open an account at money bank, american money, or j.t.t. bank.

16. In british history, Elizabeth I was admired both during and after her time.

17. The dallas cowboys play at texas stadium.

18. My grandparents drink english tea every afternoon.

19. Essex and ocean counties are located in New Jersey.

20. The monarch butterfly migrates to mexico before winter sets in.

SPEAKING APPLICATION

Discuss with a partner the importance of capitals. Suggest three ways capitalization makes reading and comprehension easier.

WRITING APPLICATION

Write a brief paragraph that contains proper adjectives. Be sure to use conventions of capitalization.

10.3 Other Uses of Capitals

Even though the purpose of using capital letters is to make writing clearer, some rules for capitalization can be confusing. For example, it may be difficult to remember which words in a letter you write need to start with a capital, which words in a book title should be capitalized, or when a person's title—such as Senator or Reverend—needs to start with a capital. The rules and examples that follow should clear up the confusion.

Using Capitals in Letters

Capitalization is required in parts of personal letters and business letters.

> Capitalize the first word and all nouns in letter salutations and the first word in letter closings.

RULE 10.3.1

SALUTATIONS
Dear **E**ric,
Dear **S**irs:
Dear **M**r. **L**evitt:
My **D**ear **C**ousin,

CLOSINGS
With **l**ove,
Yours **t**ruly,
Sincerely **y**ours,
Best **r**egards,

Using Capitals for Titles

Capitals are used for titles of people and titles of literary and artistic works. The charts and rules on the following pages will guide you in capitalizing titles correctly.

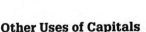

Capitalize a person's title only when it is used with the person's name or when it is used as a proper name by itself.

WITH A PROPER NAME	Yesterday, **G**overnor **W**ilson signed the bill.
AS A PROPER NAME	I'm glad you can join us, **G**randma.
IN A GENERAL REFERENCE	The **s**enator followed the progress of the debate.

The following chart illustrates the correct form for a variety of titles. Study the chart, paying particular attention to compound titles and titles with prefixes or suffixes.

SOCIAL, BUSINESS, RELIGIOUS, MILITARY, AND GOVERNMENT TITLES	
Commonly Used Titles	Sir, Madam, Miss, Professor, Doctor, Reverend, Bishop, Sister, Father, Rabbi, Corporal, Major, Admiral, Mayor, Governor, Ambassador
Abbreviated Titles	*Before names*: Mr., Mrs., Ms., Dr., Hon. *After names*: Jr., Sr., Ph.D., M.D., D.D.S., Esq.
Compound Titles	Vice President, Secretary of State, Lieutenant Governor, Commander in Chief
Titles With Prefixes or Suffixes	ex-Congressman Randolph, Governor-elect Loughman

Some honorary titles are capitalized. These include First Lady of the United States, Speaker of the House of Representatives, Queen Mother of England, and the Prince of Wales.

RULE 10.3.3

Capitalize certain honorary titles even when the titles are not followed by a proper name.

EXAMPLE   The **p**resident and **F**irst **L**ady visited with the **q**ueen of England.

Occasionally, the titles of other government officials may be capitalized as a sign of respect when referring to a specific person whose name is not given. However, you usually do not capitalize titles when they stand alone.

EXAMPLES   We thank you, **G**overnor, for taking time to meet with us.

Fourteen **s**enators voted against the bill.

RULE 10.3.4

Relatives are often referred to by titles. These references should be capitalized when used with or as the person's name.

WITH THE PERSON'S NAME   In the summer, **U**ncle **T**ed enjoys gardening.

AS A NAME   He says that **G**randmother enjoys gardening, too.

RULE 10.3.5

Do not capitalize titles showing family relationships when they are preceded by a possessive noun or pronoun.

EXAMPLES   my **a**unt   her **f**ather   Jeff's **m**other

> Capitalize the first word and all other key words in the titles of books, periodicals, poems, stories, plays, paintings, and other works of art.

The following chart lists examples to guide you in capitalizing titles and subtitles of various works. Note that the articles (*a, an,* and *the*) are not capitalized unless they are used as the first word of a title or subtitle. Conjunctions and prepositions are also left uncapitalized unless they are the first or last word in a title or subtitle or contain four letters or more. Note also that verbs, no matter how short, are always capitalized.

TITLES OF WORKS	
Books	*The Red Badge of Courage, Profiles in Courage, All Through the Night, John Ford: The Man and His Films Heart of Darkness*
Periodicals	*International Wildlife, Allure, Better Homes and Gardens*
Poems	"The Raven" "The Rime of the Ancient Mariner" "Flower in the Crannied Wall"
Stories and Articles	"Editha" "The Fall of the House of Usher" "Here Is New York"
Plays and Musicals	*The Tragedy of Macbeth Our Town West Side Story*
Paintings	*Starry Night Mona Lisa The Artist's Daughter With a Cat*
Music	*The Unfinished Symphony* "Heartbreak Hotel" "This Land Is Your Land"

Capitalize titles of educational courses when they are language courses or when they are followed by a number or preceded by a proper noun or adjective. Do not capitalize school subjects discussed in a general manner.

WITH CAPITALS

Latin   **H**onors **B**iology

History 105   **M**ath 4

Economics 313   **F**rench

WITHOUT CAPITALS

geology   **p**sychology

woodworking   **h**istory

biology   **m**ath

EXAMPLES

This year, I will be taking **a**lgebra, **E**nglish, **H**onors **C**hemistry, and **w**orld **h**istory.

Catherine's favorite classes are **a**rt **h**istory, **I**talian, and **b**iology.

She does not like **p**hysical **e**ducation and **m**ath as much.

After **E**nglish class, I have to rush across the building to **c**hemistry.

See Practice 10.3A
See Practice 10.3B

PRACTICE 10.3A Capitalizing Titles

Read each sentence. Then, write the word or words in each sentence that should be capitalized.

EXAMPLE   Tyrone Plunkett sr. is here to see you.

ANSWER   *Sr.*

1. Did you see the latest copy of *the new york times*?

2. I think lieutenant bell has some urgent news.

3. Last night, Thomas read "politics in the english language" by George Orwell.

4. In 1991, Colin Powell became chairman of the joint chiefs of staff.

5. At the vote, senator wellington was noticeably absent.

6. *Beautiful world* is a painting by grandma moses.

7. I just finished reading the novel *cold mountain*.

8. DaVinci's *mona lisa* is still the pride of the Louvre in Paris.

9. "Excuse me, mr. lopes. I would like to introduce you to ms. carlton."

10. Thomas Hardy's "hap" is one of the most emotionally charged poems I've read in class.

PRACTICE 10.3B Using All of the Rules of Capitalization

Read each sentence. Then, rewrite each sentence, using the conventions of capitalization.

EXAMPLE   t.j. thinks we should drive along st. lawrence avenue.

ANSWER   *T.J. thinks we should drive along St. Lawrence Avenue.*

11. The class will have to read Gustave Flaubert's *madame bovary*.

12. The jackson years were some of the most controversial in american history.

13. Ironically, hamburgers are not named for hamburg, germany.

14. Fans applauded sir elton john as he strolled down the red carpet.

15. It is rare that mr. and mrs. singh are late.

16. kirsten is no longer the company's liaison to japan.

17. The average new yorker walks five miles every day.

18. Pardon me, miss, but where is the nearest ATM?

19. Even the civilians saluted vice-admiral salva for his brilliant strategy.

20. A french-canadian man asked berta to dance.

SPEAKING APPLICATION

Discuss with a partner the importance of capitals in names and titles. Together, answer the following question: How does capitalizing a title show respect?

WRITING APPLICATION

Pick a personal title, such as "captain" or "doctor," and write four sentences. Two should demonstrate when the title is capitalized, and two should demonstrate when it is not capitalized.

CHAPTER 11

PUNCTUATION

Using punctuation correctly will help you to organize and clarify your writing.

WRITE GUY *Jeff Anderson, M.Ed.*

WHAT DO YOU NOTICE?

Notice how punctuation is used as you zoom in on these sentences from the story "The Red-Headed League" by Sir Arthur Conan Doyle.

MENTOR TEXT

> "You may place considerable confidence in Mr. Holmes, sir," said the police agent loftily. "He has his own little methods, which are, if he won't mind my saying so, just a little too theoretical and fantastic, but he has the makings of a detective in him."

Now, ask yourself the following questions:

- Why is the word *sir* set off by commas?
- How are commas used in the second sentence?

The word *sir* is set off by commas to show that the speaker is addressing someone directly. The second comma serves to separate *sir* from the tag line *said the police agent loftily*. In the second sentence, commas set off nonrestrictive phrases, those not needed to complete the meaning of the sentence but that add extra detail. The author uses the comma before the conjunction *but* to separate the main, or independent, clauses.

Grammar for Writers Text would be difficult to read and understand without punctuation because it shows readers how to group words. Writers have a variety of punctuation marks available to make their writing clear.

Commas are such useful things.

I, always, have, extra, if, you, need, one.

11.1 End Marks

End marks tell readers when to pause and for how long. They signal the end or conclusion of a sentence, word, or phrase. There are three end marks: the **period (.)**, the **question mark (?)**, and the **exclamation mark (!)**.

Using Periods

A **period** indicates the end of a declarative or imperative sentence, an indirect question, or an abbreviation. The period is the most common end mark.

RULE 11.1.1 Use a **period** to end a declarative sentence, a mild imperative sentence, and an indirect question.

A **declarative sentence** is a statement of fact or opinion.

DECLARATIVE SENTENCE
This is a beautiful park.

An **imperative sentence** gives a direction or command. Often, the first word of an imperative sentence is a verb.

MILD IMPERATIVE SENTENCE
Finish reading the chapter.

An **indirect question** restates a question in a declarative sentence. It does not give the speaker's exact words.

INDIRECT QUESTION
Mae asked me whether I could stay.

Other Uses of Periods

In addition to signaling the end of a statement, periods can also signal that words have been shortened, or abbreviated.

RULE 11.1.2 Use a period after most abbreviations and after initials.

PERIODS IN ABBREVIATIONS	
Titles	Dr., Sr., Mrs., Mr., Gov., Maj., Rev., Prof.
Place Names	Ave., Bldg., Blvd., Mt., Dr., St., Ter., Rd.
Times and Dates	Sun., Dec., sec., min., hr., yr., A.M.
Initials	E. B. White, Robin F. Brancato, R. Brett

Some abbreviations do not end with periods. Metric measurements, state abbreviations used with ZIP Codes, and most standard measurements do not need periods. The abbreviation for inch, *in.*, is the exception.

EXAMPLES   mm, cm, kg, L, C, CA, TX, ft, gal

The following chart lists some abbreviations with and without periods.

ABBREVIATIONS WITH AND WITHOUT END MARKS	
approx. = approximately	misc. = miscellaneous
COD = cash on delivery	mph = miles per hour
dept. = department	No. = number
doz. = dozen(s)	p. or pg. = page; pp. = pages
EST = Eastern Standard Time	POW = prisoner of war
FM = frequency modulation	pub. = published, publisher
gov. or govt. = government	pvt. = private
ht. = height	rpm = revolutions per minute
incl. = including	R.S.V.P. = please reply
ital = italics	sp. = spelling
kt. = karat or carat	SRO = standing room only
meas. = measure	vol. = volume
mfg. = manufacturing	wt. = weight

Sentences Ending With Abbreviations When a sentence ends with an abbreviation that uses a period, do not put a second period at the end. If an end mark other than a period is required, add the end mark.

Be sure to call Jack Jenkins Jr**.**

Is that Adam Martin Jr**. ?**

See Practice 11.1A

RULE 11.1.3

Do not use periods with acronyms, words formed with the first or first few letters of a series of words.

ACRONYMS

USA (United States of America)

UN (United Nations)

RULE 11.1.4

Use a period after numbers and letters in outlines.

EXAMPLE

I**.** Maintaining your pet's health

    A**.** Diet

        1**.** For a puppy

        2**.** For a mature dog

    B**.** Exercise

Using Question Marks

A **question mark** follows a word, phrase, or sentence that asks a question. A question is often in inverted word order.

RULE 11.1.5

Use a **question mark** to end an interrogative sentence, an incomplete question, or a statement intended as a question.

INTERROGATIVE SENTENCE

Do snakes hatch from eggs **?**

What time do you want me to pick you up **?**

INCOMPLETE QUESTION

Many small birds build false nests. Why **?**

I'll leave you money. How much **?**

Use care, however, in ending statements with question marks. It is better to rephrase the statement as a direct question.

STATEMENT WITH A QUESTION MARK	The geese haven't migrated yet **?**
	We are having spaghettif for dinner **?**
REVISED INTO A DIRECT QUESTION	Haven't the geese migrated yet **?**
	Are we having spaghetti for dinner **?**

Use a period instead of a question mark with an **indirect question**—a question that is restated as a declarative sentence.

| EXAMPLES | Ted wanted to know which bus to take **.** |
| | He wondered if he would be on time **.** |

Using Exclamation Marks

An **exclamation mark** signals an exclamatory sentence, an imperative sentence, or an interjection. It indicates strong emotion and should be used sparingly.

> Use an **exclamation mark** to end an exclamatory sentence, a forceful imperative sentence, or an interjection expressing strong emotion.

11.1.6 RULE

| EXCLAMATORY SENTENCE | Look at that huge vulture **!** |

| FORCEFUL IMPERATIVE SENTENCE | Don't spill the water **!** |

An interjection can be used with a comma or an exclamation mark. An exclamation mark increases the emphasis.

EXAMPLES	Wow **!** That was a great throw **.**
	Oh **!** Look what I found **.**
WITH A COMMA	Wow **,** that was a great throw **.**

See Practice 11.1B

PRACTICE 11.1A Using Periods Correctly in Sentences

Read each sentence. Then, rewrite each sentence, adding periods where they are needed.

EXAMPLE   Michael C Young published that famous book

ANSWER   *Michael C. Young published that famous book.*

1. I asked Mrs Robinson to watch my cats

2. The bus leaves promptly at 7:15 AM

3. S E Hinton wrote *The Outsiders*

4. Send the letter to Dr Paul K Wright

5. One of the candidates was a POW

6. Nellie asked me if I saw her cellphone

7. This is 18 mm of copper wiring

8. Deanna asked me if I wanted to bring my sweater

9. The forty-fourth president of the United States is Barack H Obama

10. The high-speed train can travel over 300 mph

PRACTICE 11.1B Using Question Marks and Exclamation Marks Correctly in Sentences

Read each sentence. Then, write the correct end mark for each item.

EXAMPLE   What a great new hat

ANSWER   /

11. How many sweaters does she have

12. How many books did Ernest Hemingway write

13. Did you wipe your muddy shoes on the mat

14. Surprise

15. When will Dean arrive

16. Watch out

17. What a beautiful symphony

18. What time are we eating dinner

19. Do you know where Plano, Texas, is

20. Be careful with that vase

SPEAKING APPLICATION

Take turns with a partner. Say declarative sentences, imperative sentences, and indirect questions. Your partner should listen for and identify each sentence type.

WRITING APPLICATION

Write two sentences that use question marks and two sentences that use exclamation marks.

11.2 Commas

A **comma** tells the reader to pause briefly before continuing a sentence. Commas may be used to separate elements in a sentence or to set off part of a sentence.

Commas are used more than any other internal punctuation mark. To check for correct comma use, read a sentence aloud and note where a pause helps you to group your ideas. Commas signal to readers that they should take a short breath.

Using Commas With Compound Sentences

A **compound sentence** consists of two or more main or independent clauses that are joined by a coordinating conjunction, such as *and, but, for, nor, or, so,* or *yet.*

> Use a **comma** before a conjunction to separate two or more independent or main clauses in a **compound sentence.**

11.2.1 RULE

Use a comma before a conjunction only when there are complete sentences on both sides of the conjunction. Do not use a comma if the conjunction joins a compound subject, a compound verb, prepositional phrases, or subordinate clauses.

EXAMPLE   Joe is getting married this summer, but I won't be
                         independent clause
able to attend the wedding.
           independent clause

In some compound sentences, the main or independent clauses are very brief, and the meaning is clear. When this occurs, the comma before the conjunction may be omitted.

EXAMPLES   Jonathan listened carefully but he heard nothing.

Mira would like to visit in June but she is too busy.

In other sentences, conjunctions are used to join compound subjects or verbs, prepositional phrases, or subordinate clauses. Because these sentences have only one independent clause, they do not take a comma before the conjunction.

CONJUNCTIONS WITHOUT COMMAS	
Compound Subject	Diana and Jill met for lunch at the mall.
Compound Verb	The friends chatted and laughed as they ate lunch.
Two Prepositional Phrases	My cat flew through the living room and up the stairs.
Two Subordinate Clauses	I enjoy shopping trips only if they are short and if I find what I need.

A **nominative absolute** is a noun or pronoun followed by a participle or participial phrase that functions independently of the rest of the sentence.

RULE 11.2.2

> Use a comma after a **nominative absolute**.

The following example shows a comma with a nominative absolute.

EXAMPLE   Precious minutes having been lost, I decided to call the fire department.

Avoiding Comma Splices

Remember to use both a comma and a coordinating conjunction in a compound sentence. Using only a comma can result in a **run-on sentence** or a **comma splice**. A **comma splice** occurs when two or more complete sentences have been joined with only a comma. Either punctuate separate sentences with an end mark or a semicolon, or find a way to join the sentences. (See Section 11.3 for more information on semicolons.)

RULE 11.2.3

> Avoid comma splices.

INCORRECT   The snow clumped on the trees, many branches snapped under the weight.

CORRECT   The snow clumped on the trees. Many branches snapped under the weight.

Using Commas in a Series

A **series** consists of three or more words, phrases, or subordinate clauses of a similar kind. A series can occur in any part of a sentence.

> **Use commas to separate three or more words, phrases, or clauses in a series.**

11.2.4 RULE

Notice that a comma follows each of the items except the last one in these series. The conjunction *and* or *or* is added after the last comma.

SERIES OF WORDS
The desert animals included camels, toads, gerbils, and insects.

SERIES OF PREPOSITIONAL PHRASES
The treasure map directed them over the dunes, into the oasis, and past the palm trees.

SUBORDINATE CLAUSES IN A SERIES
The newspapers reported that the service was flawless, that the dinner was impeccable, and that the band played remarkably well.

If each item (except for the last one) in a series is followed by a conjunction, do not use commas.

EXAMPLE
I visited castles and museums and forts.

A second exception to this rule concerns items such as *salt and pepper*, which are paired so often that they are considered a single item.

EXAMPLES
Every table in the diner was set with a knife and fork, a cup and saucer, and salt and pepper.

Dave's favorite dinners are macaroni and cheese, spaghetti and meatballs, and franks and beans.

Using Commas Between Adjectives

Sometimes, two or more adjectives are placed before the noun they describe.

> Use commas to separate **coordinate adjectives,** also called **independent modifiers,** or adjectives of equal rank.

EXAMPLES a tasteless , boring show

a raucous , festive , thrilling occasion

An adjective is equal in rank to another if the word *and* can be inserted between them without changing the meaning of the sentence. Another way to test whether or not adjectives are equal is to reverse their order. If the sentence still sounds correct, they are of equal rank. In the first example, *a boring, tasteless show* still makes sense.

If you cannot place the word *and* between adjectives or reverse their order without changing the meaning of the sentence, they are called **cumulative adjectives.**

> Do not use a comma between cumulative adjectives.

EXAMPLES a new dinner jacket
(*a dinner new jacket* does not make sense)

many unusual T-shirts
(*unusual many T-shirts* does not make sense)

> Do not use a comma to separate the last adjective in a series from the noun it modifies.

INCORRECT A tall , majestic , building rose above the skyline.   See Practice 11.2A

CORRECT A tall , majestic building rose above the skyline.   See Practice 11.2B

PRACTICE 11.2A **Using Commas Correctly in Sentences**

Read each sentence. Then, rewrite each sentence, adding commas where they are needed.

EXAMPLE   It snowed last night but it was all melted by this morning.

ANSWER   *It snowed last night, but it was all melted by this morning.*

1. The thunderclap startled my brother and he jumped up from the chair.

2. I washed the dishes swept the floor and put away the groceries.

3. David must have arrived on time or we would have received a phone call from the school.

4. The tubas stopped playing but the drum line continued the song.

5. The proud happy contest winner celebrated with her parents.

6. Devon bought canned peaches pears and plums.

7. I called Jake but he didn't answer.

8. She sang the anthem in a soft sweet voice.

9. Tears glistening in her eyes she clapped louder for her son than anyone else.

10. His face red with embarrassment Doug picked up the scattered papers.

PRACTICE 11.2B **Revising to Correct Errors in Comma Use**

Read each sentence. Then, rewrite each sentence, adding or deleting commas as necessary.

EXAMPLE   We took sandwiches, apples, and, juice for lunch.

ANSWER   *We took sandwiches, apples, and juice for lunch.*

11. I took an umbrella but Joe left it at Anita's house.

12. With trumpet lessons, baseball practice and play rehearsal I have no time to join that club.

13. The bus driver was running behind schedule and then the bus broke down.

14. I'm tired yet I can't fall asleep.

15. Laura can't find her homework her lunch or her new, field-hockey stick.

16. We sat around the campfire and John told a gruesome scary story.

17. Stella ate strawberries, and blueberries, and raspberries.

18. We watched the movie, and cheered at every victorious part.

19. The bread was moist chewy, and delicious.

20. Their faces glowing the bride and groom greeted their guests.

SPEAKING APPLICATION

Take turns with a partner. Say compound sentences. Your partner should tell where a comma would go if your sentences were written.

WRITING APPLICATION

Write four sentences that use commas incorrectly. Exchange papers with a partner. Your partner should rewrite each sentence correctly.

Using Commas After Introductory Material

Most material that introduces a sentence should be set off with a comma.

> **Use a comma after an introductory word, phrase, or clause.**

KINDS OF INTRODUCTORY MATERIAL	
Introductory Words	Yes, we do expect to hear from them soon. No, there has been no response. Well, I was definitely surprised by her question.
Nouns of Direct Address	Joe, will you attend?
Introductory Adverbs	Hurriedly, they gathered up their equipment. Patiently, the children's mother explained it to them again.
Participial Phrases	Moving quickly, she averted a potential social disaster. Marching next to each other in the parade, we introduced ourselves and started to chat.
Prepositional Phrases	In the shade of the maple tree, a family spread a picnic blanket. After lengthy festivities, we were all exhausted.
Infinitive Phrases	To choose the right gift, I consulted the bridal registry. To finish my speech on time, I will have to cut some examples.
Adverbial Clauses	When she asked for a permit for the fair, she was sure it would be denied. If you compete in marathons, you may be interested in this one.

Commas and Prepositional Phrases Only one comma should be used after two prepositional phrases or a compound participial or infinitive phrase.

EXAMPLES	In the pocket of his vest, he found the ring.
	Lost in the crowd and confusion, the children asked a police officer for help.

It is not necessary to set off short prepositional phrases. However, a comma can help avoid confusion.

CONFUSING	In the rain water stained the silk tablecloth.
CLEAR	In the rain, water stained the silk tablecloth.

Using Commas With Parenthetical Expressions

A **parenthetical expression** is a word or phrase that interrupts the flow of the sentence.

> **Use commas to set off parenthetical expressions from the rest of the sentence.**

11.2.9 RULE

Parenthetical expressions may come in the middle or at the end of a sentence. A parenthetical expression in the middle of a sentence needs two commas—one on each side; it needs only one comma if it appears at the end of a sentence.

KINDS OF PARENTHETICAL EXPRESSIONS	
Nouns of Direct Address	Will you have lunch with us, Ted? I wonder, Mr. Green, where they'll go for lunch.
Conjunctive Adverbs	Someone had already bought them towels, however. We could not, therefore, buy those.
Common Expressions	I listened to Jack's directions as carefully as anyone else did, I think.
Contrasting Expressions	Tom is seventeen, not eighteen. Lisa's personality, not her beauty, won Bill's heart.

Using Commas With Nonessential Expressions

To determine when a phrase or clause should be set off with commas, decide whether the phrase or clause is *essential* or *nonessential* to the meaning of the sentence. The terms *restrictive* and *nonrestrictive* may also be used.

An **essential,** or **restrictive, phrase** or **clause** is necessary to the meaning of the sentence. **Nonessential,** or **nonrestrictive, expressions** can be left out without changing the meaning of the sentence. Although the nonessential material may be interesting, the sentence can be read without it and still make sense. Depending on their importance in a sentence, appositives, participial phrases, and adjectival clauses can be either essential or nonessential. Only nonessential expressions should be set off with commas.

NONESSENTIAL APPOSITIVE	The part was played by Henry Fonda, the famous actor.
NONESSENTIAL PARTICIPIAL PHRASE	The graceful bridge, built in the 1800s, spans a lake in Central Park.
NONESSENTIAL ADJECTIVAL CLAUSE	The lake, which freezes in winter, is popular with swimmers in summer.

Do not use commas to set off essential expressions.

ESSENTIAL APPOSITIVE	The part was played by the famous actor Henry Fonda.
ESSENTIAL PARTICIPIAL PHRASE	The man wearing the white cap is my uncle.
ESSENTIAL ADJECTIVAL CLAUSE	The paragraph that Juan suggested would change the paper's thesis.

See Practice 11.2C
See Practice 11.2D

PRACTICE 11.2C Placing Commas Correctly in Sentences

Read each sentence. Then, rewrite each sentence, adding commas in nonrestrictive relative clauses, introductory material, and parenthetical expressions.

EXAMPLE   No she doesn't like the painting.

ANSWER   *No, she doesn't like the painting.*

1. Yes he came with us to the meeting.

2. After the previews ended the audience became quiet.

3. Mom what should I do with these old books?

4. When he's happy Alberto is very funny.

5. The plant the one sitting on the sill is growing healthy because it receives a lot of sunlight.

6. To arrive early for the performance we'll need to leave within ten minutes.

7. Louis Pasteur who was French was a famous scientist.

8. Waiting impatiently the man paced the hallways.

9. My little brother whose name is Kyle is in first grade not second grade.

10. Tell me what happened Marcos.

PRACTICE 11.2D Revising Sentences for Proper Comma Use

Read each sentence. Then, rewrite each sentence, adding or deleting commas as necessary.

EXAMPLE   Mickey Mantle who was a Yankee was inducted to the National Baseball Hall of Fame, in 1974.

ANSWER   *Mickey Mantle, who was a Yankee, was inducted to the National Baseball Hall of Fame in 1974.*

11. We had already paid for the tickets however.

12. Eduardo met us, before school not after school.

13. Slowly we opened the door.

14. Grinning, broadly, Warren accepted the science award.

15. My neighbor who is a chef, told us about the new restaurant.

16. Amanda please pass out these papers.

17. She was therefore chosen for the starring role.

18. The lamp which was an antique was broken in two pieces.

19. Yes Ted I heard the noise.

20. That scarf is mine I believe.

SPEAKING APPLICATION

Discuss with a partner the difference between the necessity of a comma in sentence 1 and the necessity of a comma in sentence 7. Tell what the purpose of the comma is in both sentences.

WRITING APPLICATION

Write a funny short story that includes unusual characters in an unusual setting. Be sure to use correct punctuation marks, including comma placement in clauses, nonrestrictive phrases, contrasting expressions, introductory material, and parenthetical expressions.

Using Commas With Dates, Geographical Names, and Titles

Dates usually have several parts, including months, days, and years. Commas separate these elements for easier reading.

> When a date is made up of two or more parts, use a comma after each item, except in the case of a month followed by a day.

EXAMPLES   The wedding took place on June 16, 2005, and their son was born on June 16, 2006.

The show opened on June 16 and closed two days later.
(no comma needed after the day of the month)

Commas are also used when the month and the day are used as an appositive to rename a day of the week.

EXAMPLES   Friday, August 23, was the first day of the fair.

Craig will arrive on Wednesday, May 14, and will stay until Friday.

When a date contains only a month and a year, commas are unnecessary.

EXAMPLES   I will graduate in June 2015.

Joy will visit Europe in August 2011.

If the parts of a date have already been joined by prepositions, no comma is needed.

EXAMPLE   The city's new subway system ran its first train in June of 1890.

> **When a geographical name is made up of two or more parts, use a comma after each item.**

11.2.11 RULE

EXAMPLES   My cousin who lives in Santa Fe, New Mexico, is cutting the ribbon for the grand opening.

They're going to Toronto, Ontario, Canada, for their winter vacation.

See Practice 11.2E

> **When a name is followed by one or more titles, use a comma after the name and after each title.**

11.2.12 RULE

EXAMPLE   I see that Jeremy McGuire, Ph.D., works here.

A similar rule applies with some business abbreviations.

EXAMPLE   BookWright, Inc., published a book about food.

Using Commas in Numbers

Commas make large numbers easier to read by grouping them.

> **With large numbers of more than three digits, use a comma after every third digit starting from the right.**

11.2.13 RULE

EXAMPLES   3,823 books, 205,000 gallons, 2,674,970 tons

> **Do not use a comma in ZIP Codes, telephone numbers, page numbers, years, serial numbers, or house numbers.**

11.2.14 RULE

ZIP CODE	07632	YEAR NUMBER	2004
TELEPHONE NUMBER	(805) 555-6224	SERIAL NUMBER	602 988 6768
PAGE NUMBER	Page 1258	HOUSE NUMBER	18436 Lamson Road

See Practice 11.2F

PRACTICE 11.2E > **Using Commas With Dates and Geographical Names**

Read each sentence. Then, rewrite each sentence to show where to correctly place commas in dates and geographical names.

EXAMPLE   It takes fourteen hours to drive from Nashville Tennessee to Austin Texas.

ANSWER   *It takes fourteen hours to drive from Nashville, Tennessee, to Austin, Texas.*

1. On December 7 1941, Japanese bombers attacked Pearl Harbor.

2. On February 2 2009, we visited San Antonio Texas.

3. The hospital is located in Newark New Jersey.

4. My cousin got married in Vail Colorado on August 30 2008.

5. The new girl in our class is from Nice France.

6. In July 2008, we took a cruise that left from Miami Florida.

7. Sally was born in Oklahoma City Oklahoma.

8. The test will be on Monday October 12.

9. On April 30 1803, the United States purchased the Louisiana Territory.

10. My uncle took me to see the Houston Texans play on Sunday November 23.

PRACTICE 11.2F > **Editing Sentences for Proper Comma Usage**

Read each sentence. Then, rewrite each sentence, deleting or adding commas where they are needed.

EXAMPLE   This Sunday March, 1 I'm going to New York.

ANSWER   *This Sunday, March 1, I'm going to New York.*

11. Jillian Polk M.D. spoke at the medical conference.

12. Did you drive from Atlanta, Georgia to Seattle, Washington, last summer?

13. Flora estimated that the box contained 5822 marbles.

14. Have you ever visited Madrid Spain?

15. Randall Tilde Ph.D. attended the meeting.

16. We will be on vacation from Friday September 9, to Wednesday September 14.

17. The plane had a layover in Salt Lake City Utah on its way to Sacramento California.

18. Unabridged Books Ltd. opens for business at 8:00 A.M.

19. The lawyer signed her name "Ingrid Blush J.D."

20. On March 4 1789 the U.S. Constitution went into effect.

SPEAKING APPLICATION

Take turns with a partner. Use sentences 2 and 6 as models to say similar sentences. Your partner should tell which sentence needs a comma in the date.

WRITING APPLICATION

Write four sentences that contain dates, geographical names, and large numbers, but omit all commas. Exchange papers with a partner. Your partner should add commas where necessary.

Using Commas With Addresses and in Letters

Commas are also used in addresses, salutations of friendly letters, and closings of friendly or business letters.

> **Use a comma after each item in an address made up of two or more parts.**

11.2.15 RULE

Commas are placed after the name, street, and city. No comma separates the state from the ZIP Code. Instead, insert an extra space between them.

EXAMPLE   Send an invitation to Mrs. Robert Brooks,

145 River Road, Jacksonville, Florida 32211.

Fewer commas are needed when an address is written in a letter or on an envelope.

EXAMPLE   Mrs. Robert Brooks

145 River Road

Jacksonville, FL 32211

> **Use a comma after the salutation in a personal letter and after the closing in all letters.**

11.2.16 RULE

SALUTATIONS   Dear Emily,   Dear Uncle Frank,

See Practice 11.2G   CLOSINGS   Yours truly,   Sincerely,

Using Commas in Elliptical Sentences

In **elliptical sentences,** words that are understood are left out. Commas make these sentences easier to read.

> **Use a comma to indicate the words left out of an elliptical sentence.**

11.2.17 RULE

EXAMPLE   Alan celebrates his birthday formally;

Fred **,** casually.

The words *celebrates his birthday* have been omitted from the second clause of the sentence. The comma has been inserted in their place so the meaning is still clear. The sentence could be restated in this way: *Alan celebrates his birthday formally; Fred celebrates his birthday casually.*

Using Commas With Direct Quotations

Commas are also used to indicate where **direct quotations** begin and end. (See Section 11.4 for more information on punctuating quotations.)

> **Use commas to set off a direct quotation from the rest of a sentence.**

EXAMPLES   "You came home late **,** " commented Bill's mother.

He said **,** "The rehearsal ran longer than expected **.** "

"I hope **,** " Bill's mother said **,** "the leading man doesn't forget his lines **.** "

Using Commas for Clarity

Commas help you group words that belong together.

> **Use a comma to prevent a sentence from being misunderstood.**

UNCLEAR   Near the highway developers were building a shopping mall.

CLEAR   Near the highway **,** developers were building a shopping mall.

Misuses of Commas

Because commas appear so frequently in writing, some people are tempted to use them where they are not needed. Before you insert a comma, think about how your ideas relate to one another.

MISUSED WITH AN ADJECTIVE AND A NOUN	After a dance, I enjoy a cool, refreshing, drink.
CORRECT	After a dance, I enjoy a cool, refreshing drink.
MISUSED WITH A COMPOUND SUBJECT	After the election, my friend Nancy, and her sister Julia, were invited to the inaugural ball.
CORRECT	After the election, my friend Nancy and her sister Julia were invited to the inaugural ball.
MISUSED WITH A COMPOUND VERB	He looked into her eyes, and spoke from his heart.
CORRECT	He looked into her eyes and spoke from his heart.
MISUSED WITH A COMPOUND OBJECT	She chose a dress with long sleeves, and a train.
CORRECT	She chose a dress with long sleeves and a train.
MISUSED WITH PHRASES	Reading the invitation, and wondering who sent it, Brian did not hear the phone ring.
CORRECT	Reading the invitation and wondering who sent it, Brian did not hear the phone ring.
MISUSED WITH CLAUSES	He discussed what elements are crucial to a party, and which caterers are most reliable.
CORRECT	He discussed what elements are crucial to a party and which caterers are most reliable.

See Practice 11.2H

PRACTICE 11.2G Adding Commas to Addresses and Letters

Read each item. Then, add commas where needed.

EXAMPLE   To my sweet little angel

ANSWER   *To my sweet little angel,*

1. Dear Aunt Carol

2. Yours truly
   Uncle Arnie

3. Send an invitation to Kate Myer 15 Blauvelt Avenue Rockland Maine 04841.

4. My best friend moved to Tasmania Australia.

5. Sincerely
   Tim Jones

6. Dear Amanda Sophia and Isabella

7. My pen pal lives at 1025 Willow Street San Francisco California 94102.

8. Dear Mom and Dad

9. With all our love
   Kate and Sam

10. John Barrett
    802 Main Street
    Portland OR 97222

PRACTICE 11.2H Revising Sentences With Misused Commas

Read each sentence. Then, if a sentence contains a misused comma, rewrite the sentence to show correct comma usage.

EXAMPLE   Sally likes roses but, Lily likes tulips.

ANSWER   *Sally likes roses, but Lily likes tulips.*

11. Hey, I found my mitt, in the yard.

12. The new teacher, seemed, excited, and shy.

13. Running, swimming, and, cycling are all part of a triathlon.

14. Alan's address is 1,491 Crescent Drive Chinook MT 5,9523.

15. Brian, Forrester Ph.D. is a genius.

16. My cousin Julia visited Rome, Italy in July 2009.

17. I want to stop in Little, Rock on our way to Montgomery Alabama.

18. Klever Designs, Inc. gives its employees a bonus every year.

19. To run, in a marathon takes a lot of training.

20. On March, 4 1893, Grover Cleveland became the first president to serve two, nonconsecutive, terms.

SPEAKING APPLICATION

Discuss with a partner the necessity of placing commas in addresses.

WRITING APPLICATION

Write five compound sentences with dates, lists, or multiple adjectives. Be sure to use commas properly.

11.3 Semicolons and Colons

The **semicolon (;)** is used to join related independent clauses. Semicolons can also help you avoid confusion in sentences with other internal punctuation. The **colon (:)** is used to introduce lists of items and in other special situations.

Using Semicolons to Join Independent Clauses

Semicolons establish relationships between two independent clauses that are closely connected in thought and structure. A semicolon can also be used to separate independent clauses or items in a series that already contain a number of commas.

> Use a semicolon to join related independent clauses that are not already joined by the conjunctions *and, but, for, nor, or, so,* or *yet.*

11.3.1 RULE

EXAMPLE   We explored the attic together; we were amazed at all the useless junk we found there.

Do not use a semicolon to join two unrelated independent clauses. If the clauses are not related, they should be written as separate sentences with a period or another end mark to separate them.

Note that when a sentence contains three or more related independent clauses, they may still be separated with semicolons.

EXAMPLE   The birds vanished; the sky grew dark; the little pond was still.

Semicolons Join Clauses Separated by Conjunctive Adverbs or Transitional Expressions

Conjunctive adverbs are adverbs that are used as conjunctions to join independent clauses. **Transitional expressions** are expressions that connect one independent clause with another one.

> Use a semicolon to join independent clauses separated by either a **conjunctive adverb** or a **transitional expression**.

11.3.2 RULE

CONJUNCTIVE ADVERBS	*also, besides, consequently, first, furthermore, however, indeed, instead, moreover, nevertheless, otherwise, second, then, therefore, thus*
TRANSITIONAL EXPRESSIONS	*as a result, at this time, for instance, in fact, on the other hand, that is*

Place a semicolon *before* a conjunctive adverb or a transitional expression, and place a comma *after* a conjunctive adverb or transitional expression. The comma sets off the conjunctive adverb or transitional expression, which introduces the second clause.

EXAMPLE   She never found the shipwreck; in fact, she really had no interest in scuba diving.

Because words used as conjunctive adverbs and transitions can also interrupt one continuous sentence, use a semicolon only when there is an independent clause on each side of the conjunctive adverb or transitional expression.

EXAMPLES   We visited antique shops in eight counties in only two days; consequently, we had no time for sightseeing.

We were very impressed, however, with Amy's knowledge of history.

Using Semicolons to Avoid Confusion

Sometimes, semicolons are used to separate items in a series.

Use semicolons to avoid confusion when independent clauses or items in a series already contain commas.

When the items in a series already contain several commas, semicolons can be used to group items that belong together. Semicolons are placed at the end of all but the last complete item in the series.

INDEPENDENT CLAUSES

The city, supposedly filled with gold, was a fable; and the hungry, tired explorers would only find it in their dreams.

ITEMS IN A SERIES

On their trip, my parents visited my aunt, who lives in Grand Rapids; my brother, who lives in Indianapolis; and our former neighbors, the Garcias, who live in Chicago.

Semicolons appear most commonly in a series that contains either nonessential appositives, participial phrases, or adjectival clauses. Commas should separate the nonessential material from the word or words they modify; semicolons should separate the complete items in the series.

APPOSITIVES

I sent notes to Mr. Nielson, my science teacher; Mrs. Jensen, my history instructor; and Mrs. Seltz, the librarian.

PARTICIPIAL PHRASES

I developed a fascination with space travel from television, watching live rocket launches; from school, learning about astronomy; and from movies, watching science-fiction adventures.

ADJECTIVAL CLAUSES

The toy police car that I bought has spare tires, which are brand new; a siren, which has just been installed; and flashing lights, which have new bulbs.

Using Colons

The **colon (:)** is used to introduce lists of items and in certain special situations.

> **Use a colon after an independent clause to introduce a list of items. Use commas to separate three or more items.**

Independent clauses that appear before a colon often include the words *the following, as follows, these,* or *those.*

EXAMPLES   For our class, we had to interview the following experts: an economist, a scientist, and a doctor.

> **Do not use a colon after a verb or a preposition.**

INCORRECT   Veronica always orders: soup, salad, and dessert.

CORRECT   Veronica always orders soup, salad, and dessert.

> **Use a colon to introduce a quotation that is formal or lengthy or a quotation that does not contain a "he said/she said" expression.**

EXAMPLE   Oliver Wendell Holmes Jr. wrote this about freedom: "It is only through free debate and free exchange of ideas that government remains responsive to the will of the people and peaceful change is effected."

Even if it is lengthy, dialogue or a casual remark should be introduced by a comma. Use the colon if the quotation is formal or has no tagline.

A colon may also be used to introduce a sentence that explains the sentence that precedes it.

> **Use a colon to introduce a sentence that summarizes or explains the sentence before it.**

11.3.7 RULE

EXAMPLE His explanation for being late was believable: He had had a flat tire on the way.

Notice that the complete sentence introduced by the colon starts with a capital letter.

> **Use a colon to introduce a formal appositive that follows an independent clause.**

11.3.8 RULE

EXAMPLE I had finally decided on a career: nursing.

The colon is a stronger punctuation mark than a comma. Using the colon gives more emphasis to the appositive it introduces.

> **Use a colon in a number of special writing situations.**

11.3.9 RULE

SPECIAL SITUATIONS REQUIRING COLONS	
Numerals Giving the Time	1:30 A.M. 9:15 P.M.
References to Periodicals (Volume Number: Page Number)	*Scientific American* 74:12 *Sports Illustrated* 53:15
Biblical References (Chapter Number: Verse Number)	1 Corinthians 13:13
Subtitles for Books and Magazines	*A Field Guide to the Birds*: Eastern *Land and Water Birds*
Salutations in Business Letters	Dear Mr. Gordon: Dear Sir:
Labels Used to Signal Important Ideas	**Danger**: High-voltage wires

See Practice 11.3A

See Practice 11.3B

Read each sentence. Then, rewrite each sentence, inserting a semicolon or colon where needed.

EXAMPLE Belle and Jessica see each other a lot they are good friends.

ANSWER *Belle and Jessica see each other a lot; they are good friends.*

1. Jeff woke up early otherwise, he would have missed the bus.

2. I only like three toppings on my pizza mushrooms, tomatoes, and peppers.

3. Janine, do your homework it won't take long.

4. Exercise is good for you however, remember to stretch before you start.

5. Dee only drinks one type of juice apple juice.

6. It's a pleasure to see the club's oldest member Robert Shaw.

7. Brush your teeth also, remember to floss.

8. Delivering papers, Aaron earned fifty dollars it was enough to buy the new shoes he wanted.

9. At our picnic, we had three kinds of sandwiches ham, peanut butter, and turkey.

10. I sent letters to Alex, my friend from camp Alana, my pen pal, and Naomi, my cousin.

Read each item. Then, for each item, write a complete sentence, using the item, the punctuation indicated in parentheses, and additional words.

EXAMPLE I have two tests next week (colon)

ANSWER *I have two tests next week: one in math and one in science.*

11. broccoli or spinach (colon)

12. There were all sorts of activities at camp (colon)

13. The boy began to laugh (semicolon)

14. I started reading a book by my favorite author (colon)

15. We drilled, sprinted, and ran (semicolon)

16. My dog knows three tricks (colon)

17. Joseph likes to swim (semicolon)

18. Three people attended the show (colon)

19. *The Washington Post and The New York Times* (colon)

20. Phillip, don't forget the juice (semicolon)

SPEAKING APPLICATION

Discuss with a partner the similarities between your corrections for sentences 5 and 6. Explain how the sentences would be different if commas were used instead.

WRITING APPLICATION

Write instructions for completing a task. Use at least one semicolon and two colons correctly.

11.4 Quotation Marks, Underlining, and Italics

Quotation marks (" ") set off direct quotations, dialogue, and certain types of titles. Other titles are <u>underlined</u> or set in *italics*, a slanted type style.

Using Quotation Marks With Quotations

Quotation marks identify spoken or written words that you are including in your writing. A **direct quotation** represents a person's exact speech or thoughts. An **indirect quotation** reports the general meaning of what a person said or thought.

> A **direct quotation** is enclosed in quotation marks.

RULE 11.4.1

DIRECT QUOTATION

"When I learn to ride," said the student, "I'll use the bridle path every day."

> An **indirect quotation** does not require quotation marks.

RULE 11.4.2

INDIRECT QUOTATION

The student said that when she learns to ride, she plans to use the bridle path every day.

Both types of quotations are acceptable when you write. Direct quotations, however, generally result in a livelier writing style.

Using Direct Quotations With Introductory, Concluding, and Interrupting Expressions

A writer will generally identify a speaker by using words such as *he asked* or *she said* with a quotation. These expressions, called **conversational taglines** or **tags,** can introduce, conclude, or interrupt a quotation.

Direct Quotations With Introductory Expressions

Commas help you set off introductory information so that your reader understands who is speaking.

Use a comma after short introductory expressions that precede direct quotations.

EXAMPLE My mother warned, "If you get a horse, you'll be responsible for taking care of it."

If the introductory conversational tagline is very long or formal in tone, set it off with a colon instead of a comma.

EXAMPLE At the end of the meeting, Marge spoke of her dreams: "I hope to advance the cause of women jockeys everywhere."

Direct Quotations With Concluding Expressions

Conversational taglines may also act as concluding expressions.

Use a comma, question mark, or exclamation mark after a direct quotation followed by a concluding expression.

EXAMPLE "If you get a horse, you'll be responsible for taking care of it," my mother warned.

Concluding expressions are not complete sentences; therefore, they do not begin with capital letters. Closing quotation marks are always placed outside the punctuation at the end of direct quotations. Concluding expressions generally end with a period.

Divided Quotations With Interrupting Expressions

You may use a conversational tagline to interrupt the words of a direct quotation, which is also called a **divided quotation.**

> **Use a comma after the part of a quoted sentence followed by an interrupting conversational tagline. Use another comma after the tagline. Do not capitalize the first word of the rest of the sentence. Use quotation marks to enclose the quotation. End punctuation should be inside the last quotation mark.**

EXAMPLE "If you get a horse , " my mother warned , "you'll be responsible for taking care of it . "

> **Use a comma, question mark, or exclamation mark after a quoted sentence that comes before an interrupting conversational tagline. Use a period after the tagline.**

EXAMPLE "You own a horse now , " stated my mother . "You are responsible for taking care of it."

Quotation Marks With Other Punctuation Marks

Quotation marks are used with commas, semicolons, colons, and all of the end marks. However, the location of the quotation marks in relation to the punctuation marks varies.

> **Place a comma or a period *inside* the final quotation mark. Place a semicolon or colon *outside* the final quotation mark.**

EXAMPLES "Secretariat was a great horse , " sighed Mother.

We were just informed about his "earth-shaking discovery " ; we are very pleased.

> **Place a question mark or an exclamation mark inside the final quotation mark if the end mark is part of the quotation. Do not use an additional end mark.**

EXAMPLE Larry wondered, "How could I lose the race ? "

Place a question mark or exclamation mark outside the final quotation mark if the end mark is part of the entire sentence, not part of the quotation.

EXAMPLE   We were shocked when he said, "Yes"!

Using Single Quotation Marks for Quotations Within Quotations

As you have learned, double quotation marks (" ") should enclose the main quotation in a sentence. The rules for using commas and end marks with double quotation marks also apply to **single quotation marks.**

Use single quotation marks (' ') to set off a quotation within a quotation.

EXAMPLES   "I remember Ali quoting Shelley, 'If winter comes, can spring be far behind?' " Mike said.

"The doctor said, 'Good news!' " Lainie explained.

Punctuating Explanatory Material Within Quotations

Explanatory material within quotations should be placed in brackets. (See Section 11.7 for more information on brackets.)

Use brackets to enclose an explanation located within a quotation. The brackets show that the explanation is not part of the original quotation.

EXAMPLE   The mayor said, "This bridge is a link between two communities [Dover and Flint]."

See Practice 11.4A
See Practice 11.4B

PRACTICE 11.4A Using Quotation Marks

Read each sentence. Then, rewrite each sentence, inserting quotation marks where needed.

EXAMPLE   This cannot be right, he said.

ANSWER   *"This cannot be right," he said.*

1. Karen asked, Have you studied for the test?

2. Throughout the movie, the actor repeated the same line: Be patient.

3. Darren borrowed my book, said Amanda.

4. This is my favorite song! exclaimed Mia.

5. I am not sure, said Jeff, where I put my scarf.

6. I didn't know for sure until Eric said, Let's go. Then, I knew, Cameron stated.

7. Did you see a movie last night? asked Dominic.

8. Is it possible that there is life on Mars? asked Alex.

9. Yes, I have read that book, replied Thomas.

10. Don't miss the bus! Dad warned.

PRACTICE 11.4B Revising for the Correct Use of Quotation Marks

Read each sentence. Then, rewrite each sentence, correcting the misuse of quotation marks.

EXAMPLE   "I can't believe that happened, said Chris."

ANSWER   *"I can't believe that happened," said Chris.*

11. "I thought the chapter assigned for homework was really interesting, observed Bella."

12. "Martin said, I need a ride to work."

13. "Do you have *The New York Times* delivered" every morning? asked Carrie.

14. "Is it time to leave for the market"? Tom asked.

15. "The book I am reading is fantastic! said Claire."

16. "What time," asked Hilary, will we be leaving for the airport?

17. Jamie asked "to borrow a pencil," and I said, Sure.

18. "Mom said, "Come straight home after school!" Jesse explained."

19. "Nancy gave it to her, said" Andrea.

20. "I can see the car from here, Steve informed us."

SPEAKING APPLICATION

Take turns with a partner. Say some sentences with direct quotes. Your partner should tell where quotation marks would be inserted if your sentences were written.

WRITING APPLICATION

Write three sentences: one direct quotation with any introductory expression, one direct quotation with a concluding expression, and one divided quotation with an interrupting expression.

Using Quotation Marks for Dialogue

A conversation between two or more people is called a **dialogue.**

> **When writing a dialogue, begin a new paragraph with each change of speaker.**

The sun slowly set over the western edge of the windswept beach as the waves lapped the shore.

Charlie sat in the cooling sand and talked with his brother about his plans.

"I'm going south," said Charlie. "I think I'll like the climate better; you know I don't like the cold."

"Have you packed yet?" asked Roy. "Can I have your snow boots?"

"They are all yours," said Charlie. "If I never see them again, it is fine with me."

> **For quotations longer than a paragraph, put quotation marks at the beginning of each paragraph and at the end of the final paragraph.**

John McPhee wrote an essay about a canoe trip on the St. John River in northern Maine. He introduces his readers to the river in the following way:

"We have been out here four days now and rain has been falling three. The rain appears to be ending. Breaks of blue are opening in the sky. Sunlight is coming through, and a wind is rising.

"I was not prepared for the St. John River, did not anticipate its size. I saw it as a narrow trail flowing north, twisting through balsam and spruce—a small and intimate forest river, something like the Allagash . . . ."

Using Quotation Marks in Titles

Generally, quotation marks are used around the titles of shorter works.

> **Use quotation marks to enclose the titles of short written works.**

 11.4.14 RULE

WRITTEN WORKS THAT USE QUOTATION MARKS	
Title of a Short Story	"The Jockey" by Carson McCullers "The Tell-Tale Heart" by Edgar Allan Poe
Chapter From a Book	"Dynamic Democracy" in *Freedom's Ferment* "Railroads in America" in *Travel West*
Title of a Short Poem	"Boy Breaking Glass" by Gwendolyn Brooks
Essay Title	"Self-Reliance" by Ralph Waldo Emerson
Title of an Article	"The Benefits of Train Travel" by Raul Jones

> **Use quotation marks around the titles of episodes in a television or radio series, songs, and parts of a long musical composition.**

11.4.15 RULE

ARTISTIC WORK TITLES THAT USE QUOTATION MARKS	
Episode	"The Iran File" from *60 Minutes*
Song Title	"Something" by the Beatles
Part of a Long Musical Composition	"Spring" from *The Four Seasons* "E.T. Phone Home" from *E.T. The Extra-Terrestrial* soundtrack

> **Use quotation marks around the title of a work that is mentioned as part of a collection.**

 11.4.16 RULE

The title *Plato* would normally be underlined or italicized. In the example below, however, the title is placed in quotation marks because it is cited as part of a larger work.

EXAMPLE   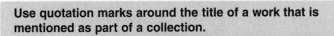"Plato" from *Great Books of the Western World*

Using Underlining and Italics in Titles and Other Special Words

Underlining and **italics** help make titles and other special words and names stand out in your writing. Underlining is used only in handwritten or typewritten material. In printed material, italic (slanted) print is generally used instead of underlining.

RULE 11.4.17

> Underline or italicize the titles of long written works and the titles of publications that are published as a single work.

WRITTEN WORKS THAT ARE UNDERLINED OR ITALICIZED	
Title of a Book	*War and Peace* *To Kill a Mockingbird*
Title of a Newspaper	*The New York Times*
Title of a Play	*The Glass Menagerie* *Long Day's Journey Into Night*
Title of a Long Poem	*Paradise Lost*
Title of a Magazine	*Newsweek*

The portion of a newspaper title that should be italicized or underlined will vary from newspaper to newspaper. *The New York Times* should always be fully capitalized and italicized or underlined. Other papers, however, can be treated in one of two ways: the *Los Angeles Times* or the Los Angeles *Times*. You may want to check the paper's Web site for correct formatting.

RULE 11.4.18

> Underline or italicize the titles of movies, television and radio series, long works of music, and works of art.

ARTISTIC WORKS THAT ARE UNDERLINED OR ITALICIZED	
Title of a Movie	*Titanic, It's a Wonderful Life*
Title of a Television Series	*Friends, Nova*
Title of a Long Work of Music	*Surprise Symphony*
Title of an Album (on any media)	*TJ's Greatest Hits*
Title of a Painting	*Mona Lisa, The River*
Title of a Sculpture	*The Thinker, The Minute Man*

> **Do not underline, italicize, or place in quotation marks the name of the Bible, its books and divisions, or other holy scriptures, such as the Torah and the Qu'ran.**

RULE
11.4.19

EXAMPLE   Adam read from Genesis in the Old Testament.

Government documents should also not be underlined or enclosed in quotation marks.

> **Do not underline, italicize, or place in quotation marks the titles of government charters, alliances, treaties, acts, statutes, speeches, or reports.**

RULE
11.4.20

EXAMPLE   The Taft-Hartley Labor Act was passed in 1947.

> **Underline or italicize the names of air, sea, and space craft.**

RULE
11.4.21

EXAMPLE   Were there horses aboard the *Santa Maria*?

> **Underline or italicize words, letters, or numbers (figures) used as names for themselves.**

RULE
11.4.22

EXAMPLES   Her *i's* and her *I's* look too much like *1's*.

Avoid sprinkling your speech with *you know*.

> **Underline or italicize foreign words and phrases not yet accepted into English.**

RULE
11.4.23

See Practice 11.4C
See Practice 11.4D

EXAMPLE   "*Bonne nuit*," she said, meaning "goodnight" in French.

Quotation Marks, Underlining, and Italics   283

PRACTICE 11.4C Using Punctuation in Titles and Dialogue

Read each sentence. Then, rewrite each sentence, adding correct punctuation where needed. If any words need to be italicized, underline those words.

EXAMPLE   Maria asked, Have you read The Scarlet Letter?

ANSWER   *Maria asked, "Have you read The Scarlet Letter?"*

1. What time is the movie? asked Nathan.

2. The movie is at 7:00 P.M. replied Juan.

3. Great, said Nathan, I'll meet you at the theater at 6:45 P.M.

4. My favorite short story is Aaron's Gift.

5. My mother reads The New York Times every day.

6. The chapter titled Cells should help you with your assignment.

7. Anne said, I just read Walker Percy's book The Moviegoer.

8. Have you read the short story The Necklace? asked Gloria.

9. Is your science project almost finished? asked John.

10. Yes, answered Heather, my project will be ready for the science fair tomorrow.

PRACTICE 11.4D Revising Punctuation in Titles and Dialogue

Read each sentence. Then, rewrite each sentence, using correct punctuation. If any words need to be italicized, underline those words.

EXAMPLE   My favorite song by the Beatles is Hey Jude.

ANSWER   *My favorite song by the Beatles is "Hey Jude."*

11. "Did you read the essay Melting Glaciers for class asked Gregory."

12. "Yes, replied Angel, I read it last night."

13. "At the end of the movie Mr. Franks forewarned is a surprising twist."

14. "I think the movie Citizen Kane has a great ending chimed Ricky."

15. "My favorite black-and-white movie is Vertigo directed by Alfred Hitchcock," said Jordan.

16. "Alfred Hitchcock wrote an interesting book titled The Murder of Monty Woolley, Mr. Franks informed the class.

17. "That painting said our teacher is by a very famous artist."

18. "It's The Starry Night a painting by van Gogh, replied Joe."

19. "I just read the short story titled Quail Seed.

20. Do you have the current issue of Popular Science?

SPEAKING APPLICATION

Take turns with a partner. Say sentences that contain both dialogue and titles. For each sentence, your partner should indicate which words should be put in quotation marks and/or italicized.

WRITING APPLICATION

Create a sarcastic character or an event that ends ironically. Write an essay that expresses your creation. Be sure to use correct punctuation marks, including quotation marks to indicate sarcasm or irony.

11.5 Hyphens

The **hyphen** (-) is used to combine words, spell some numbers and words, and show a connection between the syllables of words that are broken at the ends of lines.

Using Hyphens in Numbers

Hyphens are used to join compound numbers and fractions.

> **Use a hyphen when you spell out two-word numbers from twenty-one through ninety-nine.**

 RULE 11.5.1

EXAMPLES   thirty-three inches   forty-seven acres

> **Use a hyphen when you use a fraction as an adjective but not when you use a fraction as a noun.**

 RULE 11.5.2

ADJECTIVE   The recipe calls for one-half cup of mushrooms.

NOUN   Three quarters of the report on Japan is complete.

> **Use a hyphen between a number and a word when they are combined as modifiers. Do not use a hyphen if the word in the modifier is possessive.**

 RULE 11.5.3

EXAMPLES   The team members took a 15-minute break.

The students put 12 weeks' work into their projects.

> **If a series of consecutive, hyphenated modifiers ends with the same word, do not repeat the modified word each time. Instead, use a suspended hyphen (also called a dangling hyphen) and the modified word only at the end of the series.**

RULE 11.5.4

EXAMPLE   The eighth- and ninth-grade students came.

Using Hyphens With Prefixes and Suffixes

Hyphens help your reader easily see the parts of a long word.

RULE 11.5.5

> **Use a hyphen after a prefix that is followed by a proper noun or proper adjective.**

The following prefixes are often used before proper nouns: *ante-, anti-, mid-, post-, pre-, pro-,* and *un-.*

EXAMPLES   pre - Renaissance   mid - February

RULE 11.5.6

> **Use a hyphen in words with the prefixes *all-, ex-,* and *self-* and words with the suffix *-elect.***

EXAMPLES   all - powerful   senator - elect

Many words with common prefixes are no longer hyphenated. Check a dictionary if you are unsure whether to use a hyphen.

Using Hyphens With Compound Words

Hyphens help preserve the units of meaning in compound words.

RULE 11.5.7

> **Use a hyphen to connect two or more words that are used as one compound word, unless your dictionary gives a different spelling.**

EXAMPLES   merry - go - round   off - season
                sister - in - law   six - year - old

RULE 11.5.8

> **Use a hyphen to connect a compound modifier that appears before a noun. The exceptions to this rule include adverbs ending in *-ly* and compound proper adjectives or compound proper nouns that are acting as an adjective.**

EXAMPLES WITH HYPHENS	EXAMPLES WITHOUT HYPHENS
a well-made pair of jeans	widely distributed information
the bright-eyed children	Native American people
an up-to-date decision	Red River valley

When compound modifiers follow a noun, they generally do not require the use of hyphens.

EXAMPLE   The jeans were **well made.**

However, if a dictionary spells a word with a hyphen, the word must always be hyphenated, even when it follows a noun.

EXAMPLE   The news was up-to-date.

Using Hyphens for Clarity

Some words or group of words can be misread if a hyphen is not used.

> **Use a hyphen within a word when a combination of letters might otherwise be confusing.**

11.5.9 RULE

EXAMPLES   semi-independent, co-op, re-cede

> **Use a hyphen between words to keep readers from combining them incorrectly.**

11.5.10 RULE

See Practice 11.5A

See Practice 11.5B

INCORRECT   the special delivery-carrier

CORRECT   the special-delivery carrier

PRACTICE 11.5A ▷ Using Hyphens Correctly

Read each sentence. Then, write the words that need hyphenation, adding hyphens where necessary.

EXAMPLE   The glass is one third full.

ANSWER   *one-third*

1. Is that your new brother in law?

2. That was a thought provoking speech.

3. Heather thought it was a well conducted presentation.

4. Jones Road is a one way street.

5. Elizabeth watched the interview with the mayor elect.

6. Please measure three quarters cup of flour.

7. We were surprised by the mid April snowstorm.

8. Please make sure your information is up to date.

9. The ninth grade students performed the play.

10. By the time he is twenty one, William wants to graduate from college.

PRACTICE 11.5B ▷ Revising Sentences With Hyphens

Read each sentence. Then, rewrite the sentence, correcting any error in hyphen usage. If the punctuation is correct, write *correct*.

EXAMPLE   He was a well known writer and poet.

ANSWER   *He was a well-known writer and poet.*

11. Tanya's sister-in law is flying into town tomorrow.

12. My coworker always has lunch at noon.

13. I suppose I was mis-informed on the subject.

14. My sister plans to open a shoe store by the time she is twenty eight.

15. The six-year-old's new toy is well-made.

16. Two thirds of the students attended the game.

17. Tony will be in charge of publishing the bimonthly newsletter.

18. My grandfather is semiretired.

19. My doctor recommended an X ray.

20. The well-known actor accepted the hotly-contested award.

SPEAKING APPLICATION

Take turns with a partner. Use hyphenated words in sentences about your family and friends. Your partner should listen for and identify which words need hyphens.

WRITING APPLICATION

Write a paragraph about an event at your school. Use at least three hyphenated words.

Using Hyphens at the Ends of Lines

Hyphens help you keep the lines in your paragraphs more even, making your work easier to read.

Dividing Words at the End of a Line

Although you should try to avoid dividing a word at the end of a line, if a word must be broken, use a hyphen to show the division.

> **If a word must be divided at the end of a line, always divide it between syllables.**

EXAMPLE   The lonely children had been sending let -

ters describing their adventures at camp.

> **A hyphen used to divide a word should never be placed at the beginning of the second line. It must be placed at the end of the first line.**

INCORRECT   The fans and players will continue to sup

-port this coach as long as he wins.

CORRECT   The fans and players will continue to sup -

port this coach as long as he wins.

Using Hyphens Correctly to Divide Words

One-syllable words cannot be divided.

> **Do not divide one-syllable words even if they seem long or sound like words with two syllables.**

| INCORRECT | lod - ge | clo - thes | thro - ugh |
| CORRECT | lodge | clothes | through |

RULE 11.5.14

Do not divide a word so that a single letter or the letters -ed stand alone.

INCORRECT	a - ble	stead - y	e - vict	scream - ed
CORRECT	able	steady	evict	screamed

RULE 11.5.15

Avoid dividing proper nouns and proper adjectives.

INCORRECT	Fe - licia	Amer - ican
CORRECT	Felicia	American

RULE 11.5.16

Divide a hyphenated word only after the hyphen.

INCORRECT   We are going with my sister and my bro -
ther - in - law to visit the museum.

CORRECT   We are going with my sister and my brother -
in - law to visit the museum.

RULE 11.5.17

Avoid dividing a word so that part of the word is on one page and the remainder is on the next page.

Often, chopping up a word in this way will confuse your readers or cause them to lose their train of thought. If this happens, rewrite the sentence or move the entire word to the next page.

See Practice 11.5C
See Practice 11.5D

PRACTICE 11.5C **Writing Correctly Divided Words**

Read each group of divided words. Then, write the word in each group correctly divided with the correct hyphenation, or write it as one word if it should not be divided.

EXAMPLE   circ-le   fol-low   sub-stitute

ANSWER   *cir-cle*

1. mu-sic   boa-rd   hap-py
2. mir-ror   fever-ish   camer-a
3. fo-olish   sup-port   fan-tasy
4. sharp-ened fold-ed   merry-go-round
5. auto-mobile break-fast   serio-us
6. Camer-on   vol-ume   cush-ion
7. pluck-y   fam-ished   favor-ite
8. shak-ened   thou-ght   smel-ling
9. fla-vorful comput-er   a-long
10. for-ever   fore-leg   forl-orn

PRACTICE 11.5D **Using Hyphens to Divide Words**

Read each sentence. If the word at the end of line has been incorrectly divided, then correctly divide the word, or write it as one word.

EXAMPLE   Is Ethan planning to compet-e in the tournament next week?

ANSWER   *com-pete*

11. The teacher had us complete a self-e-valuation.
12. My favorite sandwich is peanut bu-tter and jelly.
13. My father wants to put a billiards tab-le into our basement.
14. Yesterday, my mom checked the smoke det-ectors in our house.
15. We're all going to a wedding in New Mex-ico next month.
16. My parents looked so graceful walt-zing across the dance floor.
17. After the play ended, we walked thro-ugh the park.
18. My brother and I took our niece Da-kota to see a movie.
19. The light in this room is perfect for pain-ting.
20. My father's business partner, Mr. White-hall, is coming for dinner.

SPEAKING APPLICATION

Take turns with a partner. Say five words. Your partner should tell where each word can be divided.

WRITING APPLICATION

Write five sentences that include an incorrectly divided word at the end of a line. Exchange papers with a partner. Your partner should correct your sentences so that the words are divided correctly.

11.6 Apostrophes

The **apostrophe** (') is used to form possessives, contractions, and a few special plurals.

Using Apostrophes to Form Possessive Nouns

Apostrophes are used with nouns to show ownership or possession.

RULE 11.6.1 **Add an apostrophe and -s to show the possessive case of most singular nouns.**

EXAMPLES   the wallet of the woman   the woman's wallet

the wings of the insect   the insect's wings

Even when a singular noun already ends in -s, you can usually add an apostrophe and -s to show possession. However, names that end in the *eez* sound get an apostrophe, but no -s.

EXAMPLE   The Ganges' source is in the Himalayas.

For classical references that end in -s, only an apostrophe is used.

EXAMPLES   Confucius' teachings   Zeus' thunderbolt

RULE 11.6.2 **Add an apostrophe to show the possessive case of plural nouns ending in -s or -es.**

EXAMPLE   the color of the leaves   the leaves' color

RULE 11.6.3 **Add an apostrophe and an -s to show the possessive case of plural nouns that do not end in -s or -es.**

EXAMPLE   the songs of the people

the people's songs

Add an apostrophe and *-s* (or just an apostrophe if the word is a plural ending in *-s*) to the last word of a compound noun to form the possessive.

RULE 11.6.4

APOSTROPHES THAT SHOW POSSESSION	
Names of Businesses and Organizations	the Salvation Army's headquarters the Department of the Interior's budget the Johnson Associates' clients
Titles of Rulers or Leaders	Catherine the Great's victories Louis XVI's palace the chairperson of the board's decision
Hyphenated Compound Nouns Used to Describe People	my sister-in-law's car the secretary-treasurer's idea the nurse-practitioner's patient

To form possessives involving time, amounts, or the word *sake*, use an apostrophe and an *-s* or just an apostrophe if the possessive is plural.

RULE 11.6.5

APOSTROPHES WITH POSSESSIVES	
Time	a month's vacation three days' vacation a half-hour's time
Amount	one quarter's worth two cents' worth
Sake	for Marjorie's sake for goodness' sake

RULE 11.6.6

To show joint ownership, make the final noun possessive.
To show individual ownership, make each noun possessive.

JOINT
OWNERSHIP

I enjoyed Bob and Ray's radio show.

INDIVIDUAL
OWNERSHIP

Liz's and Meg's coats are hanging here.

Use the owner's complete name before the apostrophe to form the possessive case.

INCORRECT
SINGULAR

Jame's idea

CORRECT
SINGULAR

James's idea

INCORRECT
PLURAL

two girl's books

CORRECT
PLURAL

two girls' books

Using Apostrophes With Pronouns

Both indefinite and personal pronouns can show possession.

RULE 11.6.7

Use an apostrophe and -s with indefinite pronouns to show possession.

EXAMPLES

somebody's umbrella

each other's homework

RULE 11.6.8

Do not use an apostrophe with possessive personal pronouns; their form already shows ownership.

EXAMPLES

| his jazz records | our house | her blue sweater |
| its tires | their party | whose paper |

Be careful not to confuse the contractions *who's*, *it's*, and *they're* with possessive pronouns. They are contractions for *who is*, *it is* or *it has*, and *they are*. Remember also that *whose*, *its*, and *their* show possession.

PRONOUNS	CONTRACTIONS
Whose homework is this?	*Who's* at the door?
Its tires were all flat.	*It's* going to rain.
Their dinner is ready.	*They're* going to the beach.

Using Apostrophes to Form Contractions

Contractions are used in informal speech and writing. You can often find contractions in the dialogue of stories and plays; they often create the sound of real speech.

> Use an apostrophe in a **contraction** to show the position of the missing letter or letters.

11.6.9 RULE

COMMON CONTRACTIONS			
Verb + *not*	cannot	can't	are not	aren't
	could not	couldn't	will not	won't
Pronoun + *will*	he will	he'll	I will	I'll
	you will	you'll	we will	we'll
	she will	she'll	they will	they'll
Pronoun + *would*	she would	she'd	I would	I'd
	he would	he'd	we would	we'd
	you would	you'd	they would	they'd
Noun or Pronoun + *be*	you are	you're	I am	I'm
	she is	she's	Jane is	Jane's
	they are	they're	dog is	dog's

Still another type of contraction is found in poetry.

EXAMPLES   e'en *(even)*   o'er *(over)*

Other contractions represent the abbreviated form of *of the* and *the* as they are written in several different languages. These letters are most often combined with surnames.

EXAMPLES

O'Hare

d'Lorenzo

o'clock

l'Abbé

Using Contractions to Represent Speaking Styles

A final use of contractions is for representing individual speaking styles in dialogue. As noted previously, you will often want to use contractions with verbs in dialogue. You may also want to approximate a regional dialect or a foreign accent, which may include nonstandard pronunciations of words or omitted letters. However, you should avoid overusing contractions in dialogue. Overuse reduces the effectiveness of the apostrophe.

EXAMPLES

"Hey, ol' buddy. How you feelin'?"

"Don' you be foolin' me."

Using Apostrophes to Create Special Plurals

Apostrophes can help avoid confusion with special plurals.

> **Use an apostrophe and *-s* to create the plural form of a letter, numeral, symbol, or a word that is used as a name for itself.**

EXAMPLES

A's and *an*'s cause confusion.

There are two *8*'s in that number.

I don't like to hear *if*'s or *maybe*'s.

Form groups of *2*'s or *3*'s.

You need two more *?*'s.

See Practice 11.6A
See Practice 11.6B

PRACTICE 11.6A Identifying the Use of Apostrophes

Read each sentence. Then, tell if each apostrophe is used to form a *possessive*, a *contraction*, or a *special plural*.

EXAMPLE   The dog's bed is next to the fireplace.

ANSWER   *possessive*

1. The lesson plan involved reviewing for Friday's test.

2. If he does not hurry, he'll miss the bus.

3. Ben's brother was the star of his college lacrosse team.

4. My aunt's house is one of my favorite places to visit.

5. My sister received all A's on her report card.

6. Wasn't that performance amazing?

7. Molly's brother has great taste in music.

8. Please arrive by eight o'clock.

9. Our new phone number contains two 8's.

10. Have you seen Andy's new car?

PRACTICE 11.6B Revising to Add Apostrophes

Read each sentence. Then, rewrite each sentence, adding apostrophes as needed.

EXAMPLE   Most of the students received As and Bs.

ANSWER   *Most of the students received A's and B's.*

11. Whos coming to Sunday dinner?

12. I put 6s, 7s, and 8s on the doors of the middle school classrooms.

13. Have you seen Jackies coat?

14. The neighbors cats are in our yard.

15. I had to write hundreds of cursive zs before I got the hang of them.

16. Our teacher gave us three weeks worth of homework.

17. Fidos puppies are named Moe, Larry, and Curly.

18. Cals and Drews bikes are chained to the fence post.

19. My sisters photograph is in the 2009 yearbook.

20. Shell be back with an extra blanket for the baby.

SPEAKING APPLICATION

Take turns with a partner. Say sentences with words that indicate possession, contractions, or special plurals. Your partner should identify how each word uses an apostrophe.

WRITING APPLICATION

Write five sentences that contain words with missing apostrophes. Exchange papers with a partner. Your partner should add the missing apostrophes.

11.7 Parentheses and Brackets

Parentheses enclose explanations or other information that may be omitted from the rest of the sentence without changing its basic meaning or construction. Using parentheses is a stronger, more noticeable way to set off a parenthetical expression than using commas. **Brackets** are used to enclose a word or phrase added by a writer to the words of another.

Parentheses

Parentheses help you group material within a sentence.

RULE

> **Use parentheses to set off information when the material is not essential or when it consists of one or more sentences.**

EXAMPLE   The task of cleaning the mansion **(** as she learned within the month **)** was far greater than she had believed.

RULE

> **Use parentheses to set off numerical explanations such as dates of a person's birth and death and around numbers and letters marking a series.**

EXAMPLES   James Naismith invented the game of basketball at the request of his employer, Luther H. Gulick **(** 1865–1918 **)**.

Go to the store and pick up these items: **(** 1 **)** basketball, **(** 2 **)** water bottle, and **(** 3 **)** towels.

Who played in the NBA first: **(** a **)** Larry Bird, **(** b **)** Nate Archibald, or **(** c **)** Shaquille O'Neal?

Although material enclosed in parentheses is not essential to the meaning of the sentence, a writer indicates that the material is important and calls attention to it by using parentheses.

When a phrase or declarative sentence interrupts another sentence, do not use an initial capital letter or end mark inside the parentheses.

11.7.3 RULE

EXAMPLE   Bill Frazier finally sold his vacation home **(**we used to love to visit**)** to a young couple.

When a question or exclamation interrupts another sentence, use both an initial capital letter and an end mark inside the parentheses.

11.7.4 RULE

EXAMPLE   Bruce **(**He is a fabulous chef**!)** cooked our dinner.

When you place a sentence in parentheses between two other sentences, use both an initial capital letter and an end mark inside the parentheses.

11.7.5 RULE

EXAMPLE   Newport is known for its incredible mansions. **(**See the Vanderbilt home as an example**.)** The excesses of wealth are staggering to behold.

In a sentence that includes parentheses, place any punctuation belonging to the main sentence after the final parenthesis.

11.7.6 RULE

EXAMPLE   The town council approved the construction **(**after some deliberations**)**, and they explained the new zoning laws to the public **(**with some doubts about how the changes would be received**)**.

Special Uses of Parentheses

Parentheses are also used to set off numerical explanations such as dates of a person's birth and death and numbers or letters marking a series.

EXAMPLES   Frank Lloyd Wright (1867–1959) was an innovative American architect.

Mike's phone number is (303) 555-4211.

Her research will take her to (1) Portugal, (2) Canada, and (3) Romania.

Brackets

Brackets are used to enclose a word or phrase added by a writer to the words of another writer.

> **Use brackets to enclose words you insert in quotations when quoting someone else.**

RULE 11.7.7

EXAMPLES   Cooper noted: "And with *[E.T.'s]* success, 'Phone home' is certain to become one of the most often repeated phrases of the year [1982]."

"The results of this vote [98–2] indicate overwhelming support for our proposal," he stated.

The Latin expression *sic* (meaning "thus") is sometimes enclosed in brackets to show that the author of the quoted material has misspelled or mispronounced a word or phrase.

EXAMPLE   Michaelson, citing Dorothy's signature line from *The Wizard of Oz,* wrote, "Theirs [sic] no place like home."

See Practice 11.7A
See Practice 11.7B

PRACTICE 11.7A > Using Parentheses and Brackets Correctly

Read each item. Then, rewrite each sentence, adding the items indicated in parentheses. The items can be placed in parentheses or brackets.

EXAMPLE   The boat tied to the dock will be sailing tomorrow. (*Lucky Seven*)

ANSWER   *The boat (Lucky Seven) tied to the dock will be sailing tomorrow.*

1. I helped Ryan with his chores. (washing the dishes and taking out the garbage)

2. The deed was filed away. (signed and)

3. I appreciate it, but I must refuse. (the offer)

4. That dancer is the best in the class. (the one in the purple leotard)

5. That little boy can name all fifty states. (Can you believe he's only seven years old?)

6. That tree is more than 15 feet tall. (a hemlock)

7. Allie wrote "That movie is fantastic!" (*A Hopeful Heart*)

8. Mrs. Avery drew this picture. (she is the art teacher)

9. Go to the grocery store and pick up these items: milk, eggs, and bread. (1) (2) (3)

10. During the performance, Nadia commented, "That dancer is so talented!" (Anna Willis)

PRACTICE 11.7B > Revising to Add Parentheses or Brackets

Read each sentence. Then, rewrite each sentence, adding parentheses or brackets where needed.

EXAMPLE   My sister the one who's an artist won an award.

ANSWER   *My sister (the one who's an artist) won an award.*

11. "We have created a new product a frictionless bike," said the CEO.

12. Reba is in Atlanta visiting her aunt.

13. "All seaven sic of the men were rescued."

14. The department anticipates reductions in the budget for the coming year 2010.

15. Dana's new phone number is 212 555-0808.

16. I met Bret my best friend at camp last summer.

17. Sean and Avery visited several cities Rome, Venice, and Florence during their vacation.

18. Please read this information Attachment B.

19. "My neighbor Mrs. Po do you know her?"

20. Tom broke the lamp he was painting the wall behind the lamp.

SPEAKING APPLICATION

Say a sentence that includes information that could be placed in parentheses if the sentence was written. Your partner should identify where the parentheses would go.

WRITING APPLICATION

Write five sentences. Then, have a partner tell you some additional information to add to each sentence. Rewrite each sentence, including the additional information in parentheses or brackets.

11.8 Ellipses, Dashes, and Slashes

An **ellipsis** (. . .) shows where words have been omitted from a quoted passage. It can also mark a pause or interruption in dialogue. A **dash** (—) shows a strong, sudden break in thought or speech. A **slash** (/) separates numbers in dates and fractions, shows line breaks in quoted poetry, and represents *or*. A slash is also used to separate the parts of a Web address.

Using the Ellipsis

An **ellipsis** is three evenly spaced periods, or ellipsis points, in a row. Always include a space before the first ellipsis point, between ellipsis points, and after the last ellipsis point. (The plural of *ellipsis* is *ellipses*.)

RULE
11.8.1

Use an ellipsis to show where words have been omitted from a quoted passage.

ELLIPSES IN QUOTATIONS	
The Entire Quotation	"The Black River, which cuts a winding course through southern Missouri's rugged Ozark highlands, lends its name to an area of great natural beauty. Within this expanse are old mines and quarries to explore, fast-running waters to canoe, and wooded trails to ride."—Suzanne Charle
At the Beginning	Suzanne Charle described the Black River area in Missouri as having " . . . old mines and quarries to explore, fast-running waters to canoe, and wooded trails to ride."
In the Middle	Suzanne Charle wrote, "The Black River . . . lends its name to an area of great natural beauty. Within this expanse are old mines and quarries to explore, fast-running waters to canoe, and wooded trails to ride."
At the End	Suzanne Charle wrote, "The Black River, which cuts a winding course through southern Missouri's rugged Ozark highlands, lends its name to an area of great natural beauty . . . "

Ellipses

Use an ellipsis to mark a pause in a dialogue or speech.

EXAMPLE The coach shouted "Ready ... set ... go!"

Dashes

A **dash** signals a stronger, more sudden interruption in thought or speech than commas or parentheses. A dash may also take the place of certain words before an explanation. Overuse of the dash diminishes its effectiveness. Consider the proper use of the dash in the rule below.

Use **dashes** to indicate an abrupt change of thought, a dramatic interrupting idea, or a summary statement.

USING DASHES IN WRITING	
To indicate an abrupt change of thought	The article doesn't provide enough information on Japan—by the way, where did you find the article?
	I cannot believe how many free throws my brother missed—oh, I don't even want to think about it.
To set off interrupting ideas dramatically	The pagoda was built—you may find this hard to believe—in one month.
	The pagoda was built—Where did they get the money?—in one month.
To set off a summary statement	A good scholastic record and good political connections—if you have these, you may be able to get a job in a congressional office.
	To see his jersey hanging from the rafters—this was his greatest dream.

Use **dashes** to set off a **nonessential appositive** or **modifier** when it is long, when it is already punctuated, or when you want to be dramatic.

APPOSITIVE The cause of the damage to the porch and the roof—a rare species of termite—went undiscovered for years.

MODIFIER The home-improvement editor—bored with writing about cement and grout—quit the next day.

Dashes may be used to set off one other special type of sentence interrupter—the parenthetical expression.

RULE 11.8.5

Use **dashes** to set off a **parenthetical expression** when it is long, already punctuated, or especially dramatic.

EXAMPLE Today we visited a castle—what an amazing place!—set on a small body of water out in the country.

Slashes

A **slash** is used to separate numbers in dates and fractions, lines of quoted poetry, or options. Slashes are also used to separate parts of a Web address.

RULE 11.8.6

Use slashes to separate the day, month, and year in dates and to separate the numerator and denominator in numerical fractions.

DATES She listed her birth date as 5/12/71.

The library book's due date was 10/29/08.

FRACTIONS 3/4 1/2 1/4

Use slashes to indicate line breaks in up to three lines of quoted poetry in continuous text. Insert a space on each side of the slash.

11.8.7 RULE

EXAMPLE   I used a quote from William Blake, "Tyger! Tyger! burning bright. **/** In the forests of the night," to begin my paper.

Use slashes to separate choices or options and to represent the words *and* and *or*.

11.8.8 RULE

EXAMPLES   Choose your topping: ketchup **/** mustard **/** relish.

Each student should bring a book and pen **/** pencil.

You can walk and **/** or run the last leg of the race.

Use slashes to separate parts of a Web address.

11.8.9 RULE

EXAMPLES   http: **//** www.fafsa.ed.gov **/**
(for financial aid for students)

http: **//** www.whitehouse.gov **/**
(the White House)

http: **//** www.si.edu **/**
(the Smithsonian Institution)

See Practice 11.8A
See Practice 11.8B

PRACTICE 11.8A Using Ellipses, Dashes, and Slashes Correctly

Read each sentence. Then, rewrite each sentence, adding dashes, slashes, or ellipses where appropriate.

EXAMPLE   Molly my best friend is sleeping over tonight.

ANSWER   *Molly—my best friend—is sleeping over tonight.*

1. "I think uh I'm not sure," said Sam.

2. The view from the top of the mountain What a hike that was! is magnificent.

3. The backyard is 34 of an acre.

4. Wait you forgot your sweatshirt!

5. Jen or Brendan will be asked to moderate lead the debate next week.

6. She wrote the date 5/10 09 at the top of her paper.

7. The boys Jim, John, and Jeff left the party early.

8. Everyone must have his or her passport to leave enter the country.

9. Please measure 1 2 of an inch of that string.

10. There was only one thing left to do apologize.

PRACTICE 11.8B Revising Sentences With Ellipses, Dashes, and Slashes

Read each sentence. Then, rewrite each sentence, using the appropriate punctuation to add or delete the information in parentheses to or from each sentence.

EXAMPLE   "Well, I'm not sure about that," Mark said. (Delete *about that.*)

ANSWER   *"Well, I'm not sure..." Mark said.*

11. Susan and Becky will help you. (Add *or*)

12. Mrs. Johnson's dogs are going to a vet tomorrow. (Add *Max and Casey*)

13. Several sports are offered in the fall. (Add *volleyball, field hockey, and swimming.*)

14. "Julie is a kind, generous, and funny person." (Delete *kind, generous, and*)

15. Some people are allergic to wheat. (Add *including my two best friends*)

16. Some of Mrs. Nelson's students play on the school soccer team. (Add *Jim, Bill, and Ming*)

17. Alexandra is coming to visit next week. (Add *my cousin*)

18. "This movie is funny, exciting, and full of action," said the reviewer. (Delete *funny, exciting, and*)

19. Jen and Nate will be here after school. (Add *or*)

20. After talking it over, I still can't decide. (Add *but I hope to make a decision soon.*)

SPEAKING APPLICATION

Take turns with a partner. Say a sentence to your partner. Then, have your partner add additional information to the sentence. Discuss which punctuation mark would be used if you were to write the modified sentence.

WRITING APPLICATION

Use sentences 11, 14, and 20 as models to write similar sentences. Exchange papers with a partner. Your partner should use the appropriate punctuation to add or delete information to your sentences.

PRACTICE 1 Using Periods, Question Marks, and Exclamation Marks

Read each sentence. Rewrite each sentence, adding question marks, periods, and exclamation marks where needed.

1. Can I lend a hand
2. Eek I saw a mouse
3. John Jr lives on W Main Street
4. Wow David almost set a new track record
5. Sit here, close to the window
6. The train leaves from Kensington Rd station
7. How much does that shirt cost
8. My uncle asked me if I enjoyed the class trip
9. Don't touch the wet paint
10. The umpire called a time out Why

PRACTICE 2 Using Commas Correctly

Read each sentence. Rewrite each sentence, adding commas where needed. If a sentence is correct as is, write *correct*.

1. Sheila's house the one with green shutters is the oldest on the block.
2. Mia called but Ted wasn't home yet.
3. We bought apples pears oranges and lemons.
4. The dinner was an elegant fancy event
5. No Harry didn't answer his cellphone.
6. There are 1524 names on the list.
7. Katrina lives in Galveston Texas.
8. "I couldn't find my shoe" said Joe "because the dog buried it somewhere."
9. The fair starts on Thursday, August 23.
10. Tina Smith Ph.D. is a neurosurgeon.

PRACTICE 3 Using Colons, Semicolons, and Quotation Marks

Read each sentence. Rewrite each sentence, using colons, semicolons, and quotation marks where needed. If a sentence is correct as is, write *correct*.

1. My father received a promotion consequently, he'll be managing more people.
2. He had an excuse: His laptop isn't working.
3. Who wrote the poem The Raven?
4. The train departs at 1145 A.M.
5. The sky darkened the waves grew choppy.
6. Jim asked, Whose car is parked in the lot?
7. There's one thing I forgot the gift.
8. Warning Keep Out!
9. My tooth, said young Bobby, just fell out.
10. Ash finished first therefore, he won.

PRACTICE 4 Using Apostrophes

Read each sentence. Rewrite each sentence, using apostrophes where needed. If a sentence is correct as is, write *correct*.

1. The dog wags its tail when its happy.
2. Rons listening to music so he cant hear us.
3. Ginny received three Bs on her report card.
4. The Mackenzies' house is for sale.
5. Thats my locker, not someone elses.
6. About the furniture, whats not ours, you may keep.
7. Its five oclock and somebodys knocking on the door.
8. Theirs is the best restaurant in town.

Continued on next page ▶

9. Hes not my partner because he wont dance.

10. Lets listen to the bands new CD.

 PRACTICE 5 > **Using Underlining (or Italics), Hyphens, Dashes, Parentheses, Brackets, and Ellipses**

Read each sentence. Rewrite each sentence, adding underlining (or italics), hyphens, dashes, brackets, parentheses, and ellipses. If a sentence is correct as is, write *correct*.

1. Our winter vacation starts in midFebruary.

2. Gary Paulsen wrote the novel Hatchet.

3. The article stated, "The school Elm Elementary will host the celebration."

4. My Aunt Lucy is thirty two years old.

5. Natalie's goal to come in first at the swimming finals is becoming a reality.

6. I read the Houston Chronicle every morning.

7. The poem *Paul Revere's Ride* starts with "Listen my children and you shall hear...of the midnight ride of Paul Revere."

8. My mother she's an artist has her own studio.

9. The list contains three items: 1 shoes, 2 gloves, and 3 sunglasses

10. The song—it was written by my music teacher—is about summer vacations.

PRACTICE 6 > **Using Capital Letters Correctly**

Read each sentence. Rewrite each sentence, using capital letters where they are needed.

1. planet earth is the only planet not named after a greek or roman god or goddess.

2. i plan to go to the american history museum on saturday.

3. Did o. henry write *the gift of the magi*?

4. cindy's birthday is thursday, december 12.

5. british troops were sent to capture american soldiers during the revolutionary war.

6. mrs. grady lives on lake michigan.

7. wow! what an intricate persian rug.

8. melanie asked, "is it my turn, yet?"

9. governor hill is retiring soon.

10. i went on a tour of the white house.

Modes
of Writing

Writing is a process that begins with the exploration of ideas and ends with the presentation of a final piece of writing. Often, the types of writing we do are grouped into modes according to their form and purpose.

Narration

Whenever writers tell any type of story, they are using narration. Most narratives share certain elements, such as characters, a setting, a sequence of events, and, often, a theme. The following are some types of narration:

● **Autobiographical Writing** Autobiographical writing tells a true story about an important period, experience, or relationship in the writer's life.

Effective autobiographical writing includes:

- *A series of events that involve the writer as the main character*
- *Details, thoughts, feelings, and insights from the writer's perspective*
- *A conflict or an event that affects the writer*
- *A logical organization that tells the story clearly*

Types of autobiographical writing include personal narratives, autobiographical sketches, reflective essays, eyewitness accounts, and memoirs.

● **Short Story** A short story is a brief, creative narrative.

Most short stories contain:

- *Details that establish the setting in time and place*
- *A main character who undergoes a change or learns something during the course of the story*
- *A conflict or a problem to be introduced, developed, and resolved*
- *A plot—the series of events that make up the action of the story*
- *A theme or message about life*

Types of short stories include realistic stories, fantasies, historical narratives, mysteries, thrillers, science fiction, and adventure stories.

Description

Descriptive writing is writing that creates a vivid picture of a person, place, thing, or event.

Most descriptive writing includes:

- Sensory details—sights, sounds, smells, tastes, and physical sensations
- Vivid, precise language
- Figurative language or comparisons
- Adjectives and adverbs that help to paint a word picture
- An organization suited to the subject

Types of descriptive writing include description of ideas, observations, travel brochures, physical descriptions, functional descriptions, remembrances, and character sketches.

Persuasion

Persuasion is writing or speaking that attempts to convince people to accept a position or take a desired action. The following are some types of persuasion:

● Persuasive Essay

A persuasive essay presents a position on an issue, urges readers to accept that position, and may encourage a specific action.

An effective persuasive essay:

- Explores an issue of importance to the writer
- Addresses an arguable issue
- Is supported by facts, examples, statistics, or personal experiences
- Tries to influence the audience through appeals to the readers' knowledge, experiences, or emotions
- Uses clear organization to present a logical argument

Forms of persuasion include editorials, position papers, persuasive speeches, grant proposals, advertisements, and debates.

● Advertisements

An advertisement is a planned communication that is meant to be seen, heard, or read. It attempts to persuade an audience to buy or use a product or service. Advertisements may appear in print or broadcast form.

An effective advertisement includes:

- A concept, or central theme
- A device, such as a memorable slogan, that catches people's attention
- Language that conveys a certain view of a product or issue

Common types of advertisements include public service announcements, billboards, merchandise ads, service ads, and public campaign literature.

Exposition

Exposition is writing that relies on facts to inform or explain. Effective expository writing reflects an organization that is well planned—one that includes a clear introduction, body, and conclusion. The following are some types of exposition:

● **Comparison-and-Contrast Essay**
A comparison-and-contrast essay analyzes similarities and differences between or among two or more things.

An effective comparison-and-contrast essay:

- *Identifies a purpose for comparing and contrasting*
- *Identifies similarities and differences between or among two or more things, people, places, or ideas*
- *Gives factual details about the subjects*
- *Uses an organizational plan suited to the topic and purpose*

● **Cause-and-Effect Essay** A cause-and-effect essay examines the relationship between events, explaining how one event or situation causes another.

A successful cause-and-effect essay includes:

- *A discussion of a cause, event, or condition that produces a specific result*
- *An explanation of an effect or result*
- *Evidence and examples to support the relationship between cause and effect*
- *A logical organization that makes the relationship between events clear*

● **Problem-and-Solution Essay** A problem-and-solution essay describes a problem and offers one or more solutions. It describes a clear set of steps to achieve a result.

An effective problem-and-solution essay includes:

- *A clear statement of the problem, with its causes and effects summarized*
- *A proposal of at least one realistic solution*
- *Facts, statistics, data, or expert testimony to support the solution*
- *A clear organization that makes the relationship between problem and solution obvious*

Research Writing

Research writing is based on information gathered from outside sources.

An effective research paper:

- *Focuses on a specific, narrow topic*
- *Presents relevant information from a variety of sources*
- *Is clearly organized and includes an introduction, body, and conclusion*
- *Includes a bibliography or works-cited list*

In addition to traditional research reports, types of research writing include statistical reports and experiment journals.

Response to Literature

When you write a response to literature, you can discover how a piece of writing affected you.

An effective response:

- *Reacts to a work of literature*
- *Analyzes the content of a literary work*
- *Focuses on a single aspect or gives a general overview*
- *Supports opinion with evidence from the text*

You might respond to a literary work in reader's response journals, literary letters, and literary analyses.

Writing for Assessment

Essays are commonly part of school tests.

An effective essay includes:

- *A clearly stated and well-supported thesis*
- *Specific information about the topic derived from your reading or from class discussion*
- *A clear organization with an introduction, body, and conclusion*

In addition to writing essays for tests, you might write essays to apply to schools or special programs, or to enter a contest.

Workplace Writing

Workplace writing communicates information in a structured format.

Effective workplace writing:

- *Communicates information concisely*
- *Includes details that provide necessary information and anticipate potential questions*

Common types of workplace writing include business letters, memorandums, résumés, forms, and applications.

Writing Effective
Paragraphs

A paragraph is a group of sentences that share a common topic or purpose. Most paragraphs have a main idea or thought.

Stating the Main Idea in a Topic Sentence

The main idea of a paragraph is directly stated in a single sentence called the topic sentence. The rest of the sentences in the paragraph support or explain the topic sentence, providing support through facts and details.

Sometimes the main idea of a paragraph is implied rather than stated. The sentences work together to present the details and facts that allow the reader to infer the main idea.

WRITING MODELS

from ***The Secret Language of Snow***
Terry Tempest Williams and Ted Major

Many types of animal behavior are designed to reduce heat loss. Birds fluff their feathers, enlarging the "dead air" space around their bodies. Quails roost in compact circles, in the same manner as musk oxen, to keep warmth in and cold out. Grouse and ptarmigan dive into the snow, using it as an insulating blanket.

> In this passage, the stated topic sentence is highlighted.

from **"The Old Demon"**
Pearl S. Buck

The baker's shop, like everything else, was in ruins. No one was there. At first she saw nothing but the mass of crumpled earthen walls. But then she remembered that the oven was just inside the door, and the door frame still stood erect, supporting one end of the roof. She stood in this frame, and, running her hands in underneath the fallen roof inside, she felt the wooden cover of the iron cauldron. Under this there might be steamed bread. She worked her arm delicately and carefully in. It took quite a long time, but even so, clouds of lime and dust almost choked her. Nevertheless she was right. She squeezed her hand under the cover and felt the first smooth skin of the big steamed bread rolls, and one by one she drew out four.

> In this passage, all the sentences work together to illustrate the implied main idea of the paragraph: The woman searches persistently until she finds food.

Writing a Topic Sentence

When you outline a topic or plan an essay, you identify the main points you want to address. Each of these points can be written as a topic sentence—a statement of the main idea of a topical paragraph. You can organize your paragraph around the topic sentence.

A good topic sentence tells readers what the paragraph is about and the point the writer wants to make about the subject matter. Here are some tips for writing a strong topic sentence.

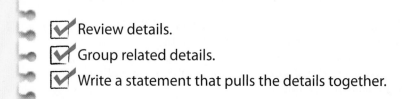

☑ Review details.
☑ Group related details.
☑ Write a statement that pulls the details together.

Writing Supporting Sentences

Whether your topic sentence is stated or implied, it guides the rest of the paragraph. The rest of the sentences in the paragraph will either develop, explain, or support that topic sentence.

You can support or develop the idea by using one or more of the following strategies:

Use Facts

Facts are statements that can be proved. They support your key idea by providing proof.

- **Topic Sentence:** Our football team is tough to beat.
- **Supporting Fact:** It wins almost all of its games.

Use Statistics

A statistic is a fact, usually stated using numbers.

- **Topic Sentence:** Our football team is tough to beat.
- **Supporting Statistic:** The football team's record is 10–1.

Use Examples, Illustrations, or Instances

An example, illustration, or instance is a specific thing, person, or event that demonstrates a point.

- **Topic Sentence:** Our football team is tough to beat.
- **Illustration:** Last week, the team beat the previously undefeated Tigers in an exciting upset game.

Use Details

Details are the specifics—the parts of the whole. They make your point or main idea clear by showing how all the pieces fit together.

- **Topic Sentence:** Our footbal team is tough to beat.
- **Detail:** There were only seconds left in last week's game, when the quarterback threw the winning pass.

Placing Your Topic Sentence

Frequently, the topic sentence appears at the beginning of a paragraph. Topic sentences can, however, be placed at the beginning, middle, or end of the paragraph. Place your topic sentence at the beginning of a paragraph to focus readers' attention. Place your topic sentence in the middle of a paragraph when you must lead into your main idea. Place your topic sentence at the end of a paragraph to emphasize your main idea.

Paragraph Patterns

Sentences in a paragraph can be arranged in several different patterns, depending on where you place your topic sentence. One common pattern is the TRI pattern (Topic, Restatement, Illustration).

- **T**opic sentence (State your main idea.)
- **R**estatement (Interpret your main idea; use different wording.)
- **I**llustration (Support your main idea with facts and examples.)

T	Participating in after-school clubs is one of the ways you can meet new people. Getting involved in extracurricular activities brings you in contact with a wide range of individuals. The drama club, for example, brings together students from several different grades.
R	
I	

Variations on the TRI pattern include sentence arrangements such as TIR, TII, IIT, or ITR.

I	This month alone the service club at our high school delivered meals to thirty shut-ins. In addition, members beautified the neighborhood with new plantings. If any school-sponsored club deserves increased support, the service club does.
I	
T	

Paragraphs
in Essays
and Other Compositions

To compose means "to put the parts together, to create." Most often, composing refers to the creation of a musical or literary work—a composition. You may not think of the reports, essays, and test answers you write as literary works, but they are compositions. To write an effective composition, you must understand the parts.

The Introduction

The introduction does what its name suggests. It introduces the topic of the composition. An effective introduction begins with a strong lead, a first sentence that captures readers' interest. The lead is followed by the thesis statement, the key point of the composition. Usually, the thesis statement is followed by a few sentences that outline how the writer will make the key point.

The Body

The body of a composition consists of several paragraphs that develop, explain, and support the key idea expressed in the thesis statement. The body of a composition should be unified and coherent. The paragraphs in a composition should work together to support the thesis statement. The topic of each paragraph should relate directly to the thesis statement and be arranged in a logical organization.

The Conclusion

The conclusion is the final paragraph of the composition. The conclusion restates the thesis and sums up the support. Often, the conclusion includes the writer's reflection or observation on the topic. An effective conclusion ends on a memorable note, for example, with a quotation or call to action.

Recognizing Types of Paragraphs

There are several types of paragraphs you can use in your writing.

Topical Paragraphs

A topical paragraph is a group of sentences that contain one key sentence or idea and several sentences that support or develop that key idea or topic sentence.

Functional Paragraphs

Functional paragraphs serve a specific purpose. They may not have a topic sentence, but they are unified and coherent because the sentences (if there is more than one) are clearly connected and follow a logical order. Functional paragraphs can be used for the following purposes:

- **To create emphasis** A very short paragraph of one or two sentences focuses the reader on what is being said because it breaks the reader's rhythm.

- **To indicate dialogue** One of the conventions of written dialogue is that a new paragraph begins each time the speaker changes.

- **To make a transition** A short paragraph can help readers move between the main ideas in two topical paragraphs.

WRITING MODEL

from **"The Hatchling Turtles"**

by Jean Craighead George

One morning each small turtle fought for freedom within its shell.

They hatched two feet down in the sand, all of them on the same day. As they broke out, their shells collapsed, leaving a small room of air for them to breathe. It wasn't much of a room, just big enough for them to wiggle in and move toward the sky. As they wiggled they pulled the sand down from the ceiling and crawled up on it. In this manner the buried room began to rise, slowly, inch by inch.

The highlighted functional paragraph emphasizes the struggle of the turtles to emerge from their shells.

Paragraph Blocks

Sometimes, you may have so much information to support or develop a main idea that it "outgrows" a single paragraph. When a topic sentence or main idea requires an extensive explanation or support, you can develop the idea in a paragraph block—several paragraphs that work together and function as a unit. Each paragraph in the block supports the key idea or topic sentence. By breaking the development of the idea into separate paragraphs, you make your ideas clearer.

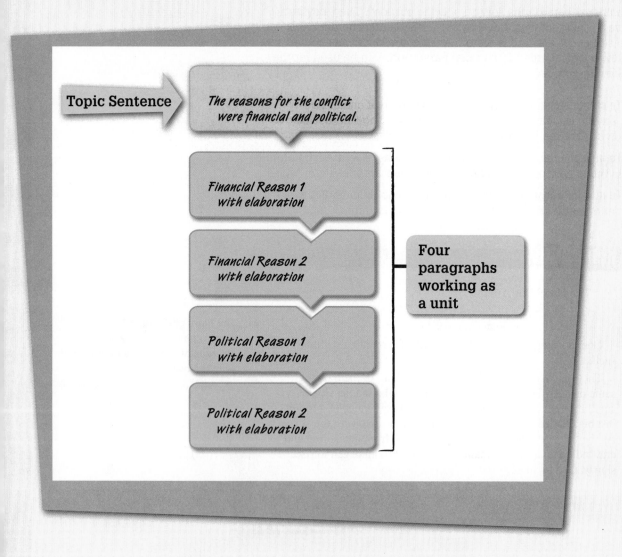

Topic Sentence → The reasons for the conflict were financial and political.

Financial Reason 1 with elaboration

Financial Reason 2 with elaboration

Political Reason 1 with elaboration

Political Reason 2 with elaboration

Four paragraphs working as a unit

Qualities
of Good Writing

The quality of your writing depends on how well you develop six important traits: ideas, organization, voice, word choice, sentence fluency, and conventions.

Organization

Organization refers to the way in which the ideas and details are arranged in a piece of writing. To enable readers to follow your ideas, choose an organization that makes sense for your topic, and stick with that organization throughout the piece of writing.

Ideas

Good writing begins with interesting ideas. Explore topics that you find interesting and that you think will interest others. Focus on presenting information that will be new and fresh to readers.

Voice

Just as you have a distinctive way of expressing yourself when you speak, you can develop a distinctive voice as a writer. Your voice consists of the topics you choose, the attitude you express toward those topics, the words you use, and the rhythm of your sentences. By developing your own voice, you let your personality come through in your writing.

Conventions

Conventions refer to the grammatical correctness of a piece of writing. Don't let errors in grammar, usage, mechanics, and spelling interfere with your message.

Word Choice

Words are the building blocks of a piece of writing. By choosing precise and vivid words, you will add strength to your writing and enable readers to follow your ideas and picture the things that you describe.

Sentence Fluency

In a piece of writing, it is important that sentences flow well from one to another. By using a variety of sentences—different lengths and different structures—and using transitions to connect them, you will create smooth rhythm in your writing.

Stages of the
Writing Process

Writing is called a process because it goes through a series of changes or stages. These five stages are:

- In **prewriting**, you explore an idea by using various prewriting techniques, such as brainstorming and questioning.

- In **drafting**, you get your ideas down on paper or on the computer in roughly the format you intend.

- Once you finish your first draft, you decide on the changes, or **revisions**, you want to make.

- Finally, when you are happy with your work, you **edit** it, checking the accuracy of facts and for errors in spelling, grammar, usage, and mechanics.

- You then make a final copy and **publish** it, or share it with an audience.

You will not always progress through these stages in a straight line. You can backtrack to a previous stage, repeat a stage many times, or put the stages in a different sequence to fit your needs. To get an idea of what the writing process is like, study the following diagram. Notice that the arrows in the drafting and revising sections can lead you back to prewriting.

Prewriting
- Using prewriting techniques to gather ideas
- Choosing a purpose and an audience
- Ordering ideas

Drafting
- Putting ideas down on paper
- Exploring new ideas as you write

Publishing
- Producing a final polished copy of your writing
- Sharing your writing

Editing
- Checking the accuracy of facts
- Correcting errors in spelling, grammar, usage, and mechanics

Revising
- Consulting with peer readers
- Evaluating suggested changes
- Making revisions

Prewriting
- Using prewriting techniques to gather ideas
- Choosing a purpose and an audience
- Ordering ideas

Prewriting

No matter what kind of writing assignment you are given, you can use prewriting techniques to find and develop a topic. Some prewriting techniques will work better than others for certain kinds of assignments.

Choosing a Topic

Try some of the following ways to find topics that fit your assignment.

● **Look Through Newspapers and Magazines** In the library or at home, flip through recent magazines or newspapers. Jot down each interesting person, place, event, or topic you come across. Review your notes and choose a topic that you find especially interesting and would like to learn more about.

● **Keep an Events Log** Every day you probably encounter many situations about which you have opinions. One way to remember these irksome issues is to keep an events log. For a set period of time—a day or a week—take a small notebook with you wherever you go. Whenever you come across something you feel strongly about, write it down. After the specified time period, review your journal and select a topic.

● **Create a Personal Experience Timeline** Choose a memorable period in your life and map out the events that occurred during that period. Create a timeline in which you enter events in the order they occurred. Then, review your timeline and choose the event or events that would make the most interesting topic.

Narrowing Your Topic

Note that narrowing a topic is not an exact science. It is part of the creative process of writing, which involves experimentation and leads to discovery. Here are some specific techniques you can use.

● **Questioning** Asking questions often helps narrow your topic to fit the time and space you have available. Try asking some of the six questions that journalists use when writing news stories: *Who? What? When? Why? Where?* and *How?* Then, based on your answers, refocus on a narrow aspect of your topic.

● **Using Reference Materials** The reference materials you use to find information can also help you narrow a broad topic. Look up your subject in an encyclopedia, or find a book on it at the library. Scan the resource, looking for specific, narrow topics. Sometimes a resource will be divided into sections or chapters that each deal with a specific topic.

● **Using Graphic Devices** Another way to narrow a topic is to combine questioning with a graphic device, such as a cluster or inverted pyramid. Draw one in your notebook or journal, and write your broad topics across the top of the upside-down pyramid. Then, as the pyramid narrows to a point, break down your broad topic into narrower and narrower subcategories. The graphic shows how questions can be used to do this.

Broad Topic: Math

How does math apply to my life?

shopping   building   Cooking

When do I use math most?

building

What building project?

building Shelves

Focused Topic:
How I use math to build a bookcase

Purpose and Audience

Every piece of writing is written for an audience. Even when you write a secret in your journal, you are writing for an audience of one—yourself. To succeed in any writing task, you have to understand what your audience wants and needs to know.

Pinpointing your purpose is also essential when you write. Sometimes you write to fulfill an assignment; at other times you decide to whom you will write and why. For example, you might decide to write a letter to your sister about your bunkmates at camp. Your purpose might be to describe your bunkmates' looks and personalities. Another time you might write a letter to your principal about cellphones. Your purpose might be to convince her to ban cellphones inside your school.

● **Defining Your Purpose and Audience** Answering certain questions can help you define your purpose for writing and identify your audience.

> • *What is my topic?*
> • *What is my purpose for writing?*
> • *Who is my audience?*
> • *What does my audience already know about this topic?*
> • *What does my audience need or want to know?*
> • *What type of language will suit my audience and purpose?*

Gathering Details

After finding a topic to write about, you will want to explore and develop your ideas. You can do this on your own or with classmates. The following techniques may help you.

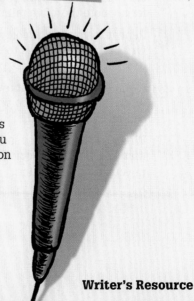

● **Interview a Classmate** Questioning a classmate can help both of you develop your topics. You can interview a friend who has a special skill. Find out how she or he developed that skill. You could also find an interview partner and question each other on an acceptable topic.

- **Fill In an Observation Chart** To come up with details to develop a piece of descriptive writing or to help you create the setting and characters for a narrative, you can fill in an observation chart. A writer created the chart that follows while wondering how to describe the school cafeteria at lunch time.

Once you have completed your own observation chart, circle the details you want to include in your piece of writing.

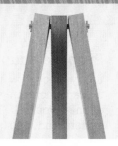

SUBJECT: *CAFETERIA AT LUNCHTIME*

See	Hear	Touch	Smell	Taste
swirl of motion	kids' voices	hot melted cheese	stuff they wash the floors with	tart juice
fluorescent lights	thuds and clunks of chairs and trays	wet plastic trays	delicious aroma of pizza	pepperoni
colors of plastic trays	scraping of chairs	cold, wet milk cartons	apple crisp baking	mild cheese

- **Do a Focused Freewriting** Freewriting can be used to either find or develop a topic. When it is used to develop a topic, it is called focused freewriting. Follow these four steps as you use focused freewriting to develop a topic:

1. Set a time limit. (Until you get used to freewriting, write for no more than five minutes at a time.)

2. Repeat to yourself the key words of your topic, and then write whatever comes to mind about them. Do not stop; do not read or correct what you write.

3. If you get stuck, repeat a word (even the word *stuck*), or write the last word you wrote until new ideas come. You can be sure they will.

4. When the time is up, read what you wrote. Underline parts that you like best. Decide which of these parts you will use in your piece of writing.

Drafting

Drafting
- Putting ideas down on paper
- Exploring new ideas as you write

In writing, an **organizational plan** is an outline or map that shows the key ideas and details that you want to include in the order that you want to include them. Following such a plan can help you structure your writing so that it makes a clearer and stronger impression on your audience.

Organizing Your Ideas

Often, a piece of writing lends itself to a particular order. For instance, if you are describing a scene so that readers can visualize it, spatial order may be your best option. However, if you are describing a person, you might compare and contrast the person with someone else you and your readers know, or you might reveal the person's character by describing a series of past incidents in chronological order.

ORGANIZATIONAL PLANS

Chronological Order	Events or details are arranged in the order in which they occur. Words showing **chronological order** include *first, next,* and *finally.*
Spatial Order	Details are given by location so that readers can visualize the scene, object, or person. Expressions showing **spatial order** include *to the right (or left), in the middle, nearby, in front of, on, beside, behind,* and *next to.*
Order of Importance	Events and details are arranged from the least to the most significant, or vice versa. Expressions showing **order of importance** include *most important, above all,* and *also.*
Logical Order	Each point that is made builds on previous information, and ideas are clearly linked. Expressions showing **logical order** include *it follows that, for example,* and *therefore.*

Introductions

The introduction to your paper should include a **thesis statement**, a sentence about your central purpose or what you plan to "show" in your paper. Here is a thesis statement for a paper on the ancient Kingdom of Ghana:

> Ghana was one of the strongest, richest kingdoms of its time.

An effective written introduction draws your readers into your paper and interests them in the subject. The way you introduce your paper depends on the goal you want to achieve and the type of writing you are doing. The following are some possibilities.

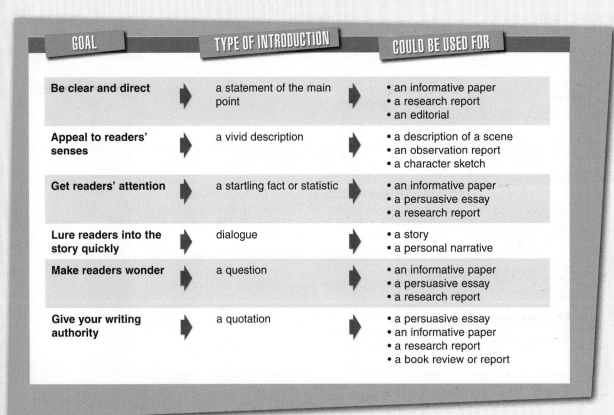

GOAL	TYPE OF INTRODUCTION	COULD BE USED FOR
Be clear and direct	a statement of the main point	• an informative paper • a research report • an editorial
Appeal to readers' senses	a vivid description	• a description of a scene • an observation report • a character sketch
Get readers' attention	a startling fact or statistic	• an informative paper • a persuasive essay • a research report
Lure readers into the story quickly	dialogue	• a story • a personal narrative
Make readers wonder	a question	• an informative paper • a persuasive essay • a research report
Give your writing authority	a quotation	• a persuasive essay • an informative paper • a research report • a book review or report

Elaboration

Sometimes what you write seems to be only the bare bones of a composition. In order to flesh out your work, you must add the right details. This process is called **elaboration**.

Certain types of elaboration are more effective for certain forms of writing, but there are no hard-and-fast rules about which type of elaboration to use. You can use facts and statistics in a poem if you want to! Some types of elaboration include the following:

Facts and Statistics	Facts are statements that can be proved true. Statistics are facts that you express as numbers.
Sensory Details	Sensory details are details that appeal to the five senses—sight, hearing, touch, smell, and taste.
Anecdotes	An anecdote is a short account of an interesting or funny incident.
Examples	An example is an instance of something.
Quotations	A quotation is someone's words—often those of an expert or public figure.
Personal Feelings	Personal feelings are thoughts and emotions that are yours alone.
Memories	Memories are recollections from the past.
Observations	Observations are things you have seen or noticed firsthand.
Reasons	Reasons are explanations of why something is true.

- **Uses of Elaboration** Here is a chart showing the types of elaboration you can use and what each is used for.

TYPE OF ELABORATION	USED FOR	
facts and statistics	essays news stories feature articles business letters	advertisements reviews research reports
sensory details	observations poems personal essays advertisements	stories plays descriptions
anecdotes	journal entries personal letters news stories	personal essays feature articles
examples	essays news stories business letters editorials advertisements poems	responses to literature book reports research reports feature articles reviews
quotations	news stories feature articles essays	responses to literature book reports
personal feelings	journal entries personal letters personal essays poems	editorials observations responses to literature persuasive essays
memories	journal entries personal letters personal essays poems	descriptions observations stories
observations	journal entries personal letters personal essays poems	reviews feature articles stories plays
reasons	essays business letters reviews book reports news stories feature articles	editorials advertisements research reports responses to literature personal essays

Conclusions

The type of conclusion you will use depends on your subject and on your purpose. Here are some ways to end a paper effectively, with suggestions on what type of writing might best suit each type of conclusion.

- **Summarize Your Main Points** Review the most important ideas you have discussed and what you have said about them. Instead of just listing them, try to present them in a creative way. This will help you remember your key ideas.

This is a great way to conclude the following types of writing:
- *observation report*
- *personal essay*
- *research report*
- *informative essay*
- *comparison-and-contrast essay*

- **Resolve Conflicts and Problems** Bring your narrative to a close by addessing unanswered questions. Did the main character survive the battle? Did the enemies become friends?

This is especially important when you are writing the following:
- *personal narrative or autobiographical incident*
- *story or fable*
- *play*

- **Recommend an Action or Solution** You have presented your readers with an issue or problem. Now tell them what they can do about it. This will enable them to do something constructive after reading.

This is a great way to conclude these writing pieces:
- *persuasive essay*
- *letter to the editor*
- *problem-and-solution essay*

- **Offer a Final Comment or Ask a Question** Talk directly to your readers. You can do this by sharing your personal feelings, asking questions, or both. This will make your readers feel more involved.

This is a great way to conclude the following:
- *personal letter*
- *persuasive essay*
- *response to literature*
- *review*

Revising
- Consulting with peer readers
- Evaluating suggested changes
- Making revisions

Revising

When you have included all your ideas and finished your first draft, you are ready to revise it. Few writers produce perfect drafts the first time around. You can almost always improve your paper by reworking it. Here are some hints to help you revise your work.

 Take a Break Do not begin to revise right after you finish a draft. In a few hours or days you will be better able to see the strengths and weaknesses of your work.

 Look It Over When you reread your draft, look for ways to improve it. Use a pencil to mark places where an idea is unclear or the writing is jumpy or disjointed. Also, remember to let yourself know when you have written an effective image or provided a wonderful example. Write Good! next to the parts that work well.

 Read Aloud Your ear is a wonderful editor. Read your work aloud and listen for dull, unnecessary, or awkward parts that you did not notice when you read your work silently. Are there any passages that you stumble over as you read aloud? Try different wordings and then read them aloud with expression, emphasizing certain words. Listen and identify which wording sounds best.

 Share Your Work Your friends or family members can help you by telling you how your work affects them. Ask them whether your ideas are clear. What is interesting? What is boring?

When it is time to revise a draft, many writers are tempted to just correct a few spelling mistakes and combine a sentence or two. Eliminating surface errors, however, is only a small part of revising. After all, what good is a neat and perfectly spelled paper if it does not make sense or prove a point? The word *revise* means "to see again" or "to see from a new perspective." In order to revise your work, you need to rethink your basic ideas.

Revising by Rethinking

Taking a close look at the ideas in your draft is the most important part of revising. Usually, you will spot some "idea" problems. When you do, it is time to get to work. Here are some strategies to help you rethink your draft.

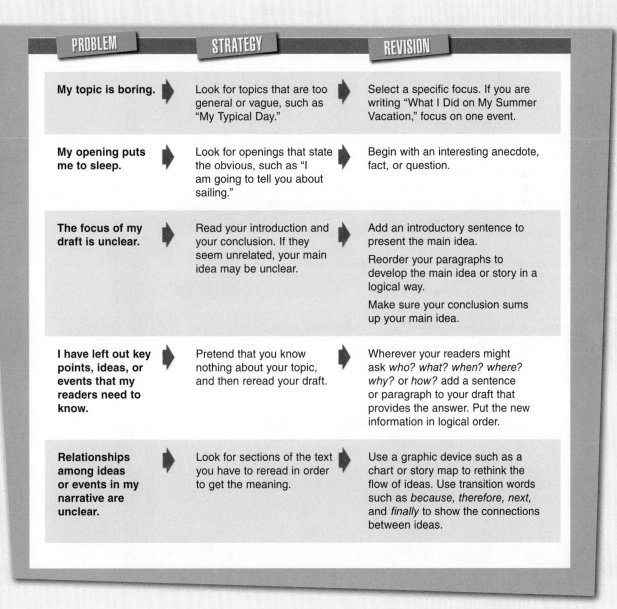

PROBLEM	STRATEGY	REVISION
My topic is boring.	Look for topics that are too general or vague, such as "My Typical Day."	Select a specific focus. If you are writing "What I Did on My Summer Vacation," focus on one event.
My opening puts me to sleep.	Look for openings that state the obvious, such as "I am going to tell you about sailing."	Begin with an interesting anecdote, fact, or question.
The focus of my draft is unclear.	Read your introduction and your conclusion. If they seem unrelated, your main idea may be unclear.	Add an introductory sentence to present the main idea. Reorder your paragraphs to develop the main idea or story in a logical way. Make sure your conclusion sums up your main idea.
I have left out key points, ideas, or events that my readers need to know.	Pretend that you know nothing about your topic, and then reread your draft.	Wherever your readers might ask *who? what? when? where? why?* or *how?* add a sentence or paragraph to your draft that provides the answer. Put the new information in logical order.
Relationships among ideas or events in my narrative are unclear.	Look for sections of the text you have to reread in order to get the meaning.	Use a graphic device such as a chart or story map to rethink the flow of ideas. Use transition words such as *because, therefore, next,* and *finally* to show the connections between ideas.

Revising by Elaborating

When you are sure your ideas are clear and in order, it is time to judge whether you have provided enough appropriate details. Remember, elaborating means developing and expanding on ideas by adding the right details. These details will help develop your ideas in clear and interesting ways.

You might choose any of the following types of details explained on page 327:

- facts and statistics
- sensory details
- anecdotes
- examples
- quotations
- personal feelings
- memories
- observations
- reasons

Revising by Reducing

Just as you need to add specific details when you revise your draft, you sometimes need to get rid of material that is unnecessary. Following are some ways you can solve revision problems by removing unneeded words.

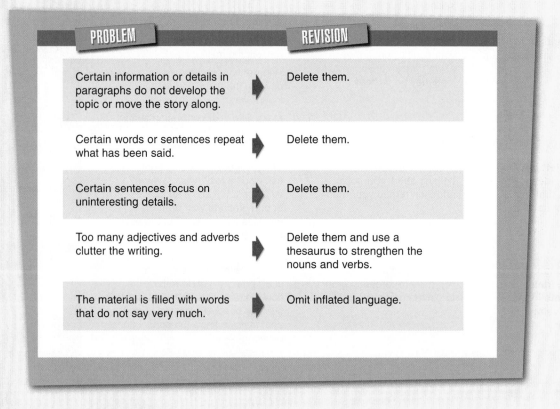

PROBLEM	REVISION
Certain information or details in paragraphs do not develop the topic or move the story along.	Delete them.
Certain words or sentences repeat what has been said.	Delete them.
Certain sentences focus on uninteresting details.	Delete them.
Too many adjectives and adverbs clutter the writing.	Delete them and use a thesaurus to strengthen the nouns and verbs.
The material is filled with words that do not say very much.	Omit inflated language.

Revising by Rewording

Choosing the right words is essential to good writing. As a final step in revising, improve your choice of words. At times, a better word will spring to mind. At other times, use a thesaurus to find words. As you rework your draft, you will reveal your own style.

The following chart can help you find the right word.

PROBLEM

Have I used the most effective word possible?

REVISION ACTIVITIES:

Choose specific nouns.
General: I wish I had some food.
Specific: I wish I had some pizza.

Choose active, colorful verbs.
General: The sick man walked to his bed.
Specific: The sick man hobbled to his bed.

Avoid the word *be*.
General: My horse is a good jumper.
Specific: My horse easily jumps four feet.

Choose the active voice.
General: Chocolate should never be fed to dogs.
Specific: Never feed dogs chocolate.

Editing
• Checking the accuracy of facts
• Correcting errors in spelling, grammar, usage, and mechanics

Editing

Editing is the process of finding and correcting errors in grammar, usage, and mechanics. When you have finished drafting and revising your paper, here is how to edit your work.

General Tips

- Look first for mistakes that you typically make.
- Proofread your paper for one type of error at a time.
- Read your work aloud word for word.
- When in doubt, use reference sources to help you.

Here are some specific editing strategies that may help you.

SPECIFIC TASKS	STRATEGY
Check Your Grammar	
Have you written any run-on sentences or fragments?	Check that each sentence has a subject and verb. Use a comma and conjunction to connect main clauses.
Do your subjects and verbs agree?	Make sure that singular subjects have singular verbs and plural subjects have plural verbs.
Check Your Usage	
Have you used the past forms of irregular verbs correctly?	Watch out for irregular verb forms such as *seen, done, gone,* and *taken.*
Have you used subject and object pronouns correctly?	Check that the pronouns *me, him, her, us,* and *them* are used only after verbs or prepositions.
Check Your Punctuation	
Does each sentence have the correct end mark?	Look for inverted word order that may signal a question.
Have you used apostrophes in nouns, but not in pronouns, to show possession?	Use a phrase with *of* to check for possession.
Have you used quotation marks around words from another source?	Avoid plagiarism by checking your notecards to be sure.
Check Your Capitalization	
Did you begin each sentence or direct quotation with a capital letter?	Look for an end mark and then check the next letter.
Have you capitalized proper nouns?	Look for the name of specific people and places.
Check Your Spelling	
Did you correctly spell all words?	Use a dictionary. Look for your common errors.

Publishing
- Producing a final polished copy of your writing
- Sharing your writing

Publishing

Once you have made a final, clean copy of a piece of writing that pleases you, you may want to share it with others. What you have to say might be important or meaningful to someone else. Here are some ways you can publish your writing—that is, bring it to the public eye.

- Submit your work to a school newspaper or magazine.

- Have a public reading of your work. Perform it in one of the following ways:
  - Over the school P.A. or radio system
  - In a school assembly or talent show
  - In a group in which members take turns reading their work
  - At your local library or community center

- If your work is a play or skit, have a group of classmates or the drama club present it.

- Work with classmates to put together a class collection of written work. You can have it copied and bound at a copy shop.

- Submit your piece to a local or national writing contest.

- Send your writing to a local newspaper or area magazine.

- Publish your own work and the writings of classmates by using a computer with a desktop publishing program.

Reflecting

Your writing can help you learn about your subject or the writing process—or even yourself. Once you have completed a writing assignment, sit back and think about the experience for a few minutes.

Ask yourself questions such as the following:

- What did I learn about my subject through my writing?

- Did I experiment with writing techniques and forms? If so, were my experiments successful? If not, what held me back?

- Am I pleased with what I wrote? Why or why not?

- Did I have difficulty with any part of the writing process? If so, which part gave me trouble? What strategies did I use to overcome my difficulties?

This resource section contains tips on writing in English and information on grammar topics that are sometimes challenging for English learners.

The numbered arrows in the side margins also appear on other pages of the Grammar Handbook that provide information on writing or instruction in these same grammar topics.

EL1

Understand the Demands of Writing in a Second Language

Talk with other writers.

When you write in an unfamiliar situation, it may be helpful to find a few examples of the type of writing you are trying to produce. For example, if you are writing a letter of application to accompany a résumé, ask your friends to share similar letters of application with you and look for the various ways your friends presented themselves in writing in that situation.

Use your native language as a resource.

You can also use your native language to develop your texts. Many people, when they cannot find an appropriate word in English, write down a word, a phrase, or even a sentence in their native language and consult a dictionary later. Incorporating key terms from your native language is also a possible strategy.

A Japanese term adds perspective to this sentence.

"Some political leaders need to have *wakimae*—a realistic idea of one's own place in the world."

Use dictionaries.

Bilingual dictionaries are especially useful when you want to check your understanding of an English word or find equivalent words for culture-specific concepts and technical terms. Some bilingual dictionaries also provide sample sentences.

Learner's dictionaries, such as the *Longman Dictionary of American English,* include information about count/non-count nouns and transitive/intransitive verbs. Many of them also provide sample sentences.

Understand English idioms.

Some English idioms function like proverbs. In the United States, for example, if someone has to "eat crow," they have been forced to admit they were wrong about something. But simpler examples of idiomatic usage—word order, word choice, and combinations that don't follow any obvious set of rules—are common in even the plainest English. If you are unsure about idioms, use Google or another search engine to find out how to use them.

INCORRECT IDIOM	Here is the answer **of** your question.
ACCEPTED IDIOM	Here is the answer **to** your question.
INCORRECT IDIOM	I had jet **legs** after flying across the Pacific.
ACCEPTED IDIOM	I had jet **lag** after flying across the Pacific.

Understand Nouns in English

Perhaps the most troublesome conventions for nonnative speakers are those that guide usage of the common articles *the, a,* and *an.* To understand how articles work in English, you must first understand how the language uses **nouns.**

Proper nouns and common nouns

There are two basic kinds of nouns. A **proper noun** begins with a capital letter and names a unique person, place, or thing: *Elvis Presley, Russia, Eiffel Tower.*

The other basic kind of noun is called a **common noun.** Common nouns such as *man, country* and *tower,* do not name a unique person, place, or thing. Common nouns are not names and are not capitalized unless they are the first word in a sentence.

EL2

PROPER NOUNS
Beethoven   Michael Jordan   Honda
South Korea   Africa
Empire State Building

COMMON NOUNS
composer athlete vehicle country
continent building

Count and non-count nouns

Common nouns can be classified as either **count** or **non-count**. Count nouns can be made plural, usually by adding the letter *s* (*finger, fingers*) or by using their plural forms (*person, people; datum, data*).

Non-count nouns cannot be counted directly and cannot take the plural form (*information,* but not *informations; garbage,* but not *garbages*). Some nouns can be either count or non-count, depending on how they are used. *Hair* can refer to either a strand of hair, when it serves as a count noun, or a mass of hair, when it becomes a non-count noun.

Count nouns usually take both singular and plural forms, while non-count nouns usually do not take plural forms and are not counted directly. A count noun can have a number before it (as in *two books, three oranges*) and can be qualified with adjectives such as *many* (as in *many books*), *some* (as in *some schools*), and *few* (as in *few people volunteered*).

Non-count nouns can be counted or quantified in only two ways: either by general adjectives that treat the noun as a mass (*much* information, *some* news) or by placing another noun between the quantifying word and the non-count noun (*two kinds* of information, *a piece* of news).

EL3

CORRECT USE OF HAIR AS A COUNT NOUN
Three blonde hairs were in the sink.

CORRECT USE OF HAIR AS A NON-COUNT NOUN
My roommate spent an hour combing his hair.

INCORRECT	five horse many accident
CORRECT	five horses many accidents
INCORRECT	three breads I would like a mustard on my hot dog.
CORRECT	three loaves of bread I would like some mustard on my hot dog.

Understand Articles in English

EL4

Articles indicate that a noun is about to appear, and they clarify what the noun refers to. There are only two kinds of articles in English, definite and indefinite.

1. **the:** *The* is a **definite article,** meaning that it refers to (1) a specific object already known to the reader, (2) one about to be made known to the reader, or (3) a unique object.

2. **a, an:** The **indefinite articles** *a* and *an* refer to an object whose specific identity is not known to the reader. The only difference between *a* and *an* is that *a* is used before a consonant sound (*a man, a friend, a yellow toy*), while *an* is used before a vowel sound (*an orange, an old shoe*).

Look at these sentences, which are identical except for their articles, and imagine that each is taken from a different newspaper story.

Rescue workers lifted **the** man to safety.

Rescue workers lifted **a** man to safety.

By using the definite article *the*, the first sentence indicates that the reader already knows something about the identity of this man. The news story has already referred to him.

The indefinite article *a* in the second sentence indicates that the reader does not know anything about this man. Either this is the first time the news story has referred to him, or there are other men in need of rescue.

RULES FOR USING ARTICLES

1. *A* or *an* is not used with non-count nouns.

   INCORRECT The crowd hummed with **an** excitement.
   CORRECT The crowd hummed with excitement.

2. *A* or *an* is used with singular count nouns whose identity is unknown to the reader or writer.

   INCORRECT Detective Johnson was reading book.
   CORRECT Detective Johnson was reading **a** book.

3. *The* is used with most count and non-count nouns whose particular identity is known to readers.

   CORRECT I bought a book yesterday. **The** book is about kayaking.

4. *The* is used when the noun is accompanied by a superlative form of a modifier: for example, *best, worst, highest, lowest, most expensive, least interesting.*

   CORRECT **The** most interesting book about climbing Mount Everest is Jon Krakauer's *Into Thin Air.*

Understand Verbs and Modifiers in English

Verbs, verb phrases, and helping verbs

EL5

Verbs in English can be divided between one-word verbs like *run, speak,* and *look,* and verb phrases like *may have run, have spoken,* and *will be looking.* The words that appear before the main verbs—*may, have, will, do,* and *be*—are called **auxiliary (or helping) verbs.** Auxiliary verbs help express something about the action of main verbs: for example, when the action occurs, whether the subject acted or was acted upon, or whether or not an action occurred.

Indicating tense with *be* verbs

EL6

Like the auxiliary verbs *have* and *do, be* changes form to signal tense. In addition to *be* itself, the **be verbs** are *is, am, are, was, were,* and *been.*

To show ongoing action, *be* verbs are followed by the present participle, which is a verb ending in *-ing.*

INCORRECT	I **am think** of all the things I'd rather **be do**.
CORRECT	I **am thinking** of all the things I'd rather **be doing**.

To show that an action is being done to the subject rather than by the subject, follow *be* verbs with the past participle (a verb usually ending in *-ed, -en,* or *-t*).

INCORRECT	The movie **was direct** by John Woo.
CORRECT	The movie **was directed** by John Woo.

Auxiliary verbs that express certain conditions

EL7

The auxiliary verbs *will, would, can, could, may, might, shall, must,* and *should* express conditions like possibility, permission, speculation, expectation, and necessity. Unlike the auxiliary verbs *be, have,* and *do,* the auxiliary verbs listed above do not change form based on the grammatical subject of the sentence (*I, you, she, he, it, we, they*).

Two basic rules apply to all uses of these auxiliary verbs. First, these auxiliary verbs are always followed by the simple form of the verb. The simple form is the verb by itself, in the present tense, such as *talk* but not *talked, talking,* or *to talk.*

INCORRECT	She **should studies** harder to pass the exam.
CORRECT	She **should study** harder to pass the exam.

The second rule is that you should not use these auxiliary verbs consecutively.

INCORRECT	If you work harder at writing, you **might could** improve.
CORRECT	If you work harder at writing, you **might** improve.

1. **Speculation:** If you had flown, you **would** have arrived yesterday.

2. **Ability:** She **can** run faster than Jennifer.

3. **Necessity:** You **must** know what you want to do.

4. **Intention:** He **will** wash his own clothes.

5. **Permission:** You **may** leave now.

6. **Advice:** You **should** wash behind your ears.

7. **Possibility:** It **might** be possible to go home early.

8. **Assumption:** You **must** have stayed up late last night.

9. **Expectation:** You **should** enjoy the movie.

10. **Order:** You **must** leave the building.

EL8

Placement of Modifiers

Modifiers will be unclear if your reader can't connect them to the words to which they refer. How close a modifier is to the noun or verb it modifies provides an important clue to their relationship.

Clarity should be your first goal when using a modifier.

UNCLEAR	Many pedestrians are killed each year by motorists **not using sidewalks**.
CLEAR	Many pedestrians **not using sidewalks** are killed each year by motorists.

An **adverb**—a word or group of words that modifies a verb, adjective, or another adverb—should not come between a verb and its direct object.

AWKWARD	The hurricane destroyed **completely** the city's tallest building.
BETTER	The hurricane **completely** destroyed the city's tallest building.

Try to avoid placing an adverb between *to* and its verb. This construction is called a **split infinitive**.

AWKWARD	The water level was predicted **to not rise**.
BETTER	The water level was predicted **not to rise**.

Understand English Sentence Structure

EL9

Words derive much of their meaning from how they function in a sentence.

With the exception of **imperatives** (commands such as *Watch out!*), sentences in English usually contain a *subject* and a *predicate*. A subject names who or what the sentence is about; the predicate tells what the subject is or does.

The Lion	is asleep.
subject	predicate

A predicate consists of at least one main verb. If the verb is **intransitive,** like *exist*, it does not take a direct object. Some verbs are **transitive,** which means they require a **direct object** to complete their meaning.

INCORRECT	The bird saw.
CORRECT	The bird saw a cat.

Some verbs (*write, learn, read,* and others) can be both transitive and intransitive, depending on how they are used.

INTRANSITIVE	Pilots fly.
TRANSITIVE	Pilots fly airplanes.

Formal written English requires that each sentence includes a subject and a verb, even when the meaning of the sentence would be clear without it. In some cases you must supply an expletive, such as *it* and *there*.

INCORRECT	Is snowing in Alaska.
CORRECT	It is snowing in Alaska.